Within the Power of
Universal
Mind

Rochelle Sparrow
and
Cortney Kane

Schiffer Publishing Ltd

4880 Lower Valley Road, Atglen, Pennsylvania 19310

Dedications

From Rochelle

This book would not have been possible without the loving support of my husband, Michael Lee Miller, my daughter, Morgan, my nieces, Tara Trotter, Katrina Duncan and their families, Susan Clendanial, Kim Ardnt, Randy Webb, Susan Schwartz, Juangian Analyst, and of course, Cortney Kane, my soul sister. With out you all, my life would be impossible.

From Cortney

Thank you Rochelle for your friendship and sisterhood. This would have never have been possible without you and our constant processing. Thank you to my husband, John, and my daughter, Paige, for your unconditional love. My sisters, Jennifer, Melanie, Whitney, and Angie. Without you I would not be who I am today. I love you.

To Our Clients

Without you this book would not have been possible and our lives would not have been as enriched. Thank you so much for your trust in our work.

Special Note For Intended Individuals

1101 1110
0125 0104

Text by Rochelle Sparrow and Cortney Kane
Artwork by Cortney Kane

Copyright © 2011 Rochelle Sparrow and Cortney Kane

Library of Congress Control Number: 2010943164

Designed by Mark David Bowyer
Type set in UniversityRoman Bd BT / New Baskerville BT

ISBN: 978-0-7643-3786-4

Printed in China

Acknowledgments

Our Manager, Marc Tetlow, with Ideal Event Management. Dinah Roseberry, our acquisitions editor. Shirley Maclaine, Dave and John with Para X Radio, *The "X" Zone* Show with Rob McConnell. *Coast to Coast* with George Noory, and the many radio shows which have given us a platform to share our work. A special thank you to Michael Lee Miller who finalized the editing of our book.

Schiffer Books are available at special discounts for bulk purchases for sales promotions or premiums. Special editions, including personalized covers, corporate imprints, and excerpts can be created in large quantities for special needs. For more information contact the publisher:

Published by Schiffer Publishing Ltd.
4880 Lower Valley Road
Atglen, PA 19310
Phone: (610) 593-1777; Fax: (610) 593-2002
E-mail: Info@schifferbooks.com

For the largest selection of fine reference books on this and related subjects, please visit our website at **www.schifferbooks.com**
We are always looking for people to write books on new and related subjects. If you have an idea for a book please contact us at the above address.

This book may be purchased from the publisher.
Include $5.00 for shipping.
Please try your bookstore first.
You may write for a free catalog.

In Europe, Schiffer books are distributed by
Bushwood Books
6 Marksbury Ave.
Kew Gardens
Surrey TW9 4JF England
Phone: 44 (0) 20 8392-8585; Fax: 44 (0) 20 8392-9876
E-mail: info@bushwoodbooks.co.uk
Website: www.bushwoodbooks.co.uk

Contents

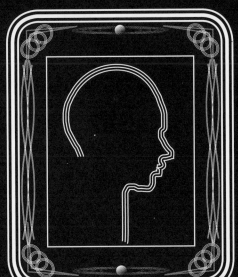

Foreword

by John Zaffis

I am a demonologist. I deal with the various and inexplicable mysteries of our world, which can be complex, dark, and unexplored. People often stigmatize me because of my ability to see things which most people do not want to see. But they exist, nonetheless.

People contact me because they are desperate and I am often their last resort. After perhaps months of denial, people tell me what is happening in their homes or in their lives. I do not deny what I see. I have an intimate awareness of who I am and all I observe around me. I am unafraid to see what is there. Because of my lack of fear in knowing myself and others, I see the authenticity of Rochelle and Cortney's work.

I believe that healing in our work with energy is underrated. Rochelle and Cortney work with unseen energy. They see your inner life with fearless clarity to help you heal, to help you understand the way energy works.

Healing is the foremost component of working with energy. Both the light and the dark. You cannot heal unless you are clear with what you are working with.

Rochelle and Cortney will make it clear what you have inside of you that keeps you from healing, that keeps you from progressing forward in your life.

~John Zaffis

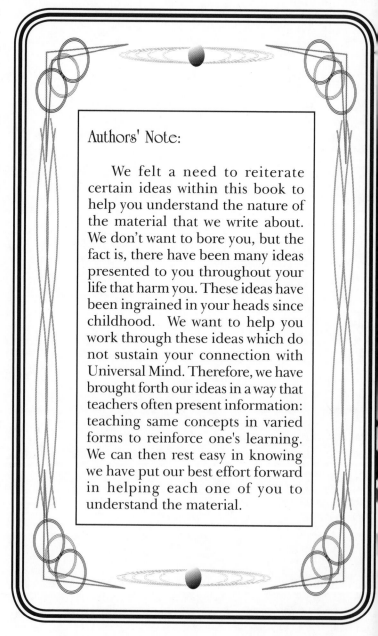

Authors' Note:

We felt a need to reiterate certain ideas within this book to help you understand the nature of the material that we write about. We don't want to bore you, but the fact is, there have been many ideas presented to you throughout your life that harm you. These ideas have been ingrained in your heads since childhood. We want to help you work through these ideas which do not sustain your connection with Universal Mind. Therefore, we have brought forth our ideas in a way that teachers often present information: teaching same concepts in varied forms to reinforce one's learning. We can then rest easy in knowing we have put our best effort forward in helping each one of you to understand the material.

Introduction

We went to a psychoanalytic salon recently. I had not attended one for many years. I went because a friend of mine was training to become a Jungian analyst in Zurich. My friend, Kim, presented a drawing for analysis. The stark pencil drawing was from a woman's dream. The woman had dreamt she had bit off the fingertips from her young daughter's hands. The image she had drawn was of a side view of her head, the blood dripping from her mouth. The other image floated in front of the bloody mouth, a disembodied hand with the tips cut off dropping from the fingers. As I watched the image, the images began to shift into a different placement. The picture came alive. The head, with its gaping mouth, centered itself, and moved toward me rapidly, seemingly to engulf me in one tremendous bite. The bitten off thumb moved into place through two lines that were drawn vertically, representing an eleven. What did the movement mean? What was I witnessing?

It occurred to Cortney and myself that the current psychological theories being presented about the image could not describe my experience. In fact, none of the theories I had been trained in while working toward my masters in social work could suffice as a working theory for what I have come to know as the reality of mind. They were obsolete. The model of the mind needed a new point of view. A view that would sustain the complexity that mind is not conventional, but a complex and intricate tool for organizing energy within many dimensions at once.

The model needed to see mind as inclusive of all energy at one time. It needed to take into account that everything everywhere was made of energy; that energy was intelligent and was capable of having its independence. Our minds and the minds of everything else within energy needed to be accounted for. The model needed to be a unified theory of all energy and therefore, all mind. We call our theory, the Psychology of Universal Mind.

Part One
Understanding Energy and Universal Law

Chapter One

What is Energy?

We saw something rather macabre on television recently. Ironically, we were sitting on my couch developing a workshop on spirit communication. It was one of those shows where people visit different countries and seek out bizarre and unusual spectacles for our entertainment, if not our enlightenment. In this episode, they went to Sedlec's Church, the all saints ossuary in Prague. Forty thousand dead form chandeliers, artwork, and altars. Its interior was laid out in intricate patterns. The patterns were made of human bones: Skulls outlined the walls, leg bones formed various squares and rectangles, and teeth decorated the ceiling. We don't think we will be calling their interior designer.

Even though this church wasn't designed how we would make a place of sanctuary, these scenes made a very important point to us: Our human forms are all equal in death. This point stood out to us because there was no hierarchy in the church—bones based on material wealth, intelligence, education, social skills, or social status. These witnesses silently spoke of their equal right to be present, regardless of their true-life circumstances. It was a humbling vision.

The truth has a way of taking your breath away by hitting you right in the gut, and putting you in your place. At the same time, truth can center and ground you. When there are hundreds of skulls staring down at you, even if you are only seeing it on your television, it can remind us that when you get right down to it, we all live and we all die. — naturally

But what is it, what really is it, that separates people when they are alive? What makes people different, what makes one person have such a drastically different life than another? Why do people feel unequal to each other, inadequate or somehow less than, let's say, the skull hanging right next to them? After all, whether we are alive or dead, we all share one essential ingredient: energy.

Everything everywhere is made of energy. Energy is made up of electrons, neutrons, atoms, protons, and particles. All energy has the same structure, no matter what it is. If you just saw the energy rather than the object itself, it would be hard to tell one thing from another. And the fact is, on a quantum level, you can't. Energy is the thing that makes us what we are and makes up everything around us. It makes up things we can see, like birds, rocks, and trees, and makes up things we can't see, like gravity.

Energy is the common bond we have with everything, even though energy can be experienced in different ways. Shamanic practice is one way to learn how to experience energy. I first heard about shamanism when I was studying for a master's in social work. I learned that people that practice Shamanism have entered energy trance states since the dawn of time. Ancient people enter these trances to journey into other dimensions and help them better their lives. While on their journey, they might learn where to hunt, become educated about plants, or heal. The tribe entered these trance states through meditative drumming.

When I learned about trances and drumming through a book someone thought I might be interested in, I became fascinated and wanted to try it. Shortly afterwards, I found out about a shamanic workshop on campus and immediately signed up. The night of the workshop, the shaman leading the workshop said he would teach us to get into a meditative state and learn about ourselves. He then passed around sage which he had lit to cleanse us and help call in our power animals which guide us from other realities we cannot see. He advised us that when we were in our trance, we were to follow whatever animal came to us three times. He suggested we not go up into the upper world of the birds and the clouds, but stay in the middle world on our earth, or go below into the earth underworld. He then told us to close our eyes and begin to breath and follow the sound of the drum.

The purpose of the drumming was to put us into a meditative trancelike state. Shortly after he began drumming, I immediately fell into a relaxed trance state. In my mind, I saw a hawk. The hawk swooped me up and I began flying alongside the hawk. Next, my body moved over into the body of the hawk and we became one. I was now the hawk. We flew so fast and so hard, I could hear and feel my wings beating and

I became dizzy from the speed. I started to become sick to my stomach. It was too much for me and I made myself come out of the trance, even though we were instructed we would naturally come out of trance once the drumming ended. Now I understood why the shaman advised us not to go to the upper world.

The shamanic experience was overwhelming. I was disoriented for days. I felt so much like a hawk, that I was not sure quite what happened to me. I would look at my hands expecting to see wings, but my hands were still there. I was sometimes confused when I was not gripping my lunch with talons. How weird.

I did not know it then, but I had shape shifted. I was the hawk and the hawk was me. Our energy had merged in a way I did not understand. Yet, inside of me, I could feel both the hawk's energy and my energy at once. The energy that makes up the hawk is the same energy that is in me. Perhaps Universal Mind, what we call God, was teaching me that I was me, even though I can shape shift into something that is not me and become one with it.

All energy has the same ability to create, to make the sky, the ocean, and the trees. What this means is that all energy has the same equal value, all energy is equally important. Our energy is not more or less powerful then the energy of the hawk. Your energy is not more or less valuable than my energy.

Since childhood I always had a very strong connection to nature. Because of my connection with nature, it was difficult for me to attribute God, Universal Mind, to a human-like person, like some people do. I never saw gender in the trees. It was impossible for me to see the inequality in a snake versus the stream or see the taller pine tree as more powerful than the small willow. I could not fathom the immorality of birds eating crickets. I saw no problems with winter coming on and the plants dying or hibernating.

By connecting with nature, I found my definition of Universal Mind.

Universal Mind is energy. The way Universal Mind behaves in the universe is organized through its own laws. The earth knows when it is ready for the sun to go down; it does not need a code of ethics. The moon knows when to come up and the crickets know when to sing. Where is the conductor? We believe there is one, but the conductor is hidden in all energy. Energy recognizes itself as connected to Universal Mind, as its own authority.

Points to Remember:

Everything everywhere is made of energy.

All energy has the same ability to create, to make the sky, the ocean and the trees.

All energy has the same equal value.

Universal Mind is energy. The way Universal Mind behaves in the universe is organized through its own laws.

Affirm:

I am energy and an equal part of the energetic world in which I live.

Experience:

Relax your body and take a deep breath and close your eyes.

Take a moment to identify what your favorite animal is.

Imagine, as you breathe deeply, that you are becoming the animal you have identified. Feel the shape of the animal and begin to move like the animal. How does the animal view the world in which it lives? What would its experiences feel like? When you are ready, open your eyes. You may want to journal your experience.

Chapter Two
The Power of Energy

When we are out of alignment and do not recognize our equal authority with all that exists, we suffer. Why do we suffer? Because we think we are different. We believe that somehow our existence is not meaningful or sufficient enough, and worst of all, we feel isolated. — YES!!

In becoming a shaman, I learned to shape shift into many animals and plants. I became a bear and traveled around the universe to see my bear relatives in China. I would then shape shift into an eagle and fly over the horizon and the clouds to perch upon the moon and watch the earth. I realized my importance, the sense of who I am never left, even though my body was in a different shape. I realized I am no less or more important than the hawk, the bear, or the eagle.

Shape shifting taught me that all energy in our universe has the same power to grow and change. What does this mean for you? The energy inside of you recognizes its own equal power and wants to expand to experience fulfillment of its power. It means that the energy within you is no more or less powerful than the energy within the richest person on earth, the president of the United States, or the grass in the park near your home.

There is, of course, more to the energy story. Yes, settle down with your milk and cookies and think of yourself as five years old. We are here to remind you of information you knew way back then.

As a five year old, you feel your energy has the same ability to behave in all of the ways that energy can. You can imagine you are your cat, or pretend you are an elephant and even believe you can fly like a bird.

In my shamanic journeys, I united my energy with the energy of the hawk and the hawk came to me. The hawk does not morally deny its existence of empowerment within the natural world. She feels the speed of the wind, the ability to see clearly, and to notice when autumn is approaching. The hawk feels everything by allowing its connection with all of nature to be experienced.

Nature teaches us to honor connections and not sever them.

Points to Remember:

All energy in our universe has the same power to grow and change.

All energy has the same ability to behave in all of the ways that energy can.

Affirm:

My energy can grow and change.

Experience:

After reading this exercise, close your eyes and take a deep breath. Relax your body. Imagine that you are walking down a long tunnel. As you do so, a small bird comes to you. You wonder what it feels like to be the bird. Slowly you feel yourself becoming smaller, your legs become thin and you feel your arms changing into wings. You see a large crystal up ahead of you. You hop to it. You look into it and see yourself as a small bird. The bird that came to you is no longer to be seen.

As you look into the crystal, you notice another animal coming up behind you. It is a tiger. You wonder what it feels like to become a tiger. Slowly you feel yourself becoming larger, your skin feels furry and you notice that you have a tail that swishes back and forth. Again you look into the crystal and see yourself as a tiger. The tiger that came to you disappears.

You begin to move past the crystal deeper into the tunnel. You see an entrance ahead of you, but it requires you to leap high into the air. You do so, and now you are out into the open. You see a small lake in front of you. You move toward it. You look into it and notice a person coming to you that looks much like your former self. As this person comes to you, you begin to wonder what it would feel like to move back into your original form and you do.

Take a deep breath. How do you feel?

Chapter Three
Energy Moves

[handwritten: Vibration]

We can understand some things about energy from the study of science. Energy constantly moves. It is hard to imagine energy moving when you are looking at the walls of a two story house. You would not want the walls of your bedroom moving around at two in the morning. But the truth is, even when energy appears still, it is moving, or it is at least vibrating. Energy moves back and forth through space like a wave in the water. Depending on how fast or slow the energetic movement is, it can discharge energy and make itself smaller, or it takes in energy and makes itself larger. Recent discoveries show that energy can exist in several dimensions at one time, not just one.

Blob Energy

[handwritten: Spiritual world right next to ours — SWB]

Think of it like this; remember the old movie *The Blob*? If you never saw it, we recommend it, even if it is a *B* grade movie. In this movie, the Blob was a huge mound of living red goo initially the size of a doghouse. It traveled around the neighborhood and ate whatever it touched, enabling it to become bigger and bigger. It ate a dog, a bush, and a person on the sidewalk. That is sort of like what vibrations can do. They can take in more and more energy, until they get bigger and bigger.

Now, what they did not show in the movie was the reverse process. What if the Blob decided to start giving up the chair, the wall, or the unfortunate moviegoer it swallowed along its merry way? You would then see it get smaller and smaller.

The thing about the Blob was that it did not just take in any old thing, even if the object was tasty and meaty. It had to swallow what came along its path; everything else was safe. If it was not in the Blob's path, it would not become part of the Blob. How come? The energy within the Blob was vibrating. The energetic vibration acted like a shield. It shielded out other energy that it did not want to take in, or take out, just by its vibration.

Energy forms its identity through movement. The identity acts like a shield and won't take on other energy that does not match its path. The clock on my desk is vibrating "clock" energy. It takes in and gives out clock energy. The stuffed animals in my daughter's room are vibrating stuffed animal energy. They take in and give out stuffed animal energy. The clock energy acts like a shield from other energy and does not become stuffed animal energy. The stuffed animal energy acts like a shield from other energy and does not become clock energy.

We think that for most of us, we are able to identify some emotions in other people. My daughter will go up and hug a child when she thinks she needs a hug, just by looking at her. Oh, I know you can say, well, the other child looked sad or was looking at her with her arms out, but I really think we are made to recognize the emotions in other people. Empathy for other people is a natural human condition. We are empathetic because we can recognize the energy in other people and we can identify the energy other people are emitting.

Ever since we were children, we were able to identify energy. We were able to feel people energy, tree energy, and couch energy. We didn't understand that was what we were doing. We just knew it. The experience inside of us was able to feel the other energy types around us.

Why? Energy creates its identity through its vibrations.

Now, you can identify energy. You just may not have been taught to use your natural ability to listen to the identity of the energy around you. You can listen and experience energy inside of you.

Let us define experience for you. As Webster states, "experience is the direct observation of, or participation in, events as a basis of knowledge." The operable word here is *participation*. This means that monitoring your thoughts, memories, feelings, senses and behaviors to affirm alignment with the identity of the energy will allow the energy to vibrate its identity through you.

You first have to identify your own energy. Once you are clear what is *your* energy and let's say, the energy of your wife or your coworker, you can then separate out your vibration from the energetic vibration of what it is you wish to identify.

You can hone your ability to identify energy, because you are focusing the identity of the energy through the power of your mind.

Correspondence

Points to Remember:

Energy constantly moves.

Depending on how fast or slow the energetic movement is it can discharge energy and make itself smaller, or it takes in energy and makes itself larger.

Energy can exist in several dimensions at one time, not just one.

Energy forms its identity through its vibrations.

Affirm:

My energy has its own identity because of my unique vibration.

Experience:

Take a deep breath, close your eyes and relax your body. Focus your mind inward. What does your energy feel like? How do you experience yourself? How would you describe your energy? Where does your energy begin? Where does it end? What is not your energy? What does dog energy feel like? What does your wife, child, or friend's energy feel like? What does the energy of your car feel like? Or, even as silly as it sounds, what about the energy of your dresser?

Chapter Four
Identifying Energy

We are going to teach you many things about your mind. Your mind is the seat for discovering your true self. It is a tool for understanding and focusing energy. You already do it all the time, if only subconsciously. You focus your energy on your job, your dog, your child, your spouse, and your house. Many of these skills you already practice, you just have to become more conscious about using the skills you already have. You can hone your skills by noticing your inward experiences of energy.

You do not need religion, the government, or the media to lead you toward self-realization. What you do need, is to pry open your mind with the awareness that your mind can bring to your true self through your experience of the energy inside of you.

The skills we are suggesting that you were born with, such as your ability to identify energy, is a natural human art. You may just not know it yet.

In our human world, the way to tune into energy is to slow our selves down through meditation. The more still we become, the more we are able to tune into energy and become aware of the energy we might not otherwise sense.

Just a point to note: How many cultural structures can you name that exist in our society help support your ability to slow down and tune into your inner experience of energy? Take a look around you, just for today, as you go about your business. We would say, not many.

Yogis have known how to read energy for centuries. They can slow down the energy in their minds to see energy that is not otherwise noticed.

We all have a natural ability to identify energy by slowing down to make ourselves more conscious of it. We can allow all of our thoughts to float by, like the waves of an ocean, and breathe deeply into what we are feeling.

You may have recognized an unseen energy within you. Why? You slowed down your mind to experience it.

What this means is that even if you do not see energy, it still exists. Like gravity and air, even if your eyes cannot identify the existence of energy, you can trust it is there. You can rely on the existence of all the identities of all energetic vibrations, even if you can't view it, taste it, smell it or feel it.

Many of us may have not been taught to focus inward and recognize our inner energy, identify our inner energy, and believe in its existence.

Now, if energy can expand and contract and change its rate of vibration to form its identity, why can't your coffee cup become a bigger coffee cup, or better yet, your one room condo change into a three bedroom house? Why? It has decided not to. Somewhere along the line, energy settled upon its identity, in joint consideration with whom and what it is, in relation to other energy.

Points to Remember:

Your mind is the seat for discovering your true self. It is a tool for understanding and focusing energy.

Even if you do not see energy, it still exists.

Many of us may have not been taught to focus inward and recognize our inner energy, identify our inner energy and believe in its existence.

Affirm:

I have a natural ability to recognize and identify energy.

Experience:

Do a quick experiment. Don't be concerned if you have heard this one before. Take a deep cleansing breath. Close your eyes after reading this paragraph and try to relax your body.

Focus on your emotional inner experience; allow your thoughts to float by. Keep breathing and focus your mind inward. Practice this exercise for at least fifteen minutes for three days. Do not be concerned if at first you are thinking about your next project at work or picking up the kids. Just continue to practice. We guarantee you one thing; you will notice something about your inward experience when you come out of the meditation that you did not notice before.

Chapter Five
Energy is Intelligent

Take a deep breath. Close your eyes after you read this exercise. Imagine for a moment that you are traveling through space. You are going to a planet, a planet filled with trees, water, and rock. This planet contains living energy that speaks to all the other energy within it. What would it look like? Open your eyes. Like earth, of course.

The harmonic alliances you see all around you, within the natural entities of earth, exist because there is natural intelligence present, a natural logic. There is also science, natural selection, DNA, and evolutionary processes. These processes exist because there is something else happening here, a built-in ability to support the logical structures of science. Why? Within energy there is already a built-in ability of awareness. This awareness can recognize both self and others.

Hence, you open your eyes and the world around you fits together. It all makes sense. Why? Energy has within it, its own mind. Energy can draw its own conclusions and form its own behaviors. Energy can make its own choices, act on its own behalf and make its own decisions. However, energy cannot exist alone; it has to have help.

What is the help, you ask? It is like help in the form of a miracle, when you think about it. We have a computer we are typing on, a light to help us see, and a comfortable chair for us to sit on. People made these three items, people who had ideas; some of these ideas were formed many generations ago. These ideas existed in the minds of their creators before they became available to help us type this word. Energy is the same kind of miracle.

The intelligence within energy takes on a decision to become its own form and identity with the help of our minds. It can't do anything with the form it takes on in your mind, unless there is the support of other energy in the world around it. This word could not be written unless there was paper. Paper would not exist unless there were plants. So, many energetic forms exist in a hidden state until they cooperate with other hidden or manifest forms of energy to bring themselves to life.

The idea of coral exists within the idea of an ocean and the many creatures who depend upon coral for their life force. The energy of the ocean and the coral talk to each other through the mind of energy, negotiate their salaries, and then draw up a contract that regulates their partnership. All energy negotiates its existence in the same way. Why have bees, if there are no plants? Why have rivers, if there is no land to contain the water? Why have music, if there is no air to carry the notes? Why have love, if there are no living things to show it to?

Our minds are tools for expressing energy. Our minds can organize energy to form an existence.

Points to Remember:

Energy can make its own choices, act on its own behalf and make its own decisions.

The intelligence within energy takes on a decision to become its own form and identity with the help of our minds.

Our minds are tools for expressing energy. Our minds can organize energy to form an existence.

Affirm:

My mind is a tool for organizing and expressing energy.

Experience:

Take a deep breath. Relax your body. Think of a creative project you would like to accomplish. Perhaps it is an art project or writing an article. What would you need to accomplish your project? Do you need to set aside time or buy a new paint brush? List all the things you would need to organize to complete your project. Now that you have your list, are you able to complete your project? What does it look like? How does it feel to complete your project? How many things on your list needed to be in existence in order to complete your project?

Chapter Six
The Law of One

The law of one helps to bring all energy together. Once the needed energy is brought together, it can move into existence.

The tree could not exist until the water and earth it needed became available. That way, the different types of energy support each other and are not left on their own to exist without other energy providing energetic help.

Do you feel as though you are one with the energy inside of you? Who you are, your talents, your skills and your abilities, are what makes you. How much do you know about you? How much are you using what you know about you? From our experience with our clients, it is not that they do not know they are talented; it is that somewhere along the way, they lost support for using what they know.

> "I know I am meant to write, but I don't understand what to write about."
>
> "I know I am meant to be a healer, but how am I going to begin."
>
> "I know I am supposed to be a musician, but it is so tough to make a living."

Our clients are not in alignment with their true self. Because they are not in alignment, they are conflicted about who they really are. The conflicts create blocks to allowing the fulfillment of their energy because they are not one with their energy. All of their energy is hidden energy waiting to come out.

From our life experience, and from our experience with our clients, abundance in great wealth and relationships is not the real issue. The issue is that people know they have something inside of them that feels like greatness, yet they do not know how to express it. They feel a sense of lack and longing that creates lack and longing outside of themselves. The issue is not one of creating abundance; the issue is one of healing. What our clients really want is to express that "something" inside of them that is unique to them and them only. They long to give themselves permission to be. In their efforts to learn how to be, they grasp onto easy solutions that do not require them to look deeply into their souls and validate what they already know about themselves.

They keep themselves in hiding. They hide in their jobs and in their relationships. They hide by experiencing a seemingly safe corner of their life, when they can have it all. And the all of what they can have is their own energy.

We believe Universal Mind exists in everything in a world that is obviously intelligent in creating itself. We believe that in your mind is the same energy that exists in what some people call God.

Life is not created from the outside in. We create our lives from the inside out. We create our lives from our inner experiences in life. We want to help you gain a clear understanding of who you are. We want to tell you what you don't want to hear. And that means that we want to help you face the denial we often see in our clients. That is, they want a magic formula to help them get what they want. And they want it in a one-hour session that does not require their own work! Multidimensional reality doesn't work like that.

> This is the formula: Inner experience works to align with universal law to help experience growth.

What did we just say? Let us break it down for you. Consider Maria's dilemma.

"My father beat me so much, some part of me can't let go of being victimized. If I am not a victim, I am responsible for me and can no longer expect anyone to rescue me. If I count on myself, I am not sure I will come through for myself. I have never practiced. I always counted on people to rescue me. Can I trust myself to become more independent?"

If something is out of alignment, as in our client Maria's case, then emotional suffering occurs. Inside of Maria was a longing for independence. She wanted to express her empowerment.

When we witness the natural world, it is ordered in the empowerment of living energy that exists within it. A window of opportunity exists for all living things to assert themselves and become what they are.

The same energy exists within us. We too just want to be who we are, no questions asked. When we experience for some reason, that we cannot, problems ensue.

Universal Mind through the plants, trees, rocks, and animals wants to express itself. The inner experience of Universal Mind lives within you through your mind. Universal Mind wants to expand. Universal Mind wants to experience life on earth. And how does Universal Mind do that? Look around. More importantly, look in the mirror.

You are important, special, and unique. You are connected to Universal Mind. And through your connection to Universal Mind, you express your uniqueness. The energetic identity of your energy can be experienced, and not just by you, but by all life.

Not only does energy have intelligence, but there is a built-in morality that states: I am me and I am allowed to be me. Simple enough? Yes. Yet, as humans, that is our number one problem, feeling free to express who we are.

When I was in my twenties, as I mentioned, I studied social work and got my masters degree. After graduating, for several years, I worked in various capacities as a therapist in a field that declared that hearing a voice was admitting psychosis. Yet, I had undeniable psychic experiences. I heard the voice of my guides.

My next job enabled me to work in a hospital as a program manager for a mental health program. My office was in a quiet wing of the hospital. No one came to this wing, except for the occasional administrators, which were few, including me. On the day I started my position, I noticed shapes of shadows going by my office door. Out of the corner of my eye, these shapes would go up and down the hall past my office.

One day, my office door was open, and I was sitting facing the door. I witnessed one of these shadows walk up to the door, pause, turn, and come into my office. I saw the head, the shape of the shoulders and the body. Then it disappeared. I freaked out! I thought about going directly to my boss, the director of the program, but thought better of it a moment later. After all, I was second in command of a well-respected mental health program in a state-regulated hospital! He might think I was in need of rest, a nice long rest. So I hid what I saw.

However, who I was continued to emerge. The energy within me wanted recognition. Hiding who I was is not healthy. We are not meant to hide ourselves. Energy wants to be seen. Healing is about being "out."

When you are working on your path, expect your past, unhealed energy to show up. And expect it to show up repeatedly in different ways. This does not mean that what you are trying to develop is blocked. It means energy that needs to be moved into alignment is there saying, "Notice me, notice me again, pay attention, I want to take over like I always have," and you are saying, "Nope sorry, I know you are there, but I want something different now." This energy can be tricky. No, I do not mean in a devil sense as in bad or wrong, but in a devilish sense.

Energy that is not aligned with Universal Law will create conflict. Energy that is not in alignment with Universal Law will also express itself to help create growth. As in my case, my energy was being hidden. Since hidden energy cannot grow, it was expressing itself by causing me emotional pain. I was being prompted through my psychological conflict to change.

Energy may reinvent itself to try to look different, as in the case of our client Andrew. Andrew was working at getting over a very difficult relationship. His past girlfriend, Sue, had been inconsistent in her feelings towards him. One day she wanted to be with him, the next day she didn't. Finally, she ended the relationship. This put Andrew into a state of severe depression. When this happened, she came around again.

Each time he saw her, Andrew went into a tailspin and called for a session. During each session, Andrew's view of Sue strengthened, what he knew was best for him was discussed during the sessions and he was helped to recognize his emotions.

The whole experience wasn't easy for him because Sue would show up in his life in many different ways. He could run into her at a post office, or where he worked, or through a mutual friend. The encounters were different, and although his emotions were strong, each time he saw her, he gained distance over the pain that accompanied these events. Eventually, he improved so much, he only felt bad for one day after seeing her, rather than feeling bad for several days afterwards.

Andrew's confidence in himself grew stronger. He became clear about the type of relationship he wanted to have in his life. He aligned himself with the energy by affirming to himself that he could get what he wanted. The negative energy that unconsciously stated "Stay with this woman, no matter what; this is all you deserve," eventually began to deplete. Why? Because it did not have support from the other energies in Andrew's mind. The old energy had to find support someplace else.

One day, Andrew began to repeatedly have disturbing dreams. The dreams were always the same. Someone came into his back yard, an intruder. Andrew murdered this person. The person was faceless and nameless. When Andrew woke up from these dreams, he would feel as though he had done something wrong and was full of shame and guilt. He did not understand the dream.

Through guidance, he was able to understand that his rage towards Sue was pointed at a former part of himself. A part of himself that felt he needed to carve out a niche in life, a niche he did not share with others, and was not supported by others. This niche was not of his space. Andrew was helped to understand that he *was* entitled to his own space, his own success, and his own love. He no longer had rage over the injustice of feeling burdened by others who were not fair to him, used him, or trespassed against him. He was also helped to understand his current thoughts of anger, that were recently showing up from his past relationship with Sue, were okay to have and he did not have to feel shame about these feelings. Lastly, he was helped to understand that in his dreams, he was murdering old energy and moving on to focus on the new energy representing his entitlement to love and success.

As can be seen, energy needs the support of other energy to make its power of existence known. In Andrew's dream, the energy of success and fulfillment were battling to become recognized. Andrew needed help to bring this energy into his consciousness to experience awareness. Now that the dreams and ill feelings towards Sue were gone, he could focus his inner experience on believing that he is "entitled to success and love."

Points to Remember:

The law of one helps to bring all energy together. Once the needed energy is brought together, it can move into existence.

Inner experience works to align with universal law to help experience growth.

Energy that is not aligned with universal law will create conflict.

Energy that is not in alignment with universal law will also express itself to help create growth.

Energy needs the support of other energy to make its power of existence known.

Affirm:

I have the ability to align the energy within me so that I may grow.

Experience:

Do an experiment. Write down each concrete situation that you currently feel unhappy with in your daily life. One example might be an unfulfilling job. Then write down all of your experiences, thoughts, beliefs, and feelings around this job or situation. Sit back and close your eyes. Then imagine that you can change your situation to any circumstance you would like. Take a deep breath. Write down all of your experiences, thoughts, beliefs and feelings around changing your situation to one you want. What conflicting experiences, thoughts, beliefs, and feelings come up that do not support the change?

Especially notice thoughts that may have come up such as, "I am afraid if I change my job (or other situation), ____ will happen." Those are the intentions and inner experiences that represent some past energetic wound that has not healed.

Chapter Seven
Knowing

Within all energy is mental energy. Mental energy is within our minds. Not just our minds; the minds of cats, the minds of plants, and even the minds of rocks. Even something like a couch, which is not alive, has within its energetic makeup mental energy. Since all energy is connected through mental energy, all energy connects like one essential mind.

We can become aware of our connection to this one essential mind and feel the connection. When we experience the feelings of being centered, grounded and balanced, we feel connected. Within mind, is a type of energy called "knowing." Our experience of connection resides in our knowing, and our knowing is connected to something bigger than we are.

Andrew's knowing was a sense of "I am entitled to my own space without intrusion. This difficult relationship happened in the past, and I do not want it to happen now." Andrew could not speak these words out loud at first, not until he woke.

Within our knowing, there is an instinctual recognition of timelessness, the divine knowledge that does not need validation from anything. Knowing connects all energy together. It has access to a huge, infinite library or computer that can calculate the exact information it must have in order for it to know. In Andrew's knowing, the answer was present. In the energy that Andrew carried, our guidance pointed out what Andrew already knew.

Energy knows within itself the identity of its own energy. The energy within a toy knows it is a toy. It knows it is a three-dimensional object in a three-dimensional world, it knows it can respond to gravity, it can have colors, it can have textures, it can be large or small, it can be hard or soft, and it can get thrown by a small child.

With help from other energy across our reality and other hidden realities that reside in knowing, the toy has taken on a form that has been jointly agreed upon.

Within our knowing, we see a toy and identify it as a toy. All people, no matter where we go on the planet, will look at the toy and say it is a toy (although the word toy may be in different languages, but a toy never the less!). We are in a cooperative state of understanding. We know what we see within the knowing of our minds. Therefore, we experience what we see through our joint agreement.

There is a place within all minds of everything that exists, a place of its own knowing of its existence and the existence of all that is. In this place within our own minds, we can focus our inward experience, our will, and our intent. It is this place, our knowing, that joins with other intelligent energy to manifest with the certainty of knowing. It knows what it knows, without explanation, education, or questioning. It exists in the realm of the mind's experience. It remembers things beyond the realms of time and space. It is within this place that our life expression takes place, but it must take place without contradictions from other energy.

We are about to go on a journey. Remember when you knew something beyond a shadow of a doubt? You just knew it. Perhaps, like our client, it was knowing that the job offer was not going to work out, even though it looked good, and paid more money. Something just did not feel right. Then he found out, two months later, the company lost their contract with the state.

Your knowing contains all the information you need to carry out your life. Andrew needed help in becoming aware of what he already knew. His entitlement was to be in the space of success, love and pride.

Once we move into our own knowing, we move into our security. We feel centered and trust our own power. We also trust the safety that resides in our knowing and trust its ability to be there. We can trust who we are.

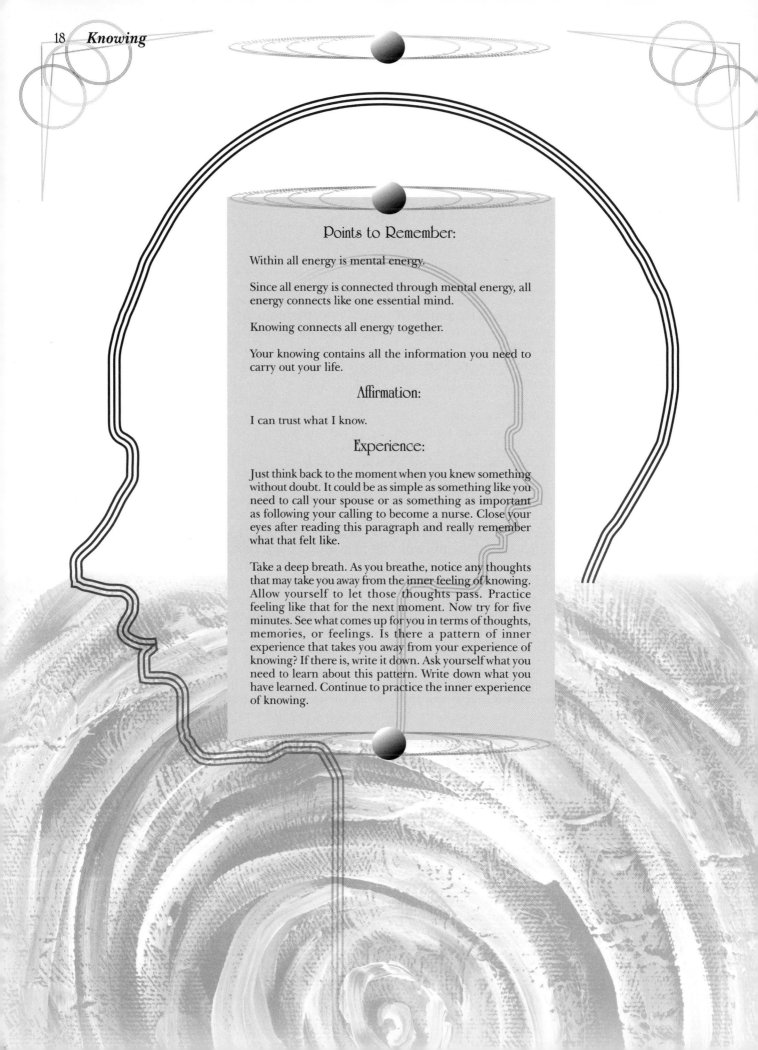

Points to Remember:

Within all energy is mental energy.

Since all energy is connected through mental energy, all energy connects like one essential mind.

Knowing connects all energy together.

Your knowing contains all the information you need to carry out your life.

Affirmation:

I can trust what I know.

Experience:

Just think back to the moment when you knew something without doubt. It could be as simple as something like you need to call your spouse or as something as important as following your calling to become a nurse. Close your eyes after reading this paragraph and really remember what that felt like.

Take a deep breath. As you breathe, notice any thoughts that may take you away from the inner feeling of knowing. Allow yourself to let those thoughts pass. Practice feeling like that for the next moment. Now try for five minutes. See what comes up for you in terms of thoughts, memories, or feelings. Is there a pattern of inner experience that takes you away from your experience of knowing? If there is, write it down. Ask yourself what you need to learn about this pattern. Write down what you have learned. Continue to practice the inner experience of knowing.

Chapter Eight
Energy is Formed by Mind

When we look at something emitting energy, we find that the energy that is being observed is shaped by our view. Our mind, our perceptions, our beliefs, and our emotions point our energy on the same course with the energy that is being observed. Our energy and the observed energy talks to each other and agree to become one form. The toy does not really become the toy until you look at it, agree with the energy in the toy that is the toy, and reach the joint decision that the toy is a toy. Then you can start looking at that teddy bear sitting on the floor.

In your mind, you and the identifying energy within the toy have reached a joint conclusion on what the toy is. You constantly make these continual conclusions each moment of each day. You are forming a reality outside of yourself by forming an inner reality that views what is happening outside of you.

Recently, two of our good friends saw the same movie, but both of them reached very different conclusions about the movie. One friend said it was devastating, hopeless about humanity, and depressing. Our other friend said it was great, offered a wonderful hopeful outcome for people from all walks of life, and she highly recommended it. Both of my friends are sophisticated and educated people, but both had very different views of the movie, because of their inner view of the world and of humanity.

How we look at things impacts what we observe. Energy exists in a hidden state until our mind helps to formulate its identity and behavior through our observation.

The "thing" we are observing, does not always have to be physical matter. It can be a situation or an event. We can be seeing something in our imagination and energy will react to it as though it is a concrete experience in reality. That means we can experience the world around us through the energy within our mind, what energy we choose to focus on, and how we observe the world around us. This also means that we can change energy, because the energy in our mind through our view can create change.

When I became a shape shifter, I experienced the energy of the hawk. I became the hawk. After this shamanic drumming experience, I became hooked on shamanic journeying. I sought out drummers to help me travel to the upper world, the middle world, and the lower world. I became ants, snakes, and elephants. As an elephant, I was really shocked at how articulate my trunk was. It was so sensitive, that I could pick up a small rock.

Journeying helped me discover how other animals and things feel. I lived their inner experiences and I believed they lived in mine. It helped me become aware that my inner experiences did not have to be sad or scary. The natural world became a role model for something different.

We create our world from the inside out from mind. We know, we keep repeating this statement, but the fact is, you have been brainwashed to believe otherwise. All energy everywhere creates its world from the inside out. And inside all energy exists the mind, the mental energy that talks to all energy everywhere and helps to form its world and ours. We exist because something else has agreed to our existence. And everything exists because we have agreed to its existence.

Why? Energy has agreed with the other energy around it about how it is going to behave and what it is going to be. Imagine what the world might be like if these joint agreements were not made. The fish would not have an ocean to swim in, the birds would not have trees to shelter in, and we would not have the air around us to breathe. The harmony in which the world is contained would not exist. We take the harmony in which we exist for granted without thought. However, if it did not exist, there would be a chaotic quagmire of energetic formations without a rhyme, reason, or purpose. Nothing would fit together.

Within the mental energy of the trees, there are millions of agreements between energies as to how the trees are going to be and how they are going to behave. Our minds also enter countless agreements with the energy around us to form our dimension.

Each day, we join with energy to form matter in our universe and make agreements to shift energy from one location to another.

Yes, we do live in a holographic universe. Our minds are constantly working with other minds and projecting these experiences out to the world around us, like one gigantic movie screen.

Like scenes in a movie, our energy is in constant communication with the energy around us. We are chattering away using the tiniest particles of our atoms, which are electrically connected to all energy within the universe, like one big circuit board. And imagine this, this energy talks to all other energy all at once within the space of knowing. The tree simultaneously knows what the bird energy is saying and vice versa. The identities of energy are constantly vibrating its known presence throughout the universe. That means that our natural language as humans is the language of energy.

When we talk, we communicate with everything in the universe through the energy we send out from ourselves. And how do we send out our energy to the universe? We do this through our experience. Our experience makes our inner and outer life possible.

Life happens through the experiences of energy formed through our minds.

Experiences occur when we are totally engaged with all of our senses and our minds with something that is occurring. When I experience something, I become an active participant. When I became the hawk, all of me was the hawk. I began to breathe heavily, my heart pounded and I began to sweat. At that moment, I was no longer me, but something more than me.

Remember, we make our lives from the inside out through our inner healing, healing our connections with who we really are.

Like Andrew, your energy constantly expands by confronting energy out of alignment and creating the third entity of energy that is in alignment. That is how you heal, through your aligning your inner experience of energy that creates fulfillment.

Points to Remember:

When we look at something emitting energy, we find that the energy that is being observed is shaped by our view.

The energy in our mind through our view can create change.

All energy everywhere creates its world from the inside out from mind.

Energy can respond to other energy around it.

Energy talks to all other energy at once.

Energy constantly expands by confronting energy out of alignment and creating the third entity of energy that is in alignment.

Affirm:

My mind can create change in the world around me.

Experience:

Think of a situation in which you feel a need for a change. Perhaps you have been trained to put a pretty face on ugly situations and ugly people. You find out your mother in-law is moving and she not only isn't a very nice woman but you live in a cramped two bedroom apartment with a husband and child. You are very upset about this. You're very upset about this but you're also aware that this is recreating a past situation in your life in which you had to put pretty faces on ugly situations and people around you. You have two choices: You can continue to try to cover it up with pink icing, or authentically express your feelings. Imagine that the energy is available for the change to happen. What changes would take place? How would those changes happen? What energy would deplete? What energy would build? How do you support the new change?

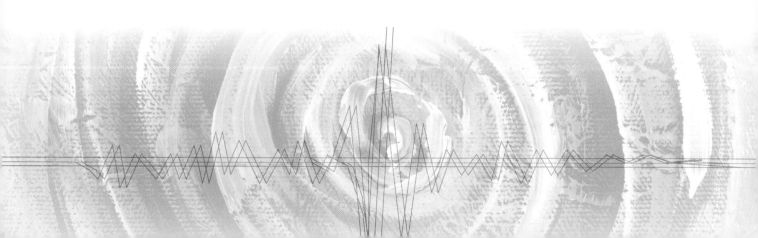

Chapter Nine
Outer Experiences Mirror Inner Experiences

Remember that knowing connects all energy together. Energy can move away from itself and observe itself from another location of energetic knowing. Therefore, energy can see its own form. Suppose you are looking at yourself in the mirror. The "you" within the mirror can actually see the "you" observing it. Yes, it is a little weird, but there is more. The "you" in the mirror can actually make intelligent choices about what it sees. It can choose to bend when you bend and make funny faces at you at the exact same time you do.

Mirrored energy has its own identity. Even though the energy is being reflected back to you in the mirror and looks exactly the same, it still has its own identity and form and it still can make its own choices. It would be like identical twins looking at each other and moving in the exact same fashion. One is mirroring the other, they look the same, but they are two different people. It is the same thing when energy mirrors other energy.

In Andrew's dream, the intruder was mirroring Andrew's unrecognized energy in himself. The intruder had his own identity, however; the intruder was still part of the energy inside of Andrew.

Our experiences outside ourselves act like a mirror for the energy inside ourselves.

In my first shamanic experience, I knew I had become the hawk, but I was still me. I had not lost my sense of who I was. Energy has a natural ability to shape shift, but still keep its own sense of itself. We can learn to tune into and share the identity of energy and other energies can tune into us and share our identity. I can shape shift and feel I am the hawk and the hawk feels my presence.

Energy that mirrors other energy never loses its connection. Energy can be very far away, such as on the other side of the world or on another planet, or it can be hidden from our view within another dimension. No matter where energy is, it can still connect with other energy by mirroring it.

Within our world, tree energy can mirror tree energy, even though there are millions of different trees, because they all emanate "tree" energy. Each tree and tree species, has its own identity and behavior, but still can mirror the essential form of energy created by "tree" energy. Water energy can mirror water energy, no matter if it is frozen in the arctic or in the form of humidity over the Pacific. It is still "water" energy. Dog energy sends out dog energy, no matter if the dog happens to be my muddy black lab or the pampered poodle down the street.

Energy is like musical chords. Each note has as its mirror the chord, as well as the chord mirrors the notes.

What this means for us is that we have an abundance of energetic mirrors to help support us. Somewhere within the universe, our experience is being mirrored. Why? The energy inside of us must form a relationship with energy outside of us to continue our progressive existence. Remember all energy everywhere makes joint agreements in order to exist.

Somewhere within the universe, we are mirroring something's experience. We are connected with all experiences that every single living thing has undergone, whether it is our own experience or not. That means that no matter what we need to help us, it is available to us within our joint experience. If we want to experience faith, courage, and hope, somewhere and somehow, another human, is experiencing exactly what we need.

How do we reach out to that experience? Through our knowledge that the experience we want is happening and we can experience it ourselves. We can choose to experience hope, faith, courage and love, no matter what situation we are in. Its existence within our experience has already happened.

Early on in my life I received many signs that Rochelle was coming into my life. They were as subtle as the street name I lived on, Sparrow Lane, or as blatant as the Sparrow tattoo on my father's arm. I did not consider the significance of the word Sparrow.

Many years later Rochelle told me that when she began therapeutic treatment, she was drawn to buy a painting of two ravens. In Native American culture, ravens witness the stark reality of our lives. I, like Rochelle, have been through many traumatic events. I needed to face the shadows within me... I wanted to know more about myself, who I was, and what I could do. I remember being a very creative child who liked to dance and act. I was also aware I had psychic abilities. As a child, I experienced the loss of many loved ones including my mother, family members, and many friends. I was grief stricken and missed all of them so much. Then I began to have vivid dreams. My mother and all of those who had passed came to me. I could see them and communicate with them. I was not sure if it was okay to tell people what I was experiencing. Later on, when I became an adult, I realized I was psychic and I hid what I knew.

I did know I wanted more from my life than the little Oklahoma town I was born into. Something was missing. So the opportunity came for me to leave my small town life behind and I did.

Eventually, I moved to Phoenix. I began to meditate. I started to receive visions. I desperately needed an outlet to channel my creativity. There was some kind of urgency inside of me to get the visions out. I had to paint them. Then something really strange began to happen. I began to see ravens all over the place. I became afraid and felt as though they were stalking me. At the time I was painting behind closed doors and hid what I was painting from my husband. The ravens continued to follow me. One day, after a raven sat on the hood of my car in the Starbucks' drive-through, I said to it, "Alright I give up; whatever you want to show me, I am willing to see."

Immediately, I left Starbucks. I had to go to Rochelle's house to drop off a book. Rochelle wanted me to see a new painting she had just bought from her weekend in Jerome. We went upstairs to her office and there was a painting of a raven shape shifting into a woman. I was stunned. I shared my story about the ravens with Rochelle and also noticed the other painting she had of the twin ravens. Rochelle noticed my interest and began to tell me her story about facing her trauma through therapy and buying the twin raven painting around the same time. To her, it meant facing all that she had hidden throughout her life. I knew that painting had great meaning to her because she told me it was the one thing she took when she left her first husband.

We started to become friends. One week later, Rochelle walked into my living room while I was painting. She looked at the paintings and asked, "You know what you're doing don't you?" I reluctantly looked up at her and said, with an attitude, "Yes." I was painting the energy I saw around people and within people. Rochelle was fascinated and walked around the living room looking at my numerous portraits. The secret was out.

From that day on, we began to develop a close relationship. We shared the many difficulties of our childhoods as well as the many triumphs of overcoming our wounds. As we grew closer, we began to see that our relationship was not usual. It felt as though we had known each other through our lives as well as many past lives.

One day, Rochelle told me the story of having a vision working with a psychic artist. She looked at me strangely. At that moment, she had an epiphany. She said to me, "You are the psychic artist." All these years, she had thought the raven in the painting represented her shadow. She realized that yes, it was her shadow, but more importantly, it was me. I was her twin raven.

Throughout our lives, we have been mirroring each other's energy. Through all the trauma, through all the work we did to achieve the truth of who we are, we had been connected. We were connected in ways that were not visible, concrete, or understandable. Yet, we knew our connection. We've been working together ever since.

Points to Remember:

Energy can see its own form.

Mirrored energy has its own identity.

Our experiences outside ourselves act like a mirror for the energy inside ourselves.

No matter where energy is, it can still connect with other energy by mirroring it.

We have an abundance of energetic mirrors to help support us.

Affirm:

My outer life mirrors my inner life.

Experience:

Notice your environment, where you live, and the quality of your life. Notice all of the daily situations during your day, the good, the bad, and the ugly. What is happening outside of you is mirroring the energy inside of you. Ask yourself how your outer life is mirroring your inward world. You may want to journal your answer. Examine your answers. Are there patterns? Are there any similarities to your parents and how they live or lived their lives? Are there similarities in the situations that you find yourself in? What do you need to notice most about your outer mirrors in the world around you?

Chapter Ten
Physical Manifestation

Once energy has reached an agreement with all the other energy surrounding it, it can be brought into physical reality. Knowing connects all energy together. Knowing is a feeling state. It is a feeling inside of the mind. Remember all energy has intelligence, mental energy. When the energy within knowing reaches a certain alignment of agreement with other energy, the energy can show itself in third dimensional reality.

We once knew a woman client who wanted a soul mate partnership. We got together with her for lunch and all she spoke of was her ex-husband. When we asked her if she had any thoughts about not being able to let go of him, she denied it, and said she had done a lot of work around letting go of her former husband. The truth of the matter was, she had not let go of her ex-husband. She had not grieved the relationship between herself and her ex-husband. She was not ready to have another relationship.

Therefore, energy must be in agreement with other energy before it can be brought into third dimensional reality. Energy must have an open pathway on the same road in order to join up. Conflicting energy blocking the agreement of alignment will also block the energy from turning into physical matter.

How can you make sure your energy is in alignment? Watch what is being lived out in your life right now and watch how the natural world around you operates. It is mirroring the energy inside of you. Energetic blocks will also be created for you to view outside of you.

Our client, Maria, was fearful about not being able to pay her bills. She was also working at a job that did not pay well. Her job was mirroring her fear about paying her bills. Once she began to focus on the experience of acceptance by herself and others, her value of herself began to increase and her expectations of employment began to change.

A past energetic wound mirrors a past energy inside of the mind. It recreates something that may have occurred long ago in this life or perhaps a past life. In present reality and time, there are several other experiences that could be lived out, but the wound must be consciously recognized first. If the wound is not recognized, it acts as an energetic block.

In Maria's case, when she was a child and organized her closet and room, her mother berated her for not being good enough. If she created her own business of healing people, she may be judged not good enough. This fear was within her unconsciousness. Unconsciously, she believed she was not good enough to help people organize their inner energy toward health.

We take for granted that our past wounds are a reflection of current reality that is "real" to us. What is true is that reality is a moment-by-moment energetic experience inside of you that becomes the mirror of reality outside of you. In Maria's case, she began to experience wanting her own private practice. Energy that was a reflection of her wound began to take on a different form.

The contrast between a developing reality (Maria's own business) and a past reality (you are not capable) became increasingly apparent. Because Maria was becoming more aware of the past energy within her wound, the energy of the past took on outside experiences that she could now see.

People who had different sales businesses in healing products began to knock at Maria's door. They offered quick income seemingly for little investment. They seemed to offer Maria her own independent business, something Maria wanted. However, the products were expensive and did not personally involve Maria's skills and abilities as a healer. These products let Maria off the hook. She could count on the products, rather than herself, to help people. These situations were a reflection of the energy within Maria that said, "You are not good enough." "You cannot do it." "No one will benefit from what you do," and "don't try so hard."

Through guidance, Maria was helped to see that the energy of the healing products business were a reflection of the past energy of her wound. Like magicians, this energy recreates itself outside of ourselves in seemingly attractive ways. They can seduce us into believing in the smokescreen of their existence to keep us involved with them. That way, they do not go away, but they keep their existence within us alive.

Yes, mental energy, energy in our mind, is alive. It seeks to express its life. It has its own intelligence and ability to think, to become a part of our life outside of us. This energy, like the energy that created the healing product business opportunities, is not "wrong" or "evil." The energy displays itself for one reason and one reason only. To show us that we can create a solution in keeping in alignment with Universal Mind: to learn, to grow, and to expand.

Points to Remember:

Energy must be in agreement with other energy before it can be brought into third dimensional reality.

Conflicting energy blocking the agreement of alignment will also block the energy from showing itself in third dimensional reality.

Energetic blocks will also be created for you to view outside of you.

Reality is a moment-by-moment energetic experience inside of you that becomes the mirror of reality outside of you.

Energy in our mind is alive. It seeks to express its life.

Affirm:

The energy within my mind mirrors the world outside of my mind.

Experience:

In the morning, when you wake up, imagine one small thing you would like to know more about. Perhaps it is a conflict at work, a medical issue with your dog, or a difficulty in your marriage. Perhaps it is to know more about your life purpose or a career decision. Ask for a mirror from the universe that can give you more information about your current situation. Now, watch for any symbols or events during the day that provide more meaning for you about the situation.

Chapter Eleven
Physical Un-manifestation

All matter is made up of energy. Energy can become matter and matter can become energy. It is just like different forms of water. Water can be frozen, it can melt and become water again, or it can evaporate into steam and disappear before your very eyes! Energy does the same thing. It can suddenly appear or suddenly vanish.

One time, my daughter lost her "blankie." *Oh my God.* The crying and screaming was enough to burst our eardrums. My husband and I tore her room apart. We looked everywhere: the closet, the dressers and the bed. It had vanished! My daughter was frantic and we were too!

Later that day, we went to the water park. I rented a water tube and gently allowed myself to roll with the waves in the wave pool. I stated to my guides and placed into my knowing that my daughter's blankie was safe and sound at home. I believed my daughter would be reunited with her blankie that night.

When we returned home, my daughter went into her room, opened her dresser drawer to get dry clothes and much to her astonishment, there was blankie! I knew it was not there before; both my husband and myself ripped that dresser apart. But there was blankie, present and accounted for and the only item in that drawer.

How did this happen? Pretend you have a bright red ball. Now throw it from one room to the next. You see the bright red ball and throw it from your kitchen to the living room and it rolls under the couch. You can't see it anymore, because it is hidden under the furniture.

Well, guess what? It is the same way with dimensions. You can't see all of the dimensions energy resides in. When energy shifts from our world to another dimension, it becomes hidden. However, the energy itself does not disappear. It shifts location.

In these different locations, energy still retains its own identity. It may be somewhere that you can't see it, but it still exists. All that we have loved and lost through death, are not truly dead. Energy lives on in ways we can't fathom or see. The existence of energy continues. Our dead pets and our dear dead loved ones have just changed their place of residence. They live somewhere else.

Even though we may not see energy in its different location and existence, it can continue to communicate. It communicates with other energy around it and even, with some of us here, in our three dimensional world. Those who have tuned into their natural human skills, which some people call psychic, like ourselves, can talk to people who have passed on and other beings in inter-dimensional space. These people and beings have retained their ability to communicate, because their form has remained intact.

Your intuition and your intuitive prompts are a form of communication with something that exists that you do not see. You can label it the spirits, your gut instincts, or your guardian angels. Regardless of the label, the communication is present. Remember, you cannot control how these spirits communicate with you.

We once had a client who was very wealthy and new to his spiritual path. His wife had recently died. His assistant contacted us and arranged an appointment. During his phone session, he wanted and demanded direct communication from his wife. He wanted to know about an exact saying they had between them. What came through was not the saying, to his great disappointment, but that she would present a sign to him within twenty four hours that she could communicate with him. The sign would involve jewelry. The next day, my client went into a closet that he had cleaned out the previous day. He knew nothing was in that closet, however, in the middle of the floor, sat his wife's jewelry box. He was shocked.

When energy depletes while it is physical, as in aging, it still retains its memory of how it was when it was young. In fact, energy remembers how it was throughout its lifespan in reality. When energy becomes disconnected from our reality, it can shift into a form from its life within our reality.

Perhaps when you communicate with your loved one who has passed on, maybe in a dream, they may appear to you as though they were young. They may sound healthy, appear vital and they are. They have taken on a preferred form from their life on earth.

Points to Remember:

Energy can become matter and matter can become energy.

When energy shifts from our three dimensional world to another dimension, it becomes hidden.

Even though we may not see energy in its different location and existence, it can continue to communicate.

Your intuition, which acts as a spiritual pull to do something, is a form of communication with something that exists that you do not see.

When energy depletes while it is physical, as in aging, it still retains its memory of how it was when it was young.

Affirm:

Even though I cannot see energy, it still exists.

Experience:

Ask for an unseen energy to communicate with you. Perhaps it may be your pet, friend, or family member who has passed over to the other side of the veil. There are many ways communication can take place. The most common way is through dreams. You may also experience seeing an item not in its usual place, feel your loved one near you, smell a scent, even feel a slight touch. All of these are signs that your loved one can talk to you, even though they live someplace else.

Chapter Twelve
Law of Relationship

The energy of your thoughts and inner experiences will form a mirrored relationship with the same type of energy it is, although it may look differently. In our work with families, the same energy often exists between all family members without their awareness.

Our client, Mark, had a strong issue with his son-in-law. Mark is a healer working on building his practice in another country. Even though he is not from this country, he feels at home there and believes the people that reside there are his true family. However, he has been working on returning to the other country for many years, and was just about to go there when he saw me.

He had blood pressure problems that were not stabilized by the medication he was taking. I immediately got "anger" and "non-recognition" from my painting the energy he was emitting. I asked him what he was troubled about. He was becoming increasingly upset with his son-in-law, who told him he wasn't going to "make it" in the business he was building overseas. Mark, in his words, "just wanted to pop him one." I got the energy of "father" and asked him if this situation reminded him of his father in any way. Mark then talked about how his father never encouraged him, supported him, or gave him any recognition for his talents. I asked Mark to do a meditation with his deceased father with the painting in view, to speak with him about his hurt.

Mark recognized that his anger was not about his son-in-law at all, but about his father. He also recognized that his son-in-law had a similar situation with his own father, who was not able to give Mark support because of his own wounds.

The energy within Mark's son-in-law matched the energy within Mark like a hand in a well fitting glove. The energy in both of them immediately moved to unite. Once Mark was able to see that the issue was not about his son-in-law, but about his father, his anger immediately dissipated and his reactions changed toward his son-in-law. The energy within Mark moved towards his father and dissolved towards his son-in-law. Energy exists in all dimensions at once. Therefore, the energy that existed within Mark was from another time

and place, but existed within the present time. Mark did not realize that the anger was not generated from his son-in-law. Once Mark understood what the issue was really about, his father, the energy within Mark changed its location and his view of the situation expanded.

Your mind helps you to determine your relationship with the energy around you.

Mental energy is within all energy. Because energy already contains mental energy, it wants to form a relationship with the energy in your mind. Think of it this way: You have a large ball. This ball has, within it, all of the energy of the universe. This ball is the mind of the universe. Inside this huge ball are billions of other balls, like golf balls. One of these golf balls is your mind.

Your mind is already connected to the energy within the Universal Mind. The energy within your mind will simultaneously recreate itself so that it can recognize itself by creating mirrors. Imagine that your mind is a red golf ball. Your mind does not see itself as red. However, what your mind sees are many red golf balls. Mirrors of red golf balls reflect the energy of your mind.

Your mind is situated inside the Universal Mind or Source to do one thing: determine the direction of energetic flow of energy toward building or toward depletion.

You are living your life, moment by moment, as the energy in your mind creates mirrored images of itself.

You are empowered through the universe to get more of what you want by being aware of the energy you want to build and deplete energy you do not want to expand. However, the energy within your mind must be in alignment with the energy you are experiencing within yourself. Contrary energy will also make its appearance outside of yourself, blocking the flow and dissolving the alignment. Why? Further awareness of your inner wounds needs recognition.

Contrary energy shows itself to you for one reason only: so that you may heal.

Back to Maria; sometimes she believes she can start her own business, sometimes she doesn't. She is blocking her energy with contrary energy, which manifests in her life as she starts and stops developing clientele.

The energy within the unconscious, subconscious, and conscious mind will equally express itself through mirrored energy. Energy does not make moral decisions. It doesn't say in its own mind, well, she really wants her own business and that is what we should create. It says, well, sometimes she does and sometimes she doesn't. The energy outside Maria reflects the energetic identity inside of Maria.

Sometimes Maria has opportunities for private clients. As we talked about before, Maria has an unconscious fear that she does not deserve her own business, that somehow she is not good enough. Her fear developed out of her parents simultaneously physically abusing her, and then rescuing her, by providing her with material items and money when she needed it. She felt that she deserved punishment because she was bad and was too inadequate to provide for herself. Her fear was projected into the space in which she wanted to have her massage business. She worried if the space would be big enough, private enough, or nice enough. Of course, she wondered if the massage room was good enough and unconsciously wondered if her talents, abilities, and skills were good enough. Maria's fears made it very difficult for her to organize her massage room. She was struggling to conquer her fear and at the same time develop trust in her truth that she deserved to be valued for her healing touch.

Your unconscious connection with energy is just as powerful as your conscious and subconscious connection. Maria criticized her lack of motivation as laziness or that there was something wrong with her. Why couldn't she get it together? Maria needed help with understanding the unconscious energy, which made it difficult for her to organize her massage room. Once she understood the unconscious energy of "I am not good enough," she was able to build up the energy of "I am good enough" and "I am safe to express who I am" without fear of danger.

Maria wanted her own business. That was the intention and the direction she was pointing the energy in her mind toward. She was clear in what she wanted, and her mind identified the experience she wanted, independence. Now, the energy within her unconscious mind needed to get in line with her conscious intent. However, something showed up that got in her way. Some of her wounded energy caused her to become unmotivated to fix up her massage space.

The fact was that she was taught to be unmotivated toward creating her own independence by her abusive parents. If she tried to accomplish anything on her own, she received criticism, or worse. To accomplish, in Maria's experience, equaled abuse.

As stated previously, one experience in Maria's life highlighted her belief of accomplishing equaling abuse. It was the day she completely took apart and reorganized her closet. Her mother bitterly criticized her and told her she was a failure.

Maria had to create a solution. To accomplish success in organizing, does not have to equal abuse, but can equal something else.

The tool to recognizing unconscious energy that is creating blocks in your life is to experience your fears, inhibitions, shame, and guilt and to become aware of their origin. Look at the blocks outside your life. They mirror your inward blocks. Open your mind and your heart to these emotions without judgment and self blame to help create a third solution. The third solution resolves energy inside of you that wants outside expression by depleting energetic blocks.

What is the third solution? It is what you want. It is the experience that you want to have in your life. What would self value feel like? Meditate, breathe, and focus on self value. Focus on the energy in total; have it be the energy you want. Shape shift into feeling within yourself a knowing of your healing ability and it will eventually shift all other energy within your unconsciousness, subconsciousness, and consciousness to align with it.

However, in order to shift the energy that is no longer serving you, you must first accept its place within you. That may mean requiring you to consciously acknowledge its existence.

Each day, my guidance presents me with energy to focus on and experience for my better good. Day after day, they were giving me "ancestral" energy. I would have the experience of the ancestors all around me and feel their presence within me.

I knew that, for years, in my therapy, I accepted my feelings about my ancestors. My mother constantly told me I was not part of the family and no one wanted me. I was aware of my feelings, and that what she said to me was not my fault. However, sometimes, what happens to us in childhood can run so deeply within us, it can affect our inner experiences in many ways. It can affect us in ways we may not be able to put into words; that we need more than the combination of a therapist and ourselves to help heal. We need the energy from the Universal Mind to help us overcome and heal our wounds. We cannot heal alone.

One day, I was getting my nails done. My guides gave me "ancestor" energy. I settled back in my spa chair and began to meditate on "ancestor" energy. I heard an audible crack with my physical ears. Layers of energy peeled away from me. First, it was a feeling of "badness," then "shame." In that moment, I realized my ancestors wanted me. I realized what my mother had told me from birth was not true, that my mother just did not want a connection with me. Now, I knew that intellectually, but I never experienced that feeling inside of me before.

That night, when I returned home, there was a card from a private detective on my door. My niece had been trying to get a hold of me for years and finally had. We had become disconnected when she was a child, because of my family addictions and dysfunction. Now, we could be united again.

You can become the experience of the energy you want to create, through the organizing tool of your mind. You can focus your mind on the energy you want inside of you, build it and crack the wall that keeps you from expansion.

Intentional Energy

Your intentions from your thoughts, feelings, and experiences must be in alignment in order for physical matter to organize into a pattern that becomes three dimensional. Your intention chooses a direction for the energy within your mind to build. It is like you are at a crossroads. On the right is one road, and on the left is another. Your mind through your intentions chooses which way to go.

Through your intentions, you can place your thoughts, feelings, and experience within the space of knowing. In knowing, all energy is connected and forms an alignment with all dimensions, both hidden and visible. Within this space, universal energetic alignments adjust, organize, communicate, form relationships and change locations. Once harmonized into similar vibrations, the energetic alliances can gain density and change location. The energy inside of you shows up outside of you.

Your knowing is connected to your mind and the Universal Mind, all at once. It is in all dimensions at once, and it knows the contents of those dimensions, because it communicates and carries within it the knowledge of those dimensions.

I could not have orchestrated the contact with my niece on my own. The energy did it for us both. All I did was focus on the energy, knew it inside of me and experienced it inside of me. The card then showed up on my door! And the blankie showed up in the dresser.

Energy becomes real, because the universe does it for you. Your part of it is to place your intentions, feelings and experiences in your mind, in your own knowing, and heal your wounds.

You know that the universe is there to support the expansion of energy inside of you. Why? The universe's job is to expand.

Then, once you placed your intentions, feelings, and experiences of the identity of what you want inside of your knowing, then a relationship with energy in the universe begins. You have turned on the switch of the mechanics of the universe to "on." The identifying energy within your knowing is released into the universe to form mirrors with other energy.

First there is Universal Mind or Source, then there is you or the Self, then there is the energy of experience. All of this energy is porous, like a colander for spaghetti. Source, Self, and Experience pour out their energy from a central point of connection as one. Think of your aura emanating energy from you. There is you, then your aura. Think of the aurora borealis at the north pole, or the aurora australis at the south pole, sending out energy into the atmosphere. All energy interfaces with all other energy by sending out an aura from a central point.

The Law of Relationship states that the three energy systems: Universal Mind called Source, Self, and Experience are what joins together inside of you to create energy outside of you.

Source, Self, and Experience is the road that brings energy from Source through you to make your life experiences real. Energy sifts through Source, Self, and Experience and pours out into our dimension, where we can see it.

Points to Remember:

The energy of your thoughts and inner experiences will form a mirrored relationship with the same type of energy it is.

You are empowered through the universe to get more of what you want by being aware of the energy you want to build and deplete energy you do not want to expand.

The energy within the unconscious, subconscious, and conscious mind will equally express itself.

The tool to recognizing unconscious energy that is creating blocks in your life is to experience your fears, inhibitions, shame, and guilt and to become aware of their origin.

The third solution resolves energy inside of you that wants outside expression by depleting energetic blocks.

We need the energy from the Universal Mind to help us overcome and heal our wounds. We cannot heal alone.

You can become the experience of the energy you want to create, through the organizing tool of your mind. You can focus your mind on the energy you want inside of you.

Intentional Energy

Your intention chooses a direction for the energy within your mind to build.

Energy becomes real, because the universe does it for you.

The identifying energy within your knowing is released into the universe to form mirrors with other energy.

The Law of Relationship states that the three energy systems, Source, Self, and Experience, are what join together inside of you to create energy outside of you.

Affirm:

I am empowered through the universe to get more of what I want by being aware of the energy I want to build and deplete energy I do not want to expand.

Experience:

Breathe in deeply and become very quiet. Relax your body and meditate. What emotional experiences are you having? Ask yourself where these emotions stemmed from. Let the memories become apparent to you. Know that you are not responsible for whatever happened to you. Practice unconditional self regard. What you are now responsible for is creating a third solution. What emotional experience would be the third solution? Is it self acceptance? Love? What would it feel like?

Chapter Thirteen
Energy Shifts

Energy can shift immediately into a different location. You are not fated to feel or be in a situation that you do not want. By shifting your energy into a different location, you immediately begin a different relationship with energy.

Like many of our clients who have had difficult childhoods, they are sometimes consumed by the trauma that had occurred when they were young. They feel they are unwanted, unloved, and abandoned. When they can shift their energy inside of them to a feeling of being lovable, they literally change the location of their inner experience. Suddenly, they are no longer experiencing a past trauma. In terms of time, they are in the present. Their minds are now in a different location. In terms of looking at themselves, they are not seeing themselves from the position of not lovable. They changed the location of the view of themselves to a different perspective, to the position of lovable. Like the ball that traveled from one room to another, the different perspective became an expanded perspective.

You already make these kinds of shifts all of the time with your energy. It is just that no one has ever explained it to you like this before.

Remember your mind as the golf ball within the larger ball? Now think of this. Your golf ball mind acts like a womb that contains the energy that can become reality. Your mind contains, or wraps around, the energy that can become physical. Your mind cannot complete the transition. Your mind organizes an experience inside of you. The experience inside of you directs other universal energy to organize outside of you. However, you won't know in exactly what way this happens, don't worry, we have no idea either.

If you were to take away your physical body, the energy of who you are would still exist. It would be like you evaporated into a cloud and you, as the cloud, contain everything needed to create what is in existence upon earth.

The cloud to create everything on earth is within your mind. This cloud, this energy, is directed by the intentional thoughts, feelings, and experiences within your mind. Depending upon which way the wind is blowing, you can change the direction of this cloud to change your experiences. Immediately afterwards, your view also changes. You see more. Ever have an "aha" moment? Since I have been in therapy for years, I can say I have had my share! It is the recognition of new information, something that instantaneously enters your mind that completely discounts what you believed was true a moment before.

Remember, your mind is a tool for organizing energy. As a tool for organizing energy, it also holds energy, just like a womb with an unborn baby inside.

One of my business associates decided that she wanted to fulfill a lifelong dream. She wanted her own production company, a company that would create the spiritual shows to help educate people about how the spirits work through us to create our life outside of us. I wanted to help her realize this dream, so each morning, we got together and channeled out messages and focused upon our energy for the day. At the time, she had a minimum-wage job, and I was still trying to transition from being a therapist into a full-time trance channel and writer.

Each day, we talked with the guides. The guides helped us confront the issues inside of ourselves that needed to be healed. We also put into our circle our intentions from the guides: an optimal job for my business associate and a transition from my current job for myself. We began to develop television programs about spirit. Some people came into our lives and stayed, while others, who were not entirely aligned with our inner healing came and left. My partner created her optimal job, which was spiritual in nature, and I made my transition. As time went by, we did all we could to ready ourselves for our production company, but we still needed one more thing: money.

Our guidance had suggested that my business associate was going to make a strong friendship within her current job situation. Well she did. And it was not only a strong friendship, because of their joint vision of educating people about the spirit, but this individual had the capital to invest in our venture. In fact, he had the full amount of capital.

Most people may have thought we were insane from the beginning. At first, we had no money, no connections to speak of and no way to get money. From a "logical" point of view, why waste our time? But being a little out of the ordinary, both my business associate and I operated from one place only; our inner connections with energy.

This means that you too can detach from the viewpoints of people around you and independently form your own experiences. You can create the substantive energy within you to change the world. And to accomplish this, you do not have to be the richest, smartest, or strongest person on earth. All you have to do is work on your healing and be clear in choosing your inner experiences that expand your view.

Dense Energy

If the energy within you is dense, strong, and creating an experience within you that you know is true, you can heal emotional wounds, diseases, and injuries. The internal power of the energetic experience within your mind can make the energy within your emotions and physical body shift into another location to make another creation. The energy that you create can be self healing. It can mirror back exactly what you need.

Okay, by now, you may be asking what we mean by shift into location. You may not get it. You may wake up and your bedroom is still the same, your wife is lying next to you, and the dog wants to go out.

The energy within your mind contains memory. Memory acts as a matrix to create a time line to understand the development of your experiences. If your experiences happened all at once, it would be hard to understand them or to sort them out.

As we have said before, your mind is a tool for organizing energy. In your mind is your memory. Your memory also organizes energy in a time line that makes sense to you. Because your memory is a organizing tool, sort of like a elaborate closet organizer, it can recall experiences that are both unconscious and conscious. It can remember times throughout your physical existence where you have healed your body, overcome trauma, and gained strength from an emotional struggle. Your memory can provide the experience of healing. And the memory we are talking about does not have to be from this lifetime.

Your memory also remembers one of your past experiences of dying in the physical, leaving this realm, and relocating to live in another dimensional space. It remembers the death and remembers awakening in other realms as whole, alive, and well.

I once had a dream. I was brought into a temple, a hall, in a white silk Chinese robe with embroidered designs. This temple was quite beautiful and I was beautifully dressed in my elegant robe. Underneath this robe, I was naked. A woman was sitting behind me. She wrapped her arms in front of me and took a knife and began to cut me. I noticed others in the hall dressed in robes were being cut the same way. I then communicated to my torturer that I wanted her to end my life. With one quick wound up my arm, I lost consciousness.

I did not know where I was. I was in this dark world, alone, and not able to see anything. I had a sense I was dead, although I did not have a clear thought that I was dead. In fact, nothing was clear. It was sort of like being in a place where all there was, was a sense of tension. I felt as though something needed to happen but I did not know how to make it happen or what was supposed to happen. I was deeply alone.

Suddenly, I awoke. I was at a long table with other people, women. I was ecstatic. I was alive. I was alive!! I could not believe I was alive! There were others at the table, but how could I tell them what just happened? They would not understand! In the background, out of my vision, I heard singing. I knew it was Quan Yin, Buddhist goddess of mercy, singing to me to come to her, although I could not see her.

Your memory can recall these times of reawakening and you can regain this experience to come alive. You can believe and know you are whole and healed, because the energy within your mind remembers itself as immortal. Your mental experience can create the healing you choose.

Remember Maria? She believed that she was unworthy of being loved and she had feelings of depression related to that experience. Maria wanted her own massage business, because she knew she had an ability to heal. She needed to make this business happen, not for money or status, but to heal her inner relationship with who she truly was. She needed to reclaim her identity.

Our outer experience reflects our relationship with our inner self. If we are disconnected with our inner self, such as if we believe we are not wanted, we will feel pain. However, we can work to heal the pain.

Our relationship with Source must also reflect the identifying characteristics of Source. We know what Source is through the concepts of universal law. We know Source wants to expand, wants to express and wants to create. If we are stuck in a belief that is not allowing us to expand, express, and create, we are not in alignment with Source. What we will be in, is conflict and pain, because we are not in alignment with ourselves, Source, and what we want to experience.

We can shift our alignment with Source, ourselves, and our experience. We can do this by practicing and becoming aware of universal law.

Universal laws are maps of the roadway of how energy flows from Source to ourselves to develop experience. In order to be able to use the map, we must begin to understand that our relationship with Source and ourselves must be direct. That means that any outside interference, such as another belief system from culture, religion, or your parents, must become null and void.

There is empowerment in your direct connection with energy. We believe that within our society, there are many cultural structures that wish to take away your empowerment. We believe these systems go to great lengths to brainwash you to disconnect from yourself and Source. We believe these organizations use fear, guilt, and shame as tools to keep people disconnected. However, we believe we have power. We have the power to heal through our inner connections.

We once did a radio show with the intention of helping people heal their physical bodies. All the listeners and ourselves formed a healing circle within our minds. We put people who wanted healing inside of the circle. Some people experienced physical shifts; for example, one lady healed her back pain. The energy generated from all of us making the healing circle crashed the radio show computers, and took us off the air. Unfortunately, we were prohibited from doing a healing circle on air again because of technological malfunctions, although we did many shows afterwards on different topics.

Energy Impacts

Like the people in our healing circle, the way you perceive the world with your energetic thoughts, feelings, and experiences can be healing to the world and people within it.

Your thoughts, feelings, and experiences impact the energy inside of you. Any impact creates a change. This change then moves out into the world around you. The vibrations you send out create mirrored relationships with other vibrations throughout three-dimensional space. Sometimes, you see these relationships form in physical reality, and sometimes you don't. Sometimes, these relationships form in such subtle ways; it almost looks like they are not there.

When I was in fourth grade, I became a sexual assault victim. When my daughter reached fourth grade, she began to have problems adjusting to school. She had difficulty sleeping at night and was very stressed about her grades. Through examination of my inner energy, I became aware of an energy I was projecting to my daughter that said, "It is dangerous to grow up." To help my daughter, and myself, I had to bring this energy to consciousness, realize where it came from, how it did not reflect the truth of the moment and begin to be aware of the reality of life. It is fun to experience living!

That night, after my energetic recognition, my daughter began to sleep and over time became much less stressed. Healing myself helped heal my daughter.

If you send out the perception to the world, that healing can happen, the impact of your intentions, feelings, and experiences form a relationship with other like energy that shifts into the experience of healing. The completion of healing relies upon a direct connection with the Universal Mind that supplies the needed energy to create a conclusion.

It is wonderful when the energy of healing creates a call to the Universal Mind or Source, and the Source ricochets a mirror back and fulfills the energetic request through the experience of healing.

The response of Source is immediate. However, our vision of how Source responded may not be clear. Because we are human, we have a very limited view of how our intended thoughts, feelings, and experiences conclude. It is like we are ants. We are able to see the bread crumb we have carried into our nest, but not be able to see how the food has nurtured the whole colony.

Because the energy within Universal Mind is whole and complete as is, all requests can be manufactured within a whole and complete form. In other words, think of this, you may have heard miracle stories of how people have survived and overcome physical obstacles, no matter what they have been. You may have read the story in the paper about the child who beat the odds with brain damage and was told he will never walk again. I knew a man who recovered from liver cancer. He declined chemotherapy because he knew he could heal himself. He uncovered the unconscious energy hiding in his liver that represented the anger against his father. His father did not accept him because he was homosexual. His father also had problems with his own sexuality that he projected upon his son. The son worked with the energy of non-acceptance and anger in meditation with Source to uncover his inward experiences. He was able to become aware of his anger and shame and change the energy to self acceptance and love.

When you read about miracles, they are situations where people drew energy from Source, as well as the energy we all place out into the world. Our beliefs that miracles are possible and that the universe can see us as whole and complete, no matter what injury we have sustained can heal us. In addition, our energy automatically helps people and Source see the situation as automatically and completely healed.

Our connection with Source, ourselves, and our experiences, makes us powerful. When we connect, we become very powerful human beings.

Higher Source

If you think you are too small to create a difference, think again. You have within you a very powerful ally, as big as the whole universe. Therefore, what you do with your energy can affect the known universe. Remember Gandhi and Mother Theresa. Both were humble individuals who created powerful changes throughout our world because of their internal connection to the limitless availability of energy within the Universal Mind.

You have limitless resources within you to create unlimited change. Your energy cannot, by its very nature, act alone. It is always connected to energetic supplies that are infinite.

It is the infinite supply of energy that people sometimes call the Universal Mind, Source, or God. Universal mental energy, Source, or God, continually act in response to our energy. That means that our roots were in the form of pure energy or mind. We come from mind. We always were, and still are, energetic mental energy. Our relationship with mental energy has not changed, but we have forgotten this relationship and think there is a disconnection between ourselves and universal energy. The reality is that, because our mental energy is the same mental energy within the universal energy, the Universal Mind cannot disconnect from us.

God and ourselves work in continual tandem to create and modify the world around us. We see with the eyes of God and God sees the world through our eyes. Together there is creation.

God responds to us through our relationships with God. If our relationship is strong in belief, certainty, and knowing, our responses will mirror the connection with greater acceleration and application. It is our certainty of God that makes creations certain. It is the power of our knowing that applies the energetic principles in force. God creates with us and we create with God. We know this and our knowing makes it so.

Points to Remember:

Energy can shift immediately into a different location.

The cloud to create everything on earth is within your mind.

You can create the substantive energy within you to change the world.

Dense Energy

If the energy within you is dense, strong, and creating an experience within you that you know is true, you can heal emotional wounds, diseases, and injuries.

The energy within your mind contains memory.

Your mental experience can create the healing you choose.

We can shift our alignment with Source, ourselves, and our experience.

There is empowerment in your direct connection with energy.

Energy Impacts

The way you perceive the world with your energetic thoughts, feelings, and experiences can be healing to the world and people within it.

The completion of healing relies upon a direct connection with the Universal Mind that supplies the needed energy to create a conclusion.

Because the energy within Universal Mind is whole and complete as is, all requests can be manufactured within a whole and complete form.

Our connection with Source, ourselves, and our experiences, makes us powerful.

Higher Source

What you do with your energy can affect the whole universe.

You have limitless resources within you to create unlimited change.

We see with the eyes of God and God sees the world through our eyes. Together there is creation.

Affirm:

Through my energy, I have a built-in relationship with God.

Experience:

After you read this exercise, close your eyes and imagine this, you are have just become a rose. A beautiful red rose. Breathe deeply and relax your body. You are in a room that is full of light. The room is your favorite color and there are flowers all around you. Take a deep breath. What does the room smell like? What does it feel like to be in this room? What emotions are you experiencing? How does your body feel? Is the room cool or warm? Take a deep breath. You have just shifted your mind to another location. By becoming the experience of the rose, you have created a relationship with other like energy that has become physical right before your eyes. Your world has changed.

Chapter Fourteen
The Universal Law of Opposites

In our work, we identify energy. As we talked about, energy has its own unique characteristics, or stamp of identification. Just like no two thumbprints look exactly the same, energy also has an identifying variation. There is dog energy, but each dog is different, just as each tree is different and each person is different.

Therefore, all energy is not the same. Why? Energy has different vibrations. Energy moves in different formations of vibrations and travels in different dimensions, sometimes in places we cannot see. Energy can also shape itself and appear flat or like a wave.

Think of it this way. We have our world. Look at a date book, notebook, or magazine lying around the house. Imagine that one page of your, let's say, magazine, is our universe. It is one page amongst several other pages. Now imagine that you have just pushed a pencil through all of the pages of your magazine, from the front towards the back. Your pencil is now going through all of the pages of your magazine.

Just imagine for a moment that the pencil is an energetic vibration. It is not only going through the page that is our world, but all of the other pages too, which are all in different dimensions. We can see the part of the pencil that is in our world, but we cannot see the parts that are in other worlds. The part of the pencil that is in other dimensions is hidden from us.

We know from science that when energy is observed, it takes on a form and can change shape.

Remember, it is our joint agreement regarding the identity of energy that helps form energy. The toy is the toy because we have all agreed upon its identity as the toy. Then, we see the toy. Our observation of energy in agreement with the Universal Mind helps form the energetic identity of the "toy."

Through our viewpoint, we help change the shape of energy and it can take on different forms. Through our agreement with the Universal Mind that the toy is a toy, we help shape energy to reveal a toy. That means that the way we look at energy, the way we observe it from inside of ourselves, can help change the shape of what we observe outside of ourselves.

The way we see the world from our experience inside of us, creates our experience of the world outside of ourselves. The Law of Opposites forms a paradoxical structure so that we constantly create life through the choice of our inner experience.

Not only do we make joint agreements about our energetic experiences, but we can make independent agreements inside our minds as to how we view our world.

We can make choices of how we see our world, because energy creates a myriad of choices that fills in all the spaces between opposing viewpoints.

Imagine you and a friend are standing on the side of the road looking at the Memorial Day parade float by. Your friend sees the beginning of the first float because she is at the opposite end of the road and you are looking at the last float go by. There are several hundred people between the two of you who create their own point of view of the same floats going by. Everyone has chosen where to stand, so that they can get the best view. And this is the most wonderful thing of all; everyone is seeing the parade differently, although they are all looking at the same parade.

The law of opposites offers us choice on how we can see our world, even when we have made joint agreements about what we see in our world.

Everyone at the parade is seeing floats go by. Some may think the floats are beautiful, some feel inspired, some grateful and, perhaps some just feel excited. The inner experience of their view colors what is seen and makes what is seen real. Your choices in how you see the world can make what you see real.

A client of ours was beginning to be pulled towards public speaking engagements. He wanted to talk about his spiritual development; however, he felt a sense of anxiety whenever he imagined talking to an audience. In one session, the guides suggested that he identified public speaking with his abusive father, a minister. Although he wanted to talk about spirituality, he felt that no one wanted to hear what he had to say. The energy of identifying with his abusive father colored the imagined outcome of his speaking engagements. The reality was that the universe supported his continuing spiritual development by helping to provide him with invitations to become a speaker at holistic events.

The universe was presenting our client with opposing choices: to talk or not to talk, to hide what he truly is or to show people who he was. Both of his views could create reality.

Energetic Speed

Energy moves at different rates of speed. Energy can accelerate or slow down. Different rates of speed create different levels of vibration. Different levels of vibration manifest differently. Higher levels of vibration in space can result in dying, but higher levels of vibration can also result in astral travel, dream states and inter-dimensional communication.

However, there are even more surprises that may not make conventional sense.

It is not the rate of the speed of the vibration which determines when it will reach its destination. It could be like this: You see two Ferraris coming down the highway. One is going 130 miles per hour and one is going 60 miles per hour. They are both going to the car wash where you work. You are expecting the Ferrari that is going 130 miles per hour to reach you first. But in the world of vibration, even though one is going faster than the other, they both arrive at the car wash at the same time.

One more surprise. Now both Ferraris have arrived at the car wash. One is in park and revving up the engine to 140 miles per hour and slowly begins to disappear. Because of the rate of its vibration, it is relocating into a different dimensional space, one in which we cannot see. Different speeds of vibration determine different vibration levels.

Remember the hidden parts of the pencil? One part is vibrating at a different rate of speed than the other.

Let's go back to our cars. Both of these experiences happen instantaneously, within a moment. One moment the Ferrari that is going 130 miles per hour is at the car wash, the next it has disappeared while parked and revving up its engine to 140 miles per hour. Because of the speed of its vibration, it has moved into another location and a different vibration level, hidden from you!

Slowed down vibrations create denser materializations. In our world, energetic vibrations are slowed down enough to create materializations that appear stable. The furniture, your car, the office, all appear concrete, you might even say "real." The truth of the matter is that the energetic vibration of these materializations is so slow that the appearances of the vibrations themselves appear to be still.

When we shift our energy inside of ourselves to a different vibration, the energy outside of ourselves also shifts. As Cortney always says, what we observe always matches the internal vibration of our energy.

What does this mean in concrete terms? Well, let me give you an example. One of our clients is working to develop a home-based healing practice. As a child, she had been physically abused by her father as her mother watched. As she worked through her issues, our client was becoming increasingly confident about her ability to have a successful practice. She shifted her internal energy to a different vibration level. Then, she began to become fearful about having enough money. She called one of her clients, who had been emotionally inappropriate with her in the past. She knew he would make an appointment and pay her. She also knew he would not pay her what she was worth and she was putting herself at risk to be emotionally bullied.

The client, as predicted, began to tell her that her healing was inadequate, not good enough and why should he pay for it? Our client began to buy into his put downs. He left, not paying her what she should have gotten and making her feel ashamed of herself for not escorting the client out of her office as soon as he began to put her down or inviting him in the first place.

What happened? When our client was a child, she watched her mother over and over again egg her father on to beat her. Our client would feel trapped with nowhere to go. She would feel she had no choice but to endure the beatings.

Believing she had no money, to her, was a concrete reality. What having no money actually mirrored was the experience of feeling trapped when she was a child. She was afraid, could not breathe and felt she could do nothing and go nowhere. Why? Because the people who were supposed to value her most did not.

Our client did not have a healthy protective mother, so she role-modeled herself after the mother she had.

She inwardly became passive, without making boundaries when someone would bully her.

Now, our client was becoming strong enough to begin to act to develop her own healing business. In valuing her healing abilities, other energy that did not value her began to become quite apparent. The contrast of valuing self and skills and not valuing self and skills became more noticeable in our client's energy inside of herself. The contrast of these different levels of energy manifested outside of our client for her to view. Why? Because our client was "mothering" her own child which was the beginning of her business. She began to mother her business in the only way she knew how, by being non-protective of her skills, abilities, and most of all, her value.

Because she literally called in this experience, she was now able to see the energy she no longer wanted to experience for herself outside of herself. She could experience the freedom of not being trapped and having choices, because that was the true reflection of reality she was currently in.

In this way, what we see is always a mirror of our internal energy. All of our client's inward experiences, such as feeling trapped, scared, and ashamed, have their own energetic vibration. Some of this energy was hidden from our client and she was not aware of it. For example, she was not aware of the un-protective mother energy "mothering" her business. Once this energy became apparent to her, because of the contrast they presented in her life, then she could choose another vibration of energy: freedom and choice.

The situations we are in and the people we are with are reflections of the energetic vibration levels inside of ourselves. We are always seeing our world from our energy inside of ourselves.

Now you may be saying, well, how do I change the energy I have inside of me? There is only one answer: by healing with the energy inside of you.

Energetic Healing

What do we mean by healing? Healing means developing the strongest connection possible between Source, yourself, and your experience. The connection will allow you the full expression of the unified alignment of the truth of who you are.

Through healing, the different levels of energetic vibration create different things.

The level of energetic vibration inside of you, helps you see the world outside of you. The energetic frequencies of your energy combine together in a harmonic level, creates a relationship with the energy outside of you. It is these different levels of energetic vibration that build or deplete events, situations, and the material world of your physical life.

It is like this, everything around you, your house, your relationships, your job, is a reflection of the level of energy inside of you. That means there is an energetic relationship between your house, your relationships, and your job.

Let's say you decided to go on vacation. The job you have continues to be the job you have, as well as your house and your friends. These all exist because together they have formed a relationship amongst themselves that is connected to you, but is also independent of you at the same time. The level of vibration of your job is harmonized with your house. Both exist independently, but both match the level of vibration of energy within you.

The energetic vibrations of multiple energy types organize themselves into different levels, or plateaus, of energy.

Think of listening to musical notes. Musical notes can be organized into different chords and the chords can be in different keys. These harmonized levels of vibrations create different experiences and can materialize into physical reality within linear time.

Everything that can be formed from a level of energy cannot happen all at once. It would not make sense to us. So what shifts into physical reality doesn't happen all at once, but one event at a time. That way, we can see what is being made from our energy.

We make different things from the same level of harmonized energy. The vacation you just went on, the job, your relationships; are all from the same level of energy. Let's talk about relationships, as an example. One client of ours, Mary, had experienced sexual abuse as a child. Because of her inner experiences, she was quite fearful of her involvement with men. It was difficult for her to trust men. Because she had now become a healer herself and had worked hard at integrating the energy of fear, she believed she had overcome energetically magnetizing difficult relationships with distant men.

She then met a man named Matthew, who she felt a deep connection. However, he was very fearful of developing a relationship with her. She wanted to know if she could heal his fear through unconditional love. The answer, however, was not to heal him, but to heal herself with unconditional love. Through her own integration of fear, she then could move into viewing the world with love from inside of herself and being attractive to and building the third solution: someone capable of becoming close to her.

One of our clients is an amateur archeologist. He travels the world seeking to solve ancient mysteries. Every one of his adventures builds upon the energy of his last adventure. His travels to pyramids in the Americas lead him to explore the pyramids in ancient Egypt, which then spurred him on to explore the coast of Alexandria for underwater treasure. Each experience opened his energy toward expanding his already-present interests.

Energy acts like music being played in a symphony. The symphony is playing the same piece of music; all is in tune, even though each musician is independently playing his instrument. Your energy is playing music with other energy, even though you may not hear the specific instruments playing, one note at a time.

Remember, we are not fated to be in our current jobs, houses, or relationships. All that we see outside of us mirrors the energy inside of us. If we are not happy with the mirror outside of us, something inside of us needs to be healed. Why? So you can open your mind to the third solution.

Right now, if you are not satisfied with what is happening outside of you, the third solution is not occurring. What is operating are two opposing opposites—what you don't want and what you do want. We automatically assume that what we want is not within our responsibility to own or to change. We believe we are fated, or that someone, or something else, is in control.

Well, we do have the ability to make a solution out of what we don't want and what we do want. How? By understanding that the energy you don't want is being manufactured by energy inside of yourself so you can see the energy outside of yourself. You need to understand the *don't want* energy by seeing it outside of yourself and becoming aware of it and focusing in on another energy, the third solution.

Becoming aware of the *don't want* energy does not require you to completely comprehend it. For example, as I mentioned earlier, I was aware of being told over and over again by my mother that I was an outcast. I could not completely tell you about all of my experiences and feelings. After all, those experiences were from years of emotional abuse, as well as physical abuse from my mother. I could tell you I was aware of feeling sad about being told I was an outcast. My guidance suggested that I focus on the energy of my ancestors. I heard an audible crack. I physically felt layers of emotions shift out of my aura. Feelings of shame and guilt left me. I realized that my ancestors wanted me. I was not rejected, like my mother told me, over and over again.

We once had a client who felt it was time to buy her dream home. She figured out what she could comfortably afford after she turned away from a beautiful house that was slightly out of her price range. She almost bought it, but listened to her inner guidance. She trusted her gut instincts. She had healed her connection with Universal Mind through her trust.

She was driving around a neighborhood she had been in several times before. She noticed a house for sale she had never noticed before, even though she had spent quite a bit of time in that neighborhood. She went up to the door and before she even entered the living room, she knew this was it. In addition, her dream house was marked down that very weekend to the price she could afford. It seemed as though this house appeared out of nowhere at exactly the time she was ready to buy it and for exactly the price she could afford.

Remember, hidden energy can suddenly shift to energy we see outside of ourselves in our third dimensional reality because emotions and thoughts can vibrate at different levels.

Energetic Experience

Emotions and thoughts harmonize together and create different energetic vibration levels that create different experiences inside and outside of ourselves.

Different energetic vibrations act as organizing tools to narrow or widen our view of our world. When feeling fear, anger, or guilt, we are quite focused on the matter we feel fear, anger, or guilt about. Our focus narrows our view of what we see. When we feel love, gratitude, or a sense of well-being, we feel open towards the world we live in and feel a sense of choice.

The narrow or wider views that we have do not mean that the views are negative or positive. Fear, a narrow energetic experience, can be quite positive, given the context of the circumstances. If you are running from a tiger, you may feel fear. There is also such a thing as feeling appropriate guilt. We can learn from guilt and use it as a tool to widen and choose our next energetic experience.

This one is for the mothers out there. A lot of mothers with older children may have experienced a child who lies about not admitting calling her friend a name. She feels guilty about this experience, and through your wise guidance, the next time she is able to admit her wrongdoing and apologizes.

We have all experienced anger. It can be a powerful organizing tool to help motivate us to assert ourselves in a situation, which needs our attention.

Like many of our clients, Laura was a healer. Like a lot of spiritual people who confuse working for money and spirituality, she allowed herself to be taken advantage of by another healer who borrowed money. After this happened for a time, she allowed her anger and resentment to focus her actions and motivate her to stand up for herself and ask him for what she needed.

What we experience inside of ourselves is the same thing we experience outside of ourselves. The experience is created from the vibration level inside of ourselves. Levels are made from different energy types that harmonize together, just like musical chords. Higher vibration levels create joy, love, freedom, gratitude, abundance, emotional openness, and emotional epiphanies. Lower vibration levels create guilt, fear, anger, resentment, shame, and impoverishment.

The lower emotional vibrations harmonize with one another and can create lower-level experiences such as illness, fear, conflicts and feelings of lack. These lower level energy types create these experiences, because they are unable to form a wider relationship with the larger Universal Mind. A wider relationship with Universal Mind makes for a wider view of what you see. A wider relationship with Universal Mind makes for a wide view of choices.

Remember our client who felt trapped because she had no money? In her view, she had no choice but to contact a client who was emotionally battering to her, because she needed the money. However, once she was able to see the situation from a different viewpoint, she became aware of her opportunities.

When you are feeling ashamed, it is very difficult to feel a wider range of emotions. The shame takes over and acts like a large blanket. It covers you and you feel as though you cannot feel anything else.

Remember the balls inside the balls? Levels of energy are like roads connecting us to the larger ball of the Universal Mind. The roads can be narrow, or wide, depending on the energy level.

Guilt, shame and fear can narrow the road to and from Universal Mind.

Remember, this is not necessarily a negative thing. You can be running from a tiger and you can be quite focused in on feeling fearful and running. The energy from your fear connects with Universal Mind and suddenly you see your work mates in front of you in the jungle who has an injection rifle. They shoot the tiger, you are safe, and the tiger is sleeping soundly. It was your fear that acted to save you. Your fear became a narrow force, opening you to a wider experience of safety.

Later on in the day, after you stopped shaking, you may begin to feel angry at the tiger's keeper, who did not latch the gate properly in the compound. You talk to the keeper and express how you feel. After you allowed yourself to let go of the anger, which created another experience of reviewing compound policy with gates, you can then feel gratitude for being alive.

Lower levels of vibration create narrow highways to and from Universal Mind and higher levels of vibrations create wider highways to and from Universal Mind. In this way, the level of vibrations act as organization tools to help provide you with an experience that reflects a narrow scope of reality, or a larger view of reality. Both views of reality can serve you, however, one view is not better than the other.

If you feel a sense of lack, look at your inner experiences of lack. Remember, we create our world in a paradoxical way, always from the inside out.

What is a lower level of vibration that you are currently experiencing that is helping to point you toward seeing a wider view?

Perhaps, some of you, as many of our clients are, were mistreated as a child. You may feel ashamed and feel fundamentally unloved. What is the wider view? What could be the opposite experience? The bigger truth about who you really are?

Creating Types of Physical Matter

As we have discussed, different levels of energy creates different types of physical matter. The denser the energy, the more solid the object appears. Think of it this way, if you only had one energy type to create a physical object, that would not be a whole lot of energy. However, if twenty energy types were added within the same space, the energy becomes thick and dense. The twenty energy types have formed a relationship with one another, they have spoken amongst themselves and decided to create an identity together with the help of the Universal Mind. In doing so, they leap into a condensed state and become physical.

The more energy added to one space, the denser the energy, and the quicker the concrete manifestation becomes.

In our world, we have countless people who have decided that the toy is the toy. Dense energy helps to create "the toy."

When inner conflicts are healed, you have more energy to place toward your desired choice. If you focus and pay attention to one matter with conviction, belief, and knowing, the more energy you are putting into a space, the denser the energy becomes, and manifestation becomes quickened.

The frequency of different levels of vibrations creates different things. High levels of vibration can help you see worlds of choice. Lower levels of energy can help you focus, organize, and choose higher levels of energy.

The higher levels of vibration carry denser energy. The higher vibration levels carry within them the vibration of joy.

Joy is a vibration which holds a great amount of worth within the Universal Mind. Why? Universal Mind values feeling and values experience. When joy is accessed through different levels of energy, the energy of joy produces physical objects quickly.

Each level creates different physical objects or events. Anger and resentment create bacteria and viruses that harm the physical body. Thunderstorms can be created by non-attachment and repression. A broken cell phone can be created by resentment. Attachment can create a for sale sign on that house you have been looking for. Commitment can create an opportunity to buy your neighbor's car. Love can create new clients for your business.

The different levels of energy already have a pre-existing relationship with the Universal Mind. The levels are already in an unseen level of creation. The world creates from energy that is in a hidden state of existence.

What we don't see inside of us, our energetic experience, creates what we do see outside of ourselves with our physical bodies.

When you tune into energetic levels with your mind, what you are seeing with your mind opens, or narrows, your vision of what you see outside of yourself. It would be like you are looking close up into the grass and all you see is the grass, the dirt, the roots and insects. You decide to step back and the image broadens and now you can see the grey tabby cat sitting in the grass. Your position as the observer has changed, and the position of what you are viewing has also changed. You both have relocated into another place where you can see more. Except that this new place is a mental space of energy. We told you this is strange, but it is a strange, strange, world!

Because you have changed the mental location of what you see, what you have been observing must also change its mental location. Remember, all energy is mental energy. Energy makes intelligent choices within its own mind independently and in relationship with all other energy. It all happens in the space of your mind!

We once had a client who had a very difficult relationship with her husband. He was diagnosed with obsessive compulsive disorder and could obsessively put her down without concern about her feelings. Of course, this behavior was all about him and he did not like his behavior, yet my client had difficulty rising out of the shame that he triggered. Both her parents severely emotionally abused her when she was a child. Once she was able to integrate the shame from her parents and no longer buy into it, she was able to allow his comments to roll off her like water off of a duck's back. Why? She viewed the situation differently. He was talking about himself, not her.

Because she was viewing her husband through anger, she saw a narrow view of herself as a victim. You can also change the level of your vibration if you are experiencing a narrow view of yourself. If you are looking at an object with anger, you will see very little of the object. It is like your view has narrowed and become fuzzy. With anger, your attention has narrowed to see very little else, other than anger. Anger helps you focus on the very thing you are angry about. Our client was angry at herself for feeling like a victim.

We once knew a woman who was very angry at her brother. All she saw was his mistreatment of her. She forgot about the times he had been kind to her and helped her. She even forgot that he was mad because of the way she had treated him! Anger became a numbing way out for her to view her relationship with her brother.

Different levels of vibrations create denser physical objects. The denser the object, the more levels of vibrations the object contains. Physical objects in three-dimensional reality often carry infinite levels of vibrations.

If you can imagine a huge tree, like the tree of life standing in front of you, fabulous with all of its green branches and leaves. Imagine all of us on earth are looking at the tree from our own positions. We are all putting out different levels of vibrations that make the tree the tree. Energy bonds together from all of us, from everything from the earth, plant and animal kingdoms alike, to make the tree. We all harmonize together with the Universal Mind and voila! The tree is made.

The tree also sees you. From all of its energy, it now recognizes your energy, too. And together you and the tree can see each other.

By now you might begin to understand it. The only thing that truly sees is the mind. And the mind is joined with all other minds, from everything everywhere, together with the Universal Mind.

It is the way your mind sees that can change your life. It is the experience inside of your mind that you can choose to change. Together, with all minds and with the Universal Mind, you can see your life change.

Mind Changes

Energetic mental changes can affect physical matter. Physical matter can be depleted from different levels of vibrations.

Once a vibration is ignored, it ceases to vibrate. Its energetic vibration depends upon your recognition to help form its existence. Now, your recognition does not need to be a conscious recognition. If you shut your eyes for a second and tune into all of the species of plants on earth, it will not take a rocket scientist for you to sense the millions of species of plants on earth. You have a sense of their existence. Even if you could not name ten species of trees that exist on earth, you still feel their existence, even if you cannot see their existence with your physical eyes. However, once an unconscious agreement exists within you to cease recognition of a certain type of vibration, the vibration ceases to vibrate. You do not see it, its observation is no longer observed and it is destroyed, meaning it changes its location to another dimension.

Now, once a vibration is ignored and no longer seen, it can become attached to other vibrations in another location.

For example, a moment can seem forever in terms of time. In the energy of the moment, the moment can decrease its level of vibration and change into a feeling of forever.

Think of this, you are waiting for a bus that is within your view. The bus will be here in one moment, but within your mind, the energy within the moment has already turned into a feeling of the bus taking forever. The energy within the moment has been taken over through the energy of impatience and changed into forever, which physically affects the bus. Can we see it physically affecting the bus? Not always. Perhaps it is moving more slowly, perhaps something just broke within the engine, we don't always know. Does the power within your energy always have immediate consequences? No. Perhaps, there are ten people at the bus stop who are feeling like you do, "This bus is taking forever," which creates relationships with your energy, which then affects the bus. Perhaps there has been energy within people at that bus stop for a month, all communicating the same thing, "This damn bus takes forever!" which then harmonizes with the current levels of energy to affect the bus and the bus breaks down.

We don't always know the outcome of what affects our energy has. What we do know is that there is an effect.

What about the woman who finally was ready to buy her dream house? The owners had lowered the price of the house that very weekend, because they were really ready to sell it. The elderly owner had bid on another house and now desperately needed to sell their two-story home. Both the owner's and the buyer's energy harmonized perfectly.

Remember, that energy is like musical chords. Several notes make up one chord. The energy of the moment is attached to the chord of time and so is the energy of forever. Both the energy of the moment and the energy of forever can change its location and relationship within the energy of time.

Also remember that all energy is connected to different dimensions all at once. That means that energy can change location in terms of its attachment to different dimensions. Sometimes, these different dimensions are not seen from our three-dimensional space.

Time is one of these dimensions that you cannot see, but it exists nevertheless. All physical matter in our space has an unseen relationship with time. That means that matter has to exist in time in our three-dimensional world.

Let's say you went into a deep meditative state, where the dimension of time no longer existed. You feel like you are in a dream state, some things feel like they are happening all at once. You feel as though there is an instantaneous building of physical objects and an instantaneous depletion of physical objects, because your attention to your experience is being refocused on different things in your dream in the span of one moment.

The same type of situations can happen within physical reality. Your attention has now shifted to experiencing the bus as momentarily arriving. So you begin to feel patient. The impatience has been destroyed, because the experience of the impatience is no longer experienced. The bus arrives on time without incident.

Not only that, but the ten other people with you suddenly have shifted into feeling relief at seeing the bus turn the corner towards them. They are no longer feeling the experience of frustration that could have affected the bus.

Our minds can affect the bus through the view of its experience. We can destroy physical matter through our mental experience in three dimensional space by focusing on different mental experiences. If our energy joins with other energetic forces and creates a dense energy formation, the bus can be physically affected.

This, of course, does not mean we can go around breaking down buses! What it does mean is that the experience of our mind can create destruction in our three-dimension reality by adding our energy to other existing levels of energy.

Imagine an old-fashion scale, perfectly balanced with sand on each side. You decide to add your ten grains of sand to the right of the scale. You have added weight to the right of the scale. The right hand side of the scale moves down.

We can create physical change through our mental experiences with the addition of our energy.

We once had a client who literally helped to create a car accident! She and her husband only had one car. One morning, after driving her husband to work before dawn, she became very angry about continually driving him to work at five am. As she was driving through an intersection, her car was hit on the side by a hit and run driver. She was asking for another solution to her dilemma by becoming increasingly angry. She wanted to heal her anger. She and her husband decided to get another car, while the damaged car was being fixed in the shop. She was convinced that her anger about this situation created the physical destruction of her vehicle.

Different Levels of Vibrations

Events, both big and small, can be created from different levels of vibrations.

Different levels of vibration can change location. Vibrations can join together, like musical chords and these chords can be combined together to create songs or symphonies. The density of the vibrations, or the more chords added to the song/symphony, can affect the size of the events.

Vibrations create activities. The activities depend upon the formation of energetic vibrations.

Let's go back to the bus example. Different physical destructive outcomes can be made from the different levels of vibration. People at the bus stop are experiencing different levels of impatience. Perhaps the bus just gets a flat tire, rather than breaking down entirely.

Events are materialized from the effects of the different levels of the energetic vibrations.

We perhaps may know of this happening, for example, the tragic incident of an earthquake which has hit a town with little resources. One of the things that was happening in a small town in Turkey, was the residents of the town had focused in on bringing resources to their town for months. Although the event of the earthquake had devastating effects upon the town, it helped to generate resources for the town through worldwide attention.

Perhaps your car has broken down for the second time. Your apprehension about money and the lack of it has caused an effect on your energy. It has been difficult to get out of bed. In turn, this energy of not being able to move, has affected your car.

All of our vibrations create events. Even though we may not recognize how our energy affects events, our energy still has had a hand in its creation. Our energy also helps to create major events, such as wars and peace.

The war in Iraq was created from our country's view that there were weapons of mass destruction present within that country. The energetic view from our country helped create war. The war was created, which has now fostered efforts and events related to making peace.

What we are pointing out are the many probabilities of energy and its completion outside of you.

Inside of you, the vibration level of your thoughts and feelings can define your connection to Universal Mind.

Your thoughts and feelings are always connected to many different dimensions at once. Remember

the ball within the ball? Your mind is always within Universal Mind. No matter what you think and what you do, you are always connected to Universal Mind, sometimes called God, Universal Mind, or Source even if you don't think you are.

Not being connected to the Universal Mind is like trying to not be connected with time. It is impossible. In your human form, you are within plain reality, and because of this, there are many parts of you, including your mind, which is connected to unseen realities.

You are a human, yet you are within dimensional realities at once. Your energetic vibrations of your reality within the reality of your connection to God can change the connection you have with that reality.

If you feel afraid of God, angry at God, or believe that God does not exist, your connection with God will be experienced as minimal, because your inner experience of connection is minimal. Please remember that everyone does have a different view of God, so just because your view is different than ours, that does not matter; it is still important and valid and connects you to Universal Mind.

If, however, you believe in the existence of God, the more you will see that connection presented throughout your life. The more thoughts and feelings you have towards God's existence, the more power God has to act through the vibration level of your broad connection.

Your knowing is the key toward your connection with God. Within your knowing lies the vibration level that creates the space for your knowing to know. Through your knowing, you can change the location from the energetic vibration level to enter the realm of God in another dimension. And in God's realm, your knowing resides and God sees you, because you see God. Through this joint recognition, you and God have joined hands and created your connection. Through the created connection between you and God, you have access to the power within God.

When the energy between you and God have been joined as one, you can access God's power. Through Universal Mind, you can know of God's existence and you can move with this power to create experiences. And, like Buddha, you can do it all within the power of your mind.

Points to Remember:

Through our viewpoint, we help change the shape of energy and it can take on different forms.

The Law of Opposites forms a paradoxical structure so that we constantly create life through the choice of our inner experience.

Your choices in how you see the world can make what you see real.

The situations we are in and the people we are with are reflections of the energetic vibration levels inside of ourselves.

Through healing, the different levels of energetic vibration create different things.

It is these different levels of energetic vibration that build or deplete events, situations and the material world of your life.

Energetic Experience

Different energetic vibrations act as organizing tools to narrow or widen our view of our world.

The more energy added to one space, the denser the energy, and the quicker the concrete manifestation becomes.

Universal Mind values feeling and values experience.

When you tune into energetic levels with your mind, what you are seeing with your mind opens, or narrows, your vision of what you see outside of yourself.

The only thing that truly sees is the mind.

Mind Changes

Once a vibration is ignored, it ceases.

You do not see it, its observation is no longer observed and it is destroyed, meaning it changes its location to another dimension.

All physical matter has an unseen relationship with time.

We can create physical change through our mental experiences with the addition of our energy.

Inside of you, the vibration level of your thoughts and feelings can define your connection to Universal Mind.

Through the Universal Mind, you can know of God's existence and you can move with this power to create experiences.

Affirm:

I can create choices for myself through my connection with Universal Mind.

Experience:

Remember the previous exercise in tuning into your knowing? Find that space within your mind of knowing. Take a deep breath. Go deeper within your knowing. Imagine there is a road that travels into the experience of your knowing. You travel upon the road and you make the experience of knowing larger. You feel it even more. You feel the certainty and security of your knowing. Continue to breathe. Allow yourself to feel the totality of what it feels like to be within this emotional space. How would you describe it? What kinds of energy are there? How would you identify the energy? How many different types of energy are there? Is there information present for you in this space? Can the information help you to make choices? Continue to feel this space and breathe. How would you identify the energy of Universal Mind. What does Universal Mind feel like to you? Breathe in. Are you able to feel the energy of Universal Mind within the space of knowing?

Chapter Fifteen
The Universal Law of Wholeness

Everything in the universe is whole and complete, just as it is.

Your car is your car. It does not need anything more to be your car. And what is even more fascinating, is that the molecules that make up your car are whole and complete, just as they are. So no matter how you think about the pieces of your car, the door, the engine, the headlight, each item, each thing, it is whole just as it is. It does not need anything else to complete itself. The headlight is a headlight. You can add parts to it or even subtract parts from it, but it still remains whole. Fascinating, huh?

So you can remove every part of your car and the parts still remain whole. Nothing can make it incomplete. Conversely, you can add more and more parts to your car to make it a fancier car, but it is still a car.

This means that the entirety of who you are—no matter what you have been through, or what you have suffered, you are whole and complete just as you are. You have the ability to open and notice your wholeness right now, right here. There can be no lack in who you are, in fact, you can only be whole, regardless of how you perceive yourself.

All of those messages that some people receive and ponder on, such as "you are not good enough," "you are not as good as your brother/sister," or "you do not measure up" are not possible. Universal law determines your completion in wholeness right now.

Universal law guarantees your equality through your wholeness with every other thing in the universe. There is not one thing lacking within you; it is only your point of view that has misunderstood the true you.

Of course, you can expand your point of view of who you are and begin to consciously know more about yourself. How? By removing the experiences inside of you through healing the things that block your view of your true self. The interesting thing is that you are finding out about things that have already been present within you, because you are already whole and complete, just as you are.

Because everything is whole and complete just as it is, there is always a rift in terms of time between what is felt as whole and complete and what has already been presented as whole and complete from God. So, in our world, everything is whole and complete just as we see it, however, in our mind's eye, we might not view it that way. Our relationships, our careers, our house, may present us with challenges for growth because we live where time is present.

Therefore, growth is a choice we make to bring on something different, other than wholeness or completion. Growth is a choice to help us know something about ourselves that we did not know before, not to complete ourselves, but to experience more of who we are.

The universe sees us in a finite state. It is hard to imagine, but imagine for a second that the Universal Mind observes us as being complete right now. Remember that time is not relevant for the Universal Mind. Universal Mind exists in a state of no time. So here we are, already in a state of wholeness and not even seeing it!

Since we are whole and complete, just as we are, the energy within us exists in a state of immortality. Again, please remember that no time exists within the Universal Mind.

Because we are in time, we are in a continual state of energy recognition and energy non-recognition. That means we are in a continual state of change.

It is our changes in energetic vibration that quest for a state of balance. It is the balancing of energy that helps form the experience of completion and it is the imbalance of energy that helps us seek the experience of completion.

We are born with the ability to create completion by knowing its existence is already present. All we have to do is balance energy to bring the completion of our healing into reality. And we balance energy by consciously recognizing what energy is blocking the flow of energy into balance.

This means that energy naturally flows and it flows to create balance. It also means that we can change the energetic flow by changing blocks that prevent energetic flow.

When we are not in balance, we experience ourselves in psychological conflict. We feel a sense of conflict through non-balance and we are motivated towards balance to resolve conflict. We can deny our sense of non-balance and put up a false front, or we can work to heal ourselves.

We cannot tell you how many times we have talked with a client through guidance and they have waited to hear what we had to say and then stated, "I knew that." We have talked to people about their life purposes, their true vocation, their talents, and their abilities. Our clients are telling us they already have a sense of their own wholeness. What they are looking to complete is how to use what they already have. Somewhere along the path, they became lost. And they lost their sense of direction. They know there is more to who they are, but want to know how to make use of what they know.

What they are asking us is how to help them find a direction. They are asking for a path back to themselves, so that they may begin to use what they know about themselves. They need to integrate the fear, the shame, and the anger within them, so that they can begin to express themselves and who they are.

Fear, shame, and anger hides people from expressing who they are. People feel these feelings, hide them, and then unknowingly hide the reality of who they are. They experience confusion as to why certain things are happening in their lives, why they are not building their career, why there are conflicts in their relationships and why they feel alone. Part of what is occurring is that they have hidden their energy; because of this, their inner energy cannot build outside of themselves.

People do not need to know how to create their lives from the inside out through energy. We really have that down to a science. We build energy naturally. What we *don't* have down to a science is how to heal.

We have wars, famine, lack of health care, problems at work, bad relationships, and peculiar illnesses. We know all about making things through our energy. We do not know how to look into ourselves and walk in balance. Many of us are just babies desperate to learn.

Energy Shape Shifts

Energy was born with the ability to become. And to become what it wants to become. Odd, you say? Well, it gets odder. Because the mind within energy can make all of these choices; well, guess what, all of the choices within creation are within one energetic vibration. Energy has the ability to shape shift.

Energetic vibration acts in entirety, all on its own. Because each energetic vibration is whole and complete, just as it is, it can make independent choices. It can say I want to be a green car, a blue convertible, or a red SUV. Or, it may say, I want to be a banana, or a jet flying to Switzerland.

When I take out-of-body shamanic journeys, I can shape shift into an elephant, a worm, or the tallest mountain. My energy, because of its intelligence, has the ability to change its form.

Energy is a paradox. It is its own form and identity, but it is the whole universe at the same time. Because we are made of energy, we are ourselves, yet we are the whole universe at the same time. Therefore, we can shape shift into anything in the universe because we are of the universe.

Because energy is intelligent, it has its own understanding of itself and the world around it. It can see. And because energy can see, it can think. And because it can think, it can choose. It can behave independently by making choices to act independently from other vibrations.

Energetic vibration can become emotions. It can see itself as freedom energy. It can experience itself as love. It can feel and see itself as dead. Energy can choose to be objects, such as your kitchen cabinet, or choose to participate in an event and create a hurricane. The choices energy makes, occur because the energy is independent. Its own independence allows it to have choice, and its movements vary according to its choices.

How do we know this? We have experienced energy making choices to shape shift into thousands of forms throughout years of experience. You too, have had the same experience. Think of your dreams, where you have become someone or something other than yourself, where you have watched yourself from afar.

Yes, energy moves. Energetic vibrations can choose locations. It can choose this dimension to reside within to be seen, felt, and heard by us. It can choose to attach to one similar energetic vibration to form larger or smaller energetic vibrations, such as a large or small house, or it can choose another similar energetic vibration, such as a tent. It can choose to form relationships without becoming any less independent, such as one grain of sand on the beach, or it can join other energetic vibrations to become a formation of energetic vibrations, such as the ocean.

Because energy is independent and can act on its own, we can trust in its ability to be whole and complete, as is.

We can direct our inner experiences to be whole and complete as they are, even when we are in a state of building experiences into reality that may not yet match our inner reality. You can experience unconditional love right now for yourself inside of yourself, even though your mind may have some work to heal your past experiences.

Energetic Links

How can you shift from one vibration to another? Energetic vibrations can attach to other vibrations, making larger and more encompassing vibrations.

Energy can act like its own internet. It can link up with one energy right after another, forming a huge, dense vibration of energy. It is like a thick cloud of energetic vibrations that can be seen, felt, or heard.

The denser the energy, the larger the impact, or the more varied the experience.

As we have discussed, energy becomes dense through focus, awareness, clarity, and experience. The more emphasis placed upon the energy through inner experience, the more it builds.

Often, in our meditation, we will experience "freedom" energy and "love" energy. The more we concentrate on those two energy types, the more we experience the energy inside of us.

Remember that energy forms its own choices. Exact outcomes cannot be controlled. The good news though is that personal outcomes can occur because you have chosen the third solution to heal.

Okay, so what does this mean for you? You can direct mental energy by choosing a focus for experiencing the energy while detaching from the outcome. You are freed up from wondering about how something is going to occur, just that it is.

My friend is a spiritual person. She works hard every day to heal her connection with Universal Mind through trust in its existence.

Energy chooses the creation of its own outcomes. It will choose how to show up as a spiritual experience.

Once the energy balances with other energy to form a relationship, it begins to unfold its identity. It begins to meld its identity with other complimentary energy. It acts like a mirror, a looking glass for other energy to see itself.

How does this happen? By your choice to heal your connection with energy. You trust in its ability to be present, to be intelligent and to form its own existence outside of you through Universal Mind. You have given up control.

Healing

A few years ago, we were honored to be part of a Native American peyote ritual. A Native American medicine woman hosted the ritual, who we have profound respect for. We felt, that at that time in our lives, we were ready to participate in this spiritual experience.

The Native Americans consider Peyote a healing medicine for the spirit. I asked the medicine to show me my connection with my guides and with other people. The medicine showed me a vision of a spider woman above a friend's body. Spider woman began to weave webs, several of them at once, and quite fast. She then showed me how the webs turned into a sea of water in which we all lived. She showed me that we are surrounded by energy, and that it lives all around us in the air we breathe.

All energy has its own web. And like the strands of a web, when energy vibrates, all of the web experiences the vibration. It is communicating with all energy at once.

Energy does not need to be recognized as independent energy in order to be heard. It can join with other like energy to form a structure of energy, and that structure of energy gets heard. For us, in the human world, we do not have to separate out the dust particles that form clouds in order to see the clouds. It is the same way with energetic frequencies.

Energetic frequencies can mirror one another and be heard as one structure. Energetic vibrations can cover huge dimensions of space and can communicate throughout the universe. At the same time, energy does not have to exist as part of a structure in order to be heard. If we chose to, we could separate the dust particles and recognize each dust particle for what it was, a dust particle. It emanates the energy of what it is in a way we can observe it. It is the same way with energetic frequencies. It can be heard emanating its own vibration.

Vibrations talk to each other by tuning into a station, just like a radio station. Each station exists throughout Universal Mind. Spider Woman showed me that energy exists in different webs. Each web is like its own station. In our minds, the sound of our inner experiences travel across our mind in a way we cannot separate from one portion of our mind to the next. We experience our experiences happening within our mind simultaneously. That means that the fastest form of energy is mental. It means that our thoughts, feelings and experiences can instantaneously race across the universe and communicate. It also means that we can trust that our thoughts, feelings, and experiences are constantly in connection to something larger than us—Universal Mind.

Universal Mind communicates with all energy. It communicates over the expanse of the universe by tuning into thought, emotional, and experience frequencies. It feels the existence of all energy, either independently or jointly, throughout the universe.

Because of the nature of mental energy, we cannot be removed from being seen and heard by Universal Mind. We are being continually recognized, moment by moment, by Universal Mind.

Try just for a second to separate yourself from your experience of reading this book. Even if you are a most enlightened being, it is impossible to separate yourself from your inner experience.

Remember your mind as a golf ball within a larger ball? Your mind always is in existence with other minds.

In the 1960s, there was a popular phrase that said, "Expand your mind." Well, guess what? Your mind already is, has already been, and will always be in a state of expansion. All you needed to do was see it.

Energy Leaps

Energetic vibrations can leap from one dimension to another dimension, even when that dimension is hidden from us.

How? Energy can suddenly change vibration. One minute it can be vibrating at one level, and the next minute, it can change into another level. This means that vibrations are in a constant state of change. These changes create appearances, and/or disappearances, within several dimensions at once, some of which we cannot see.

The energy that comes from us can change into a physical form without us being aware of it. We can also shift our energy into other dimensions unseen by us, without our conscious awareness. The good news is that we don't have to be aware of how it all comes down, just that it does. What we can do is be aware of the language of our energy.

What are you saying to the Universal Mind through your language?

Energy communicates and can leap into other spaces, time zones, physical realities, and non-physical realities. This vibrating energy can then form relationships with one another to build denser energy, faster or slower frequencies, or work independently. Energy may choose to emanate its identity through its

vibration by staying in one place, yet be in all places at once, like the energy of Universal Mind.

Energy is not only able to choose its location, but it is able to chose its identity within that location. In our world, a tree is choosing this reality and identifying itself with its energy as a tree.

Energy can shift location through its intentional will. Because our minds are made of energy, you can shift energy though that intentional will. You can mentally intend, through the choosing of your mental experience, what it is you are about to inwardly experience.

Sometimes the doing is just being. The tree believes it is a tree and continues to be that experience moment by moment.

There are also shifts that energy can take that look like physical movement in space. For example, a cat can be remembering when it was chasing a mouse yesterday. At the same time, it leaps onto the floor. In the cat's mind, his memory is not happening yesterday, but happening right then and there. He is chasing the mouse.

When you are in moments where it may be difficult for you to shift your inner experience, there is a block present that must be healed. If you are caught in a web of sadness, as with one client whose husband needed healing from past abuse issues, her sadness needed more recognition and more moving into, rather than out of, in order to heal. She needed to consciously become aware of what her sadness was about, before her sadness could shift into something different. For her, she needed to be with her sadness and experience her emotions before she could shift.

Since we create our lives from the inside out, the energy inside of us lets us know, through our inward experiences, what must be healed. If we are not feeling free to experience something we wish to experience, our inward world needs examination.

We need to know more about what is blocking us from our outward experience, so that the inside of us can move forward. We can find this out by looking at what is being created outside of us as a mirror and by focusing in on the energetic experience inside of us that helps us heal.

Energetic Consciousness

Sometimes energy chooses to become consciously aware of itself; even if that part of itself is very far away. It would be like if you reached out your arm in front of you. Suddenly, you become aware of your hand, which is touching the fence. You're not focused on your arm, which is of course attached to your hand, and you don't notice your arm's experience, but you do notice your hand, which has landed on wet paint!

Energy can behave in the same way. It can suddenly become aware of a part of itself that is very far away, when that part gains your attention. Suddenly, like our hand, it feels itself in another part of space! That is why when we tune into our consciousness, it does not feel like we can put it all into a square box. There are parts of it we cannot define that are here, there and everywhere; we just cannot pinpoint it in terms of space or time.

Even though a part of ourselves can be far away, we can still sense its existence. We feel ourselves as connected to something else, but what that "else" is, remains indefinable. It is a part of ourselves that we recognize as someplace else. Where, what, and how remains hidden from our view, but we know a piece of us is somewhere beyond our concrete reality.

The piece that is someplace else, communicates information back to us that can be translated into our reality. Remember the wet paint? The hand feels the wet paint and we suddenly realize something is different in our environment. The same thing happens in our consciousness. Our energy from our consciousness brings back information from other realms, realms we can't identify and realms we are not focusing upon with our awareness. We become aware of this energy when we have sudden spiritual impulses, epiphanies, or insights. Sometimes we call these experiences an awakening.

We awaken to a part of ourselves that is already someplace else and can communicate with us. That piece of us is divine, immortal and in a space and time that is not three dimensional. It is a piece of us that recognizes our existence and recognizes us as a part of itself.

That piece of your energy that is very far away, also recognizes itself as not in our world. We feel it as unconscious or subconscious energy, as energy that is momentarily nonexistent or one step moved from awareness in our world. As we retrieve the knowledge from our unconscious and subconscious, this energy becomes alive, and we bring it forth into birth.

This part of ourselves that is aware someplace else recognizes us as not in its world. It experiences us as subconscious and unconscious energy. It too brings back awareness of us and experiences our energy as life. It becomes conscious of us.

In this interchange of balanced knowledge, we gain energetic solutions to our most difficult dilemmas, we solve problems, we become more aware that there is energy in existence that we cannot place within our intelligence with a label, criteria, or definition. We just

know it exists. We feel its existence. And in this feeling, we can sense its belonging to us in a connection we can't place.

The energy that is far away from us, still reminds us that we are connected in ways that make us all one energy. In our oneness, humanity has, in common, our shared memories and present feelings of being in other places not of this earth. We feel energetic movements in places far away from us that remind us we are more than the self we see in the mirror. We experience a longing to connect to this energy, so that our view of who we are quells our longing to be home.

Energy is felt in one place at one time in three-dimensional space. You feel you are on earth and the rest of where you are, you cannot pinpoint. However, what remains for you to know is that you sense that all of who you are is not within the physical limitations of your body. Your mind becomes the vehicle to be able to drive you to know more about where your consciousness lies. Your mind reaches out and seeks out places far away from your physical body to help you know more about the parts of itself which are not here, are not in three-dimensional space. It can direct you to recognize its existence in other realms, and allows you to be open to more than just three-dimensional reality.

Your mind can bring you connection and awareness of other energy that is hidden from you. Your mind can bring to life this energy so that you can live more completely.

In my shamanic journeys, I traveled out through my third eye. I moved the core of my consciousness out of my physical body. I connected with power animals who became my guides. A worm led me into tunnels deep into the earth. I shape shifted into the worm. I felt the dark wet earth, experienced the sensitivities of the worm, who felt the slightest of vibrations. I traveled fast into the depths of the hot mud, until it became molten lava. I learned to breathe in lava and breathe out lava. The fire goddess Pele came to me. She beckoned me to come to her with a wave of her arm. I did, and as I got closer, her mouth opened. I entered her mouth, which led to the dark caverns of tunnels that sped me deeper underground like being on a bobsled run. I started to see a gleaming golden light. It attracted me as I sped forward. Within one turn, I was sitting in the golden room. It was filled with gold coins.

In my journeys, I learned that going into the depths of our emotions can appear and perhaps feel dangerous. However, emotions don't kill you and I survived going into the depths of Pele's hungry mouth. I found that through meeting the challenges posed by going deeper into my emotions, that gold awaited me. The bounty of gold represented my experience of myself as powerful, strong, and capable of knowing the other side of fear.

We are capable of experiencing energy in other worlds that train us that the energy is our world can be seen differently. We can look back at our world from this hidden dimension and know more about it than we ever could from our limited sight.

Energetic Language

As we have mentioned many times, energy is like musical chords. Each chord is made of notes. When played on an instrument, the chords create a vibration that sings the song of its many notes. The level of the vibrations is harmonized to create the energy itself. Then, the identity of the vibration is clear, because of the music it makes.

The best way to think of energy is this. You know when you feel sad, happy, or angry. You can feel it and automatically identify the feeling. Energy acts in the same way. You can feel the energy and identify it. Most of us are just not used to listening to energy.

Each vibration has its own form, it has a shape that we cannot see. This shape can be linked to many different shapes or it can be independent in its shape. Let's go back to the car. The car door has many different parts, all different sizes and shapes, and yet they can link together to form one shape, the door.

These shapes harmonize and fit together to create one large vibration, or stand alone in vibrating its identity. In that way, energetic vibration is always identified by other energy.

There is no energy within Universal Mind that does not have an identity.

We, as people, are able to identify energy by what we see, feel, hear, taste, think, and experience. We are also able to identify energy through our natural ability to be able to sense and experience the existence of energy. Even when we do not see energy, we may be able to experience it. Through this experience of sensing energy, we can identify what we sense.

When we listen to the many forms of energy around us, it heightens our awareness. We might know something is wrong with someone we love, even though we may not be able to say what. We may experience the forms of the energy and can identify it as "something wrong." Or we may feel that the job we just did is going to be well reviewed by our supervisor. We just know it. Perhaps we feel something good is going to happen today. However, we may not know these things, we may just be paying attention to our inner experience.

Independent energetic vibration talks to all the energy around it. It may choose to create a relationship with the energy around it, or stay alone, however, its identity remains clear.

Energy, no matter how many relationships and forms it links to, always has its original identity. The apple you ate this morning is still an apple even though it has taken on a different form. The door handle on the car door is always the door handle. It can be attached to your Honda or be lying on the garage floor, but it is still a door handle.

As we have talked about, God, or Universal Mind, is able to consciously hear all energy within its realm through life. All energy, no matter how many relationships it has formed, or the lack of relationships it has formed, is recognized by Universal Mind. Each identity and the choice of forms it has taken on is also recognized by Universal Mind. This means that no matter how small or large the energetic vibration is, it is seen by Universal Mind. The energy of an ant is recognized equally as well as the tallest pyramid on earth.

God witnesses everything and everybody.

Universal Mind is aware of energy we are unconscious about. It experiences what we are not aware of, all at once. Universal Mind strives to birth new energetic forms through us, through spiritual prompts and insights.

Through our natural motivation to create, we bring forth new forms of energetic vibration. Because we experience time, we can create new forms of energy within time. We experience a separation in between energetic forms. The car going down the street has not reached the red light. One minute later, it reaches the red light. We can see, in terms of time, the separation between events. Universal Mind does not perceive the same separation.

For Universal Mind, there is no separation between events. The mind of God finds it impossible to create new energetic formations. It is like one giant womb holding all the energy of creation without separation. All energy ever created is already within Universal Mind. All energy is already connected to Universal Mind. However, through time, Universal Mind can witness and experience what can be created through energy.

We are natural born creators through the necessity of the mind of God to know more about what it can create with energy.

Imagine, for a moment, that everything you are seeing right now has all turned into music. It would probably sound to you like an orchestra tuning up. It would be difficult for you to pick out any one tune, or perhaps, any one instrument.

Now, the orchestra is done tuning up and begins to play Beethoven. Suddenly, it makes sense to you; you are able to hear and experience the music as it is being played. It is the same way with Universal Mind. We are the instruments in which Universal Mind can hear and experience life. In that way, we make the unconscious conscious for Universal Mind.

Even though Universal Mind can identify all energy at once and be aware of all energy at once, it cannot consciously recognize independent forms of energy without its creation.

By necessity, we need the energy of Universal Mind to help us create and Universal Mind needs our creation to know its own energy.

Energy from Universal Mind can take any form, however, it cannot take the form of our experience created through linear time. This means that our human lives and our experiences are extraordinarily important. It means that our importance to the Universal Mind to know who it is, is sacred and our experience divine.

Let's go back to the orchestra. It is tuning up and everyone is playing at once. Imagine there is no conductor to direct the orchestra to stop tuning up and play Beethoven. Well, God does not have a conductor.

We were created from the belief within Universal Mind that it needed a way to organize itself, so it could see what it was. It could not create the conductor, but it could create the energy that formed the conductor. In this way, we became partners with Universal Mind with our joint intent to create and know more about creation. It also means we are truly creators in partnership with Universal Mind, for not only ourselves, but for God. We know ourselves with help from Universal Mind and the Universal Mind knows itself through us. Therefore, creation is formed.

Points to Remember:

Everything in the universe is whole and complete, just as it is.

Universal law guarantees your equality through your wholeness with every other thing in the universe.

Because everything is whole and complete just as it is, there is always a rift in terms of time between what is felt as whole and complete and what has already been presented as whole and complete from God.

Because we are in time, we are in a continual state of energy recognition and energy non-recognition. That means we are in a continual state of change.

It is our changes in energetic vibration that quest for a state of balance.

We feel a sense of conflict through non-balance and we are motivated towards balance to resolve conflict.

Energy Shape Shifts

Energy was born with the ability to become.

Energy is a paradox. It is its own form and identity, but it is the whole universe at the same time.

Yes, energy moves.

Energetic Links

Energetic vibrations can attach to other vibrations, making larger and more encompassing vibrations.

You can direct mental energy by choosing a focus for experiencing the energy while detaching from the outcome.

Energetic frequencies can mirror one another and be heard as one structure.

Energy does not have to exist as part of a structure in order to be heard.

The fastest form of energy is mental.

Universal Mind communicates with all energy.

Energy Leaps

Energetic vibrations can leap from one dimension to another dimension, even when that dimension is hidden from us.

Energy can suddenly change vibration.

Because our minds are made of energy, you can shift energy though your intentional will.

When you are in moments where it may be difficult for you to shift your inner experience, there is a block present that must be healed.

Energetic Consciousness

Sometimes energy chooses to become consciously aware of itself—even if that part of itself is very far away.

Our energy from our consciousness brings back information from other realms, realms we can't identify and realms we are not focusing upon with our awareness.

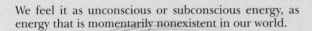

We feel it as unconscious or subconscious energy, as energy that is momentarily nonexistent in our world.

Your mind can bring you connection and awareness of other energy that is hidden from you.

Energetic Language

The identity of the vibration is clear, because of the music it makes.

When we listen to the many forms of energy around us, it heightens our awareness.

God, or Universal Mind, is able to consciously hear all energy within its realm through life.

By necessity, we need the energy of Universal Mind to help us create and Universal Mind needs our creation to know its own energy.

We were created from the belief within Universal Mind that it needed a way to organize itself, so it could see what it was.

We are truly creators in partnership with Universal Mind, for not only ourselves, but for God.

Affirm:

I have an ability to heal and connect with my true self and God.

Experience:

Breathe deeply. Relax your body. Feel the earth supporting your physical body. Now, notice that your body had everything it needs to support itself upon the earth. You can feel the stability of the ground below your feet. You can breath the air. There is food to nurture you. Notice that there is not one thing missing from your ability to support yourself within this moment. Now shift your awareness to a memory. It could be of a family member, when you were a child, or having a wonderful time on your birthday. Remember the warmth of this moment. During this time, you felt connected and you felt joy in your connection. Relive the moment in your memory, as though you were experiencing it now. Hold the moment in your mind. What is different in your experience as you went through this exercise in how you felt an hour ago? How much of your joyful experience can you recreate? Are you able to hold on this experience? Or are other experiences taking over? If other experiences are taking you away from your feeling of joy, what do you need to heal?

Chapter Sixteen
The Universal Law of Variety

In our healing processes, we recognized our ability to shift energy.

We eventually stopped hiding the many secrets of our past, because they were not our secrets to hide. In that way, I brought my stepfather to justice. It was my very normalcy that kept me sane. I shifted from the energy of self blame to the realization of inward power and strength.

No matter how bad you think a situation is, think again. It can be changed. Shifts into different views can occur.

I had always heard about the power of secrets and how they can make people sick. I had never considered my secrets as changeable. The power of denial kept me safe from other views, however, other views other than the one I held, confronted me every day.

Since my traumatic experience ceased with the death of my stepfather, information regarding sexual abuse began to present itself in the media. Almost weekly, exposure about this criminal act presented itself, continually supporting a different view of myself, other than the one that I had held for so long. Secrets hold our selves accountable, just by the very nature of hiding energy. Once energy becomes exposed, another view makes itself apparent.

The honest and deliberate recognition of energy allows energy to be seen. The varieties of energy can be recognized in the form of inspired thought, intuition, knowing when you need another's viewpoint for support, or healing. You can also recognize, without denial, what is happening in your life around you.

When we see, without blinders, the constant variety of the energetic choice around us, we see the true nature of Source. Source wants to continually create. We are the manufacturers. We see the presence of change and react to change. The varieties of energy are already present. We are motivated to see the choice and take on the choice as our own. The choice was always there.

I was never at fault for what happened to me. The choice to hold my stepfather accountable was always present. My view changed and I embraced the choice.

There are always built-in choices that are available for you to choose. So no matter how stuck you think you are, the truth is that you can't be stuck in a world full of choice. It is actually impossible. The mechanisms of the universe are constantly working to make you unstuck. And, like a spinning wheel, the universe is in constant flow.

Because the energy in the universe flows, variety through change is the stable energy within the universe. That means for you, your feeling of "being stuck" cannot be a stable force. Look around you. Whether you are in a car, sitting in your living room, or on a beach, you are witnessing thousands of items, living energy or events that contain energy. The variety of energy you are witnessing would be impossible for you to talk about, or to count. It would take a week to describe all of the energy contained in the items on your desk. Yet, the universe provides all of the energy to create the variety of objects sitting upon your desk. That means that creation is always present, because it goes hand in hand with variety. This also means something else; the law of variety guarantees the presence of choice.

If you are feeling stuck, ask yourself what the advantages are in being blind to the wider choices in your life. What are you protecting yourself from? How do you really feel about changing your present situation? What do you need to give up? What do you need to take on?

We are reminded again of our friend who we were having lunch with. The total focus of her conversation was about her ex-husband and his new girlfriend. At the time, she was reading many books about how to create your soul mate. She was also going through exercises to teach herself how to love herself more. She told us, over and over again, that she wanted her new relationship to come in. Yet, the main topic of lunch was her poor ex-husband and how he treated her in the past. Obviously, she was stuck.

Often times, being stuck means feeling afraid. Ask yourself if you feel afraid and what it is you are afraid of? Dig deep. Is your fear attached to an old pattern or belief? Is there shame involved? Or are you holding someone, or something, other than yourself responsible for your fear? Both of these situations keep change from happening and keep you trapped. Both situations keep you blocked from being in the flow of universal variety. These blocks keep your energy entombed. If your energy is entombed, it is deadened. Deadened energy feels hopeless and powerless.

You can empower yourself to see the variety of choices in your life that you really do have. Heal the blocks of thoughts, emotions, and experiences that keep you from experiencing the wider view. Stand up. Stand up right now and turn around. There are 360 degrees of views you can witness when you turn around. It is the same thing within your mental choices. You have an infinite variety of choices to see.

What do you need to surrender to in order to see them?

Energetic Change

A friend of ours was working on being within feminine energy. She was just allowing herself to feel feminine and receptive. Being a warrior type, always doing and trying to do things for others, she found that giving up control of situations was rather difficult for her. Barbara had trouble just being.

Knowing how energy works, she decided to just allow herself to be in feminine energy.

For Barbara, healing her connection with her feminine energy allowed for different responses than the ones she was previously getting.

Changing energetic vibrations allows relationships with energy to change. In fact, changing energetic vibrations guarantees that relationships with energy will change. Energy has no choice but to respond to energetic change.

And once energetic vibrations change, the changes can affect emotions, events, and the physical environment you live in.

Let's go back to Barbara. Barbara was in a restaurant, one of her favorite restaurants, with her father, James. James was confirming for Barbara what she already knew, she needed to change her energy to be more feminine, more receptive. At the time, Barbara was also having difficulty in her relationship with her husband. Not only was she somewhat concerned about

money, but she was concerned that her husband was not going to find his way in his own healing journey with alcohol. Although he was attending Alcoholics Anonymous, she was having a hard time just allowing him to control his own process without her influence. She wanted to take over and do it for him.

She knew she was struggling with this issue, but how could she let it go? She felt sad, shut down, and consumed with worry that if she did let go, he would not reach sobriety. She wanted his healing to be her will, not his will that directed his path.

Her father told her exactly what she needed to hear. Her husband needed the space to heal himself, to figure out his own way and to count on his will, not hers. She slowly let go of the sadness and moved into a state of feminine, receptive energy. As she did so, the waitress went to remove a glass from the table next to them. The glass spontaneously shattered into pieces.

Often what we see, what we want to obtain, cannot be had until we shatter the glass walls around us of our old energy that keeps us trapped. We think we see out of these walls, but it is the illusion of these walls that keep our energy from change and flow.

The energy changes without our doing anything other than being in the new energy we want. It requires us to hold a mental space inside of our minds that is holding the new energy. It requires us to be responsible for being the new energy, feeling the experience and allowing the energy to flow to us and through us.

How does change happen? The energy makes the change through us. And, like Buddha, we allow the energy to be.

Remember when we talked about how fear can narrow the focus of energy, or how love can open energy to create choice?

Through the caring and love of my analyst, the viewpoint I had regarding myself of an abused person, and what I had endured, changed. Susan helped to open my mental view.

Changing the energetic vibration inside of your mind opens, or narrows, the flow of energy. Open energy can create more energy to flow through you. Raising the frequency of energetic vibrations defines the change that can happen.

The frequency of vibration creates its own level of change.

Like water settling in a glass, energy settles and balances outside of you to match the energy inside of you.

We create our lives from the inside out. If our inner experience and view is joy, joy is created on the outside of ourselves also. What form joy takes on for us to see, we cannot control. However, what we do control is this: the recognition of the emotional issues inside of us that ask for our attention to heal.

A client of ours began to develop kidney issues. He asked for our guidance as to why his kidney's hurt. My guidance suggested that he must look at how his father had ignored him while he was growing up and how he did not have emotional support during that time. He must also stop vying for recognition from others, when others do not see who he is as a healer.

During his next session, he confided in me that his kidneys were still hurting. He also went on to describe a meeting with a group of people who did not recognize his healing ability. He felt ashamed and confused about their inability to listen to what he had to say and continued to expound his spiritual views for them to honor.

Again, guidance pointed out to him that he now must recognize his inner experience in regards to his father's lack of support, so that he can allow himself to support and validate his true identity. In doing so, he would free himself from looking for outside approval from people who would not provide it for him.

Our client eventually began to recognize and pay attention to his inner emotions, without defenses to feel those emotions. As he did so, his kidney pain disappeared.

Energy can shift automatically. What is newly created can shift automatically as well.

A good friend of ours, Sherry, was despondent about not finding "the man." Unfortunately, she had been on many dates, but they were all really boring.

Sherry changed the frequency of her vibration from being shut down with hopelessness to one of being open in hope. The level of frequency of her inner experience created an outer energetic change. Hope defined her outer experience.

Remember, frequency levels of energetic vibration can broaden the connection with the Universal Mind. A broader connection will result in expanded building of energetic change. It would be like making a congested four-lane freeway into a six lane freeway. The opened connection allows for more cars to move merrily along, without bumper-to-bumper delays, allowing you to be on time for your hair appointment.

Energy and Mind

Because your mind is an organizing tool for energy, energy reacts to your mental experience. Your mind is capable of organizing energy in many ways. It can take in energy by focusing and creating a relationship with energy, it can move energy by changing the focus upon energy, it can change the level of energy frequency by building a higher level of frequency and it can deplete the energy frequency by intending a lower level of frequency. Your mind can also step back or forward and create a different location for viewing energy.

Seem complex?

Not really. It is just that you may never have heard it in this way, even though you naturally do this already! But I bet you are getting the picture. Your mind is a conductor that is able to conduct the energy that flows through it. Just like being at the symphony, your mind is able to tap on the music stand and grab the attention of the musicians to play a certain tempo, key, and score. And just like the conductor, your mind does not have control over how brilliantly the violinist plays his solo, but it can help direct how the violinist plays.

In tandem, the conductor and the violinist organize how the music is played. You, as the conductor, can organize how the energy flows through your mind, because energy reacts to your mental direction.

Your mind creates a path for energetic vibration. Your mind can encounter all sorts of energy, but your mind determines what energy you allow to flow through it.

Imagine that you have a boss that has had a bad day. He had a very bad day. So bad, he begins to take it out on you. He criticizes the work you did on a vital report about finances within the department.

Your mind can react in several ways. You can take into your mind his anger toward you and feel inadequate, be quiet, and not say anything. You can feel betrayed by his behavior and allow the energy of distrust to flow through your mind and tell him off. You can feel upset by his behavior and say, "I am upset by how you are treating me, come back when you are calmer." Or perhaps you feel the energy of compassion flow though you and you say, "Hey, Bill, I know you're not that upset about the report, what is really going on here?"

What determines the energetic flow of your response? You do. It is your responses to the world around you that can help you see what energy you are taking in and reacting to. There are no right or wrong answers here.

Begin to notice how you react to your life situations.

What energy do you take in? What energy do you allow to flow through you? Are there other types of energy you focus on to flow through you?

You have the power to change the energetic flow from any situation you encounter in your life, no matter what it is.

This means that your mind can shape energy. It can shape energy to any form your mind can direct. These forms are energetic vibrations your mind experiences as real-life situations.

We are suggesting that energetic vibrations and mental experiences are the same. And as the same thing, energetic vibrations and mental experiences create life experiences. Energy on the inside of you is the same as energy on the outside of you. We know we are repeating ourselves, but the fact is, you may have been brainwashed to think differently, and we want to make sure that you understand it correctly.

Energetic vibrations can also be blocked from your mind. You can block lower vibrations from flowing, or you can block higher vibrations from flowing. Your mind can conduct energy by matching the level of vibration it encounters outside of you in your life. You can narrow your energetic reactions to your boss's criticism by becoming angry, or you can open your energy towards your boss through compassion. Both anger and compassion are being presented as choices through the life situation your boss is presenting to you.

How is both the energy of angry and compassion present outside of you in this situation with your boss? The universal law of variety guarantees that all energetic choices are available for you to choose from. What a smorgasbord of reactions you can create for yourself. And remember, your reactions are a mirror for the energy inside of you.

The choices that are given to you are meant to help you heal. If you continually take in criticism from your boss as something that is your fault, you will take in the experience of criticism until another choice is made. If you begin to recognize your boss reminds you of your critical father and that was your father's issue, you can then begin to heal your response toward your boss. How? By no longer personalizing your boss's response towards you. Ultimately, you differentiate the energy between yourself and your boss and you create freedom for yourself by knowing that your energy is not your boss's energy, nor your critical father's energy. You are freed to experience more of your own energy. You have opened up your energetic choices to respond in a different manner, rather than experiencing guilt, shame, and/or anger towards yourself. You are now ready to focus on a different response.

Energetic vibration can be moved forward through your focus. Your own knowing and experience can direct energy, which then quickens the energetic flow through you to the world around you. As a conductor of energy, you can direct the traffic flow of energy through your mental organization.

Your mind can change energy. But even before your mind changes energy, it must identify the energetic vibration within it.

We, as people, know a language deep inside of us. We can talk in this language without saying one word. We can feel and know and experience this language without listening to anyone's voice, without hearing someone talk and without learning anything at all about speaking. We know this language inside of us, because it is the same language everything everywhere speaks. It is the language of energy.

Let's go back to the situation with the angry boss. Your mind has identified the energy from your boss as anger. You can react, as our friend Randy did, with compassion. His angry boss responded to Randy's inquiry into what was the matter, by telling him what was really going on. He was upset because his wife was going to have to have breast cancer surgery. Randy, who happens to be psychic, knew something else was happening in his boss's life.

We are all psychic. We are all energy readers. It is a part of our natural human ability to understand and know energetic communication. It is our inherent right to use this language to help us negotiate our world.

Energy continually reacts and changes the energetic flow within your mind. You make choices, like the conductor, of what energy you want to flow in and flow out of your mind. Energy must respond to your choices. In this way, energy is continually reorganized and reshuffled inside of your mind to reflect the energy inside of your mind. It is an instantaneous process. You automatically identify energy and change energy without your even realizing it! In fact, it is so natural to you, it does not require your awareness or any thought at all. It happens because who you are is really energy. You can have blonde hair, brown eyes, dark skin, light skin, and any type of nose, but the fact is, we are all the same. We are energy.

Our mind, with Universal Mind, helps us recognize our energy through how we create with our energy. What we see around us is really us. We are it; we are the twenty-four/seven "us" channel, making each of us special. In fact, we are so special, that the way we use our energy is very significant.

Think back to Randy's boss. Randy's boss has a very difficult time talking about his feelings and his private life. It would be hard for him to come into work and say, "Randy, I am really having a tough time today. I just found out my wife needs surgery. I just found out she has breast cancer."

In reality, because he was in shock about his wife's condition, it was really hard for him to formulate words. He may have felt powerless and inept. Perhaps he subconsciously wanted Randy to feel his experiences of being powerless and inept, perhaps because he felt powerless and inept regarding his impact upon his wife's condition.

Randy, who is not only psychic, but also a therapist, reacted in a way that helped Bill see how he was feeling. It helped clear the gunk out of the road so that Bill could talk about how he was feeling more directly and give Randy the information about his wife. The interaction between Randy and Bill became one of healing, creating a connection for both people, rather than a feeling of anger and powerlessness. It helped Bill to let other people in the office know what was going on in his personal life and allowed Bill to receive the support from his coworkers that he really needed.

Energy reacts to mental vibrations because mental vibrations are intelligent. Look at the lamp in your living room, if you have one, if not, picture one in your mind. The electricity comes from your house socket into the lamp and creates light. The lamp is engineered to define the resource of energy to create light, but what really makes the light? Your vacuum cleaner and your computer does the same thing. Most important of all, so does your mind. Your mind connects with intelligent energy and chooses to direct its intelligence.

This means that you can make the intelligence within energy work for you and not against you. It means you can focus energy because you recognize its ability to react intelligently towards your focus.

Think back to the lamp. The intelligence within the energy of electricity creates light. How smart is that? We just don't recognize its IQ, because we don't pay attention to it. We are so used to the brilliance of energy that we don't consider it at all! But there it is, all around us, very busy doing what it does naturally.

But, wait! The good news is, so are we.

Yes, we have the power to interact in an aware and intelligent way with energy. We have the power to interact with energy in the same way we choose to interact with people. So, if a stranger walks across the street and attempts to talk to you, you can choose whether or not you talk back. On occasion, we have people call up and want us to spontaneously talk to them about their concerns with metaphysics, without an appointment or without consideration about what we are doing at that moment. We have a choice to continue the conversation or ask them to make an appointment for a session. We have a choice to block the interaction, or continue to let the interaction flow.

Your interactions with energy can operate in the same way. You can block, within your mind, certain energy from occurring. Ever have this experience with a child or friend? They are insistent about wanting something, and you say no, more than once, without eye contact. You just keep on moving without that eye contact! It is the same way with energy, you don't budge in your mind toward allowing an energy into it that you don't want. You block it and you can feel the presence of the block in your mind.

You don't even have to say a word for this block to form. It is created through your intentions, inner experiences, and knowing you want a block to happen.

You can block energy anytime and anywhere and direct the block toward any situation on the planet.

Energy is very flexible. Did you ever play with a slinky toy when you were a kid? The slinky is a metal coil-shaped toy that can go down stairs. You could also twist it in many ways. You could do the same thing with salt water taffy at the fair. Twist it and turn it and pull it till it gets really, really thin. Or you can push it all together in one lump ball and make it really thick. Energy is the same way.

It is flexible and soft and reacts to your healing, inner intentions, experiences, and knowing in an immediate and flexible way.

You can block a situation from happening through healing and the block will begin immediately.

Now, remember, in some situations, you may not be able to see the outcome in a physical, concrete way. The outcome is determined through your relationship with Universal Mind. Nonetheless, your energetic blocks may have profound effects.

It may start to begin to sound like the conscious use of your energy carries along with it a lot of responsibility? Well, it does. I think that is why many people have chosen not to know about it, really know about it, for a long time. We kind of have been skipping along, having a grand ole time, dabbling in this, and dabbling in that. But to really, really know about energy, well, that means being aware of ourselves in a way we have not experienced consciously before.

Are you ready to learn more about energy? We know you are. We are facing problems on this planet that will not be resolved until each one of us, including you, own your own power.

We believe in you, your energy, and your ability to be aware of your energy. You can make your life and your world a better place by understanding how the energy within you works and you can make your energy work for you.

Energetic Balance

Picture the symbol of Yin and Yang. You may want to find the symbol in a book or through the Internet on a computer. This symbol represents a perfect balance of energetic waves, yet the symbol carries within it a small circle of the other half's energy, one small circle black, and one white. In such a balanced state, if there was just the slightest movement, an imbalance would immediately occur.

Energy creates imbalances through movement and then seeks to reunite through relationship and shift into balance through additional movement. The movement from balance into imbalance helps to reorganize energy so that energy can change.

Changes happen because energy can become unbalanced. Change can help accommodate new changes.

Our friend Tammy told us about a situation where a performer's nude pictures of herself were placed on the Internet without her permission. The performer stated, "Well, now I get to see what I am made of, don't I?" She looked at the challenge as one she could overcome. Because of this life event, she decided to use parts of herself, such as courage and fortitude, she did not know existed.

If our lives were always in balance, we would not be on a path of discovery to find out who we are. We would just be moving along on the same road, without it ever becoming bumpy. We would not find out more about ourselves then we were already aware of. Challenges would not present themselves to help us grow.

Imbalances in energy present challenges. The momentum of energy seeks to acquire balance. Think of a dam. One side of the dam is full of water, which the dam has made into a lake, the other is just a small trickle of river. The dam breaks and the water will seek its lowest level.

The energy within you will seek to level itself out through healing. If there is a conflict present, if you are at a job you do not like, you will seek to correct the energy within you to a greater harmony. It could be as simple as changing your attitude, or changing your job entirely. It could be a series of inner changes, such as finally recognizing the need to begin your own business and focusing upon the confidence to do so. Regardless, the energy within you will present itself over and over again throughout your work day, and throughout your life, until the energy becomes balanced.

Energy will also seek to use creativity as a tool in order to become balanced. Energy builds and depletes through imbalance.

Say, for example, that you are at a job that you do not like. Harry, one of our clients, hated his job. He had ideas about a product he had invented, but was unsure about how he could market it. He could market it, but he was being challenged to believe and trust in his product's marketability. Until he creatively healed his inner experiences about his product, his product was going to remain on the shelf (unless someone else also created a similar product). Harry had to believe that other people were going to believe in his product and buy it, too!

Energy seeks to build. Energy seeks to know itself through the creativity gained within its own expansion. Harry now had to trust in parts of himself that he had not counted on before. He had to trust and heal his connection with his courage, value, and confidence. How did the story end? Harry did market his product, it was successful, and he quit his job.

Energy seeks to revitalize itself through creative change.

How many of you out there are artists, writers, athletes, or musicians? What do you engage in that feels creative to you? It can be as relaxing as fly fishing, or as perhaps labor intensive as painting a portrait. What is it inside of you that really feels timeless, fun and inventive? What is the energy doing inside of you? Creative energy creates a relationship with life force energy through the Universal Mind. It literally sparks life into your physical brain.

There have been videotaped experiments conducted (which I do not condone) with mice. The mice are given laser zaps which create trauma in their brains. The mice have strokes and are then paralyzed. Their neurotransmitters then gather around the trauma to heal the trauma and the internal bleeding stops. Other neurotransmitters take over and the brain heals. You can literally see sparks of light occurring in the mice's physical brain as it heals.

We have the same capacity to heal ourselves through the drive of energy to seek balance. And we can use this momentum within energy to know more about who we are and the power within who we are.

Mind and Variety

The Universal Mind, wants to know who it is, by building itself outward and viewing its own energy. Stand up. Put your hands at your side. Look forward. You can't see yourself. Now, lift up your hand so that you can view it. Look at your hand closely; you can see it. It is the same thing with the Universal Mind. It senses it has a hand, in fact, the Universal Mind can feel it. But it doesn't quite know what it is and what it can do. So it creates us, a part of its energy, so that the Universal Mind can know more about who it is. We provide the Universal Mind with consciousness and self awareness. Who we are, the energy within us, balances out the energy within the Universal Mind, so that the Universal Mind, becomes consciously aware of its own energy. It sees the hand. The Universal Mind not only sees the hand, but it can view what the hand can do.

The flow of energy from the Universal Mind intends to create self awareness. Because we are part of the Universal Mind's energy, the flow of energy through us from our unconscious is intended to help us become aware. Through our dream states, the symbolic language of energy talks to us, so that we can know more about our state of energy.

The energy within the Universal Mind always has to have variety present within it, because it is constant in its building. You cannot have expansion without variety. It would be an impossibility. The Universal Mind constantly provides us with a variety of vibrations to experience, so that we can discover more about the vibrational experiences.

Remember Miles Davis? He was a very inventive jazz player. He had a set of notes available for his use. He learned them, like any other musician. But, unlike any other musician, he took what he learned and used it in a very different way.

Your creativity, the way you play an instrument, write, paint, or perhaps help other people heal, is going to be very different from any one else on the planet. The way you use your energy is uniquely governed by you and is like your own specialized thumbprint. It cannot be copied and it cannot be duplicated.

We are constantly given notes, or energy, from Source to use as our very own energetic experiences. We can take this energy and do what we wish with it through our creativity. We can create variety for ourselves, because our creativity allows us to create variety.

Because we are creative individuals, it is impossible for us to be stuck in one vibration experience. We can

always expand our choices, because we are creatively prompted to do so through the Universal Mind.

Even if you are experiencing repeated traumas and you seem to be unable to get out of psychological patterns that repeat themselves, they are repeating themselves for one reason only: so that you can make a different choice through self awareness into a different experience.

Take Diane, one of our clients, for an example. She had a traumatic childhood. Her father continually emotionally abused her and belittled her. He also physically battered her. She grew up traumatized and scared of men. She repeated the pattern of abuse by marrying young at eighteen to escape her situation. Although her new husband seemed charming at first, he quickly changed after the marriage. He too began to belittle her and hit her, for not taking care of the house and for not having dinner on time. Inside of herself, Diane felt he was right, she was to blame for his behavior, that somehow, she just didn't do things right. However, these thoughts were not right.

Some of you might blame Diane for getting into such a mess, especially after her horrible childhood. But there is another reason why Diane repeated the pattern. She needed to find another way out of her past vibrational experience. She had to come to terms that she was not at fault for his behavior, no matter what she was doing within the relationship.

Her shame about her childhood was replaced with self value about her worth. She was able to work through the energy that her husband repeatedly dished out to her and look at his behavior in a different way. She was able to step back from his criticisms and see that he intended to make her feel inadequate. She also began to see that he felt a need for her to be inadequate, so that he would not have to view his own inadequacy. Through her broader view that she gained through healing, Diane began to let go of the relationship. Over time, she eventually divorced him.

Patterns are presented again and again within a person's life, until they are able to see another way out. If the patterns were left unrepeated, the energy would remain static, stable, and unhealed.

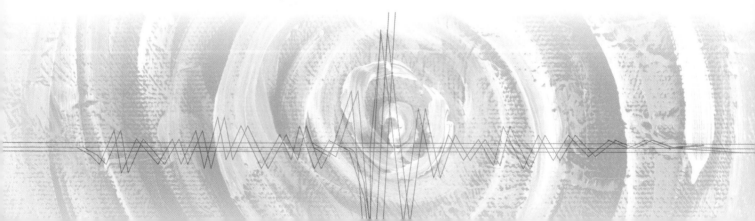

Points to Remember:

Shifts into different views can occur.

Once energy becomes exposed, another view makes itself apparent.

The varieties of energy can be recognized in the form of inspired thought, intuition, knowing when you need another's viewpoint for support, or healing.

When we see, without blinders, the constant variety of the energetic choice around us, we see the true nature of Source.

Because the energy in the universe flows, variety through change is the stable energy within the universe.

The law of variety guarantees the presence of choice.

You can empower yourself to see the variety of choices in your life that you really do have.

Changing energetic vibrations allows relationships with energy to change.

The energy changes without our doing anything other than being in the new energy we want.

Energy can shift automatically. What is newly created can shift automatically as well.

Energy and Mind

Because your mind is an organizing tool for energy, energy reacts to your mental experience.

Your mind creates a path for energetic vibration.

Your mind can shape energy. It can shape energy to any form your mind can direct.

Energetic vibration can be moved forward through your focus.

Energy continually reacts and changes the energetic flow within your mind.

You can focus energy because you recognize its ability to react intelligently towards your focus.

Yes, we have the power to interact in an aware and intelligent way with energy.

Energy is very flexible.

Energetic Balance

Energy creates imbalances through movement and then seeks to reunite and shift into balance through additional movement.

Changes happen because energy can become unbalanced.

Imbalances in energy present challenges. The momentum of energy seeks to acquire balance.

Energy will also seek to use creativity as a tool in order to become balanced. Energy grows and expands through imbalance.

Energy seeks to know itself through the creativity gained within its own expansion.

We have the same capacity to heal ourselves through the drive of energy to seek balance.

Mind and Variety

The flow of energy from the Universal Mind intends to create self awareness.

The Universal Mind constantly provides us with a variety of vibrations to experience, so that we can discover more about the vibrational experiences.

Because we are creative individuals, it is impossible for us to be stuck in one vibration experience.

Patterns are presented again and again within a person's life, until they are able to see another way out.

Affirm:

I have a variety of experiences I can choose from.

Experience:

You may want to grab your journal for this exercise. Take a deep breath. Focus on a pattern that reoccurs in your life. It could be a recurring problem with your mother. Perhaps you quit job after job without satisfaction. Again, you find yourself in the same old conflict with a coworker. Write down the pattern. Notice where the pattern occurs, what emotions it brings up, what happens before the pattern starts up. Write down your answers. Think back to your past. Are there any similarities in your pattern and events in your past? Write down the similarities. Now, write down the changes you need to make to help yourself heal the pattern. These changes are in your control. Perhaps you need to become less defensive when your mother criticizes you and begin to not buy into her comments about your child rearing. Maybe you need to stand up to your interfering coworker and let them know you do not appreciate their behavior. Perhaps you need to begin to believe that you are smart enough to further your education and to get the job you do want. What steps do you need to go through to help yourself make the changes? Write those down as well. You are now blocking the old energy from forming. Now, when do you begin?

Chapter Seventeen
The Universal Law of Containment

There is an overriding force in the universe, sometimes people call it God, that helps move the energy in creation in the right direction. The law of containment states that all the energy in the universe is within Universal Mind and Mind moves energy in the right direction.

So, you ask, what is the right direction? The right direction, as far as energy is concerned, is flow. Energy likes to create flow through balance and imbalance. Although you may be intent on buying a new house, your energy may be saying to the universe that you are afraid of commitment. Energy does not understand that you really want that new house and, so, let's go ahead and get the house for you. Your energy states, "I am afraid of buying that new house." The energy in the world around you may present to you circumstances that validate your fear over and over again, mirroring your inner fear. Why? So that you can consciously begin to be aware of your fear and consciously heal your fear. The "right" direction for energy within this case is to change fear towards expansion. Fear that is not fear becomes faith, courage, or trust. The energy of fear can flow into a direction of expansion, which means broadening energy that was within a narrow mental space.

The right direction also might be narrowing energy from a broader, more open space. Remember the keeper and the tiger? The keeper experienced fear by running from the tiger, which, of course, is the reaction we would probably have! He recognized energetic circumstances in his world that were threatening his life.

Energy direction is supported by the flow from the Universal Mind and it is always toward one thing: change. And change guarantees one thing: The force behind change can only be the Universal Mind.

You have the power to access this force whenever you choose to change the flow of your energy. You have the power to know that the creative flow of the Universal Mind moves through you with the power to change any circumstance, no matter what it may be. You have the power to unite with this force through the enlightened knowing that this force exists through you, so that you can become the powerful force you already are.

Wholeness of Mind

You are whole and complete, just as you are, because you have access to all of the energy that exists within the Universal Mind. Remember the golf ball within the large ball? You cannot be anything but whole, because your existence is connected to the larger Source of energetic vibration.

And because of your connection to the Universal Mind and your unique vibration, the Universal Mind recognizes you. Your vibration is like your very own thumbprint. No one has your thumbprint, except you.

The energetic flow from the Universal Mind guarantees that you have access to creative forces which make you complete, just as you are. We watched a television show recently about a woman who was a mechanic. She was born without arms and legs, however, she had artificial hands attached to her shoulders and was able to move herself around on a skateboard. Of course, many people may have considered her disabled, but she considered herself anything but disabled. She worked and was about to get married. She saw herself whole and complete, just as she was.

This woman opened herself to the creativity that was available to her from the energy inside of her and operated her life from a place of strength and power. It was obvious that she saw herself as empowered and able to live her life freely in the way she chose. She was not a victim and did not see herself a victim, although she could have easily lived her life as one.

When things happen, we have several choices. We can whine and cry and stamp our feet about life's circumstances, and it is our right to do so. It is also our right to choose to do something else, because we view our life from a different stance. Being a victim when we have choices available; is a choice.

Now, we are not saying there are not circumstances that happen that truly victimize people, such as child abuse. There are circumstances that occur that take away choice. What we are saying is that it is our choice to continue to be a victim once we become able to make choices and we are responsible for our choices.

It is our choice not to use the power within the Universal Mind to help us heal, create our choices and act on our choices. We do not have to remain in a position that does not empower us because all of the forces of empowerment lie within us.

We are powerful. We have been brainwashed to believe we are disabled by outside, not inside forces. We have been disabled by outside forces that do not validate our inner goodness through our inner, not outer, connections with God.

Our sovereign right to be independent, to deeply recognize our connectedness to the Universal Mind, to validate and operate from that connection, is our inherent right as human beings. It is our natural right to know our wholeness through our connection and to know that through our connection lies our true worth as people.

We are divine, and through our divinity, we are whole, no matter our circumstances, current conditions and the family we were born into. All of these energy types are external views that can be changed through our inward perception with the creativity of the Universal Mind. We are truly this free, we are truly this alive, and we are truly this connected.

God Feels

No one, not anything, be it plant, animal, or human, has your unique set of vibration energy. And through your energy, God experiences your presence.

Your existence, your personality, all of who you are, is felt consciously by God all of the time, no matter where you are, or what you are doing. Because your existence is recognized, you are considered. Because you are considered, all of your energy all of the time is responded to by God. You are in the creation mode 24/7 constantly flowing with the energy through the Universal Mind.

No matter how alone you feel, or think you are, you are not. It is virtually impossible to be alone with so much attention given to you! You are the star attraction, because no matter how many billions of energy types exist in the universe, there is only one *you* that is recognized.

You are always being recognized, no matter how you feel or how you are vibrating. If you are in a good mood, bad mood, or anything in between, your energy is constantly vibrating; me, me, and me. In our most alone moments, in our greatest crisis, and our worse disasters, God sees our energetic vibrations.

What that means for us is that we can count on being recognized by the Universal Mind, no matter what our circumstances are. We are heard, seen, and felt by the Universal Mind through the language of our vibrations.

It is impossible for us to be left unseen. It is impossible for us to believe we can hide our energy.

We continually vibrate our energy, so who we are is continually experienced, not only by God, but by all energy everywhere. We broadcast "the me" channel all the time, every minute, no matter what the show.

Like us, God too is broadcasting "god" energy 24/7. The language of the Universal Mind is symbolic. God may speak in music, art, writing, athletic performances, nature, healing, miracles, or any energy that is creative.

Creative energy expresses one thing: building energy. Expansive energy is energy that is flowing out to create a broader flow of energetic choice. That spark, the flow of ideas, that creative juice that is rolling through your mind; that is the energy from the Universal Mind. That is what God is, the flow of energy through you so that you can know more about who you really are through your own acts of creation. In that way, you know and mirror God's energy back to God, so that God can consciously recognize its own energy. Your creation, meaning your very life, is divine.

We remember a friend of ours, Ally, talking about another friend of hers. Her friend stated that she believed she was a Goddess. Ally told her that even though you may feel like that, you are not a worshipped and immortal Goddess. The fact is, we do not have to take on the powerful identity of something we are not to own our powerful identity.

While we may not be Gods or Goddesses because we are human and mortal, we are just as divine and powerful nonetheless. As divine people, our daily actions become sacred and our lives holy.

Are we this important? Do you have the courage to believe you are equal to the presence of God? Yet, it is our very belief that somehow we are not good enough, okay enough, or wise enough, that has rendered us purposeless and our activities senseless.

Some of us have been brainwashed to believe we cannot be present with the energy of God, so we do not embrace the full power of God's presence. And yet, we can feel the creative Source of empowerment that the presence of the Universal Mind provides for us. When we believe we are not equal to this presence, we do just that: create inequality. And in our inequality, we are ashamed of who we are, rather than embrace what we are. For those of us who have been brainwashed in this way, it is our shameful belief of inequality that has caused aggression, fear, and disconnection with others.

If we are to truly create peace, end hunger, and provide justice, we must own our divine right to be equal with God. We must know our equality like we know it is our right to breathe, to eat, and to exist. It is our inner conflicts in owning the power of equality that has created conflicts outside of us that are unequal.

We can resolve those conflicts. We can resolve them now. We can accept the presence of God within us, feel the connection through our creative energy and build the knowledge of who we really are.

The Third Solution

Types of energy are made through the combination of your energy with the energy of the Universal Mind. You cannot make new energy, but you can make something new with the energy already available to you. In this way, energy from yourself and the Universal Mind continues to birth creative views of reality.

By the very nature in which we are made, we are placed into a position where we must recognize our connection with the Universal Mind in order to create from our connection. When our connections are narrowed by fears, which are not reactions to our environment, we sever our connections.

Think back to the tiger. It is a good plan to feel fear in a fearful situation. But what about one of our clients who was fearful of a long-term relationship, because she was unconsciously afraid of long-term sexual intimacy leading to sexual abuse? Her fear did not serve a good purpose.

Remember, no one within the universe has your energy. Although the stars, planets, and the world around you are made up of the same energy we all are, because we are all one, the fact is that you are you and you have your individual thumbprint. Your energy with the energy within the Universal Mind will always create something unique. This means that with every moment of your existence, something within you and the Universal Mind creates another something that is entirely singular.

One plus one does not equal two, it actually equals three! The third something is an expansive choice of energy through the combined efforts of the Universal Mind and the power of your energy.

You are always in a position of creating change. You can always manifest something other than what is within this moment to have something different. The combination of energy between you and the Universal Mind connects, expands, and makes a different view for you to see.

A client of ours, Joyce, was looking to become involved in a relationship. She did meet a man, but jumped into the relationship with both feet, treating him as though he was already romantically involved with her. When he panicked and began to back away, she was advised to treat him like a "friend." Her view of the situation changed, as she put it, she "clicked in" and she was able to change her attitude towards him. He then relaxed and began to connect with her more.

When we open our mind, we allow the energy from the Universal Mind to flow through us. We gain the ability to clearly see a different path, one that was not thought of before, perhaps one we didn't even think was useful and we were resistant to seeing. However, when we finally do see the view, we are often astounded at the simple clarity we find in what we see.

There is an acceptance of this new view, because we already sense within our knowing the possibility of its existence, making it real. Eureka! Of course, that is the answer, that is the ticket, how else could it be?

The connection between your energy and the Universal Mind's energy always creates. You cannot have creation without your energy or the energy within the Universal Mind. Different types of energy cannot be made without this joint effort.

Intent and its Purpose

Remember that your mind is a tool, a way of organizing energy. Like a well-organized closet, it puts energy into categories and organizes energy in a way that makes it useful to you. Can you imagine going into your closet with nothing organized? One shoe is way up high on a shelf and the other, who knows where, hidden under a pile of clothes on the floor. You could not easily take out the clothes you need to get ready for work if they were not on hangers. Not without a lot of extra work. Your mind naturally organizes the energy within it without much conscious thought.

If it did take all of your thinking to organize the energy within it, you could not function, there would not be enough time! Imagine thinking, well, now I have to breathe, lift my arm, turn my head and blink my eyes! Your brain would get fried up in one minute!

We are saved from those conscious uses of energetic tasks through the use of our intent. Our intent immediately organizes our energy in a conscious way that pulls together all of the energy within us that we may not be conscious of. In this way, you can intend what energy to use within your mind and within the Universal Mind.

Since nothing creative can be made without the energy of the Universal Mind, your intention pulls together the creative flow of energetic resources from yourself and the Universal Mind. Together, your intention organizes the energetic flow of joint energy toward a creative endeavor of joint intent. It is the formation of your intent that acts a tool to govern the direction of joint universal flow.

Your intent does three things at once. It recognizes energetic flow, embraces the joint power that is within flow, and conducts flow towards a conclusion. You are able to take your intent, take the energy that is already organized within your mind, like a well-organized closet, and say, hold on folks, this is where we are going next, yeee ha!

The energy that is available to you within this closet is limitless. Imagine that. Limitless supplies of shoes and pocket books! Certainly our dream come true! No matter how often you would go into that closet, like a cornucopia, more great shoes appear! The types of energetic choices are infinite!

Balanced Energy

By owning and accepting God's energy within us, we can expand our energy, empower ourselves, and raise the frequency of our energetic vibrations. In this way, we balance our energetic vibrations with the energy within the Universal Mind. We become dense and strong with all of the energy within the Universal Mind. We have the power to embrace this energy and to use this energy for the greater good of ourselves and the world around us.

By balancing our energy with the energy within the Universal Mind, we automatically access realms beyond our three-dimensional world. Because of the equation of the vibration, we develop relationships with energy that exist beyond our world. This energy may not be able to form a relationship with our energy before, but the ascension of our vibration made the relationship possible. Once the frequency of our energy expanded, our view changed locations and what we saw and experienced became different. We suddenly could see and interact with energy that we could not interact with before.

As I progressed upon my journey as a trance channel, I began to see things in the physical realm that I had not witnessed before. Colors flashed in from the astral world on a daily basis. Entities from around my home, I saw skirting across the parking lot. Orange arms appeared in front of me, telling me something about a person I was working with. All of these experiences became non-frightening to me, although I would initially become startled. I knew I was

allowing the world of the spirit to enter my experience, because the energy around fear was not narrowing my experience. I was balancing my energy with other energy in other dimensions, so that my experience of other dimensions became commonplace.

The energy that finds expression through other energy is a combination of our energy, the Universal Mind energy and other energy from hidden dimensions. Remember that we are all one. The energy that comes through from other dimensional realities creates their energy with the Universal Mind as well as we do. They form a relationship with us, because the frequency of our vibration has allowed this relationship to form.

We interact with this uniquely created energy to know more about who we are as energy. We experience other worldly energy to know more about ourselves. In this way, we are empowered to shape our world with the creative gift of knowledge in the never ending process of making the unconscious where God lives, conscious.

Universal Mind Responds

Your energy is always connected 24/7 to the energy within the Universal Mind, it cannot be separated. We can prove it to you. Close your eyes, take a deep breath, focus in on your awareness, be really conscious of it. Now, try to separate it from the sea of energy around you. What happens?

You may find out that your consciousness is pretty flexible, you can stretch it out here, there and everywhere, move it deeper inside of you, but you can't cut if off from the sea of energy surrounding you. In fact, try as you might, but it is impossible!

Belief in your connection to the Universal Mind is not needed for connection to the Universal Mind to happen. Your mental energy guarantees this connection, whether or not you consciously accept the connection. Your mental energy already assumes that the Universal Mind is a part of its energy, so conscious belief or recognition is not needed. It would be like believing in your arm. Okay, I have an arm, it does not require my belief to exist. You can see how ridiculous that is!

Just like your arm, the Universal Mind assumes its connection to you. And because the connection is assumed, so is the continual response to your energy. The Universal Mind must respond to you, because, like your arm, it is attached to you.

You are a part of the Universal Mind and the Universal Mind is a part of you. So, even if you are not moving your arm towards that cup of green tea, your mind still recognizes its presence. There is not one moment where your arm is not recognized by you, taken into account, and responded to as a part of you.

The Universal Mind responds to you continually, because there is no other way for it to exist. The existence of the Universal Mind counts on your presence. Your arm cannot exist without you. In the same way, the Universal Mind counts on your presence for it to be.

Remember, we are equal with the Universal Mind. We are important, so important, that the existence of the Universal Mind counts on us for it to flow with life force. And because it counts on us for life force, it must respond to our life force in order to continue creation of the life force.

So yes, we evolved, from the start, along with the Universal Mind. The memories of our existence in our knowing are aware of our connection and our involvement. Our knowing is aware of the continual presence of the Universal Mind and counts on this presence to help us live.

Of course, the Universal Mind is unable to be unresponsive to your energy. The only way it would not respond, would be if the Universal Mind suddenly was not there. It would be like your trying to ignore your arm and not respond to it. Try to pretend that your arm does not exist when it does.

Points to Remember:

There is an overriding force in the universe, sometimes people call it God, that helps move the energy in creation in the right direction. The law of containment states that energy must move in the right direction with the help of God.

The right direction, as far as energy is concerned, is flow.

Energy direction is supported by the flow from the Universal Mind and it is always toward one thing: change.

Wholeness of Mind

You are whole and complete, just as you are, because you have access to all of the energy that exists within the Universal Mind.

God Feels

Your existence, your personality, all of who you are, is felt consciously by God all of the time, no matter where you are, or what you are doing.

That spark, the flow of ideas, that creative juice that is rolling through your mind; that is the energy from the Universal Mind.

That is what God is, the flow of energy through you so that you can know more about who you really are through your own acts of creation.

Your creation, meaning your very life, is divine.

Some of us have been brainwashed to believe we cannot be present with the energy of God, so we do not embrace the full power of God's presence.

The Third Solution

Types of energy are made through the combination of your energy with the energy of the Universal Mind.

It is our inner conflicts in owning the power of equality that has created conflicts outside of us that are unequal.

By the very nature in which we are made, we are placed into a position where we must recognize our connection with the Universal Mind in order to create from our connection.

Your energy with the energy within the Universal Mind will always create something unique.

The connection between your energy and the Universal Mind's energy always creates. You cannot have creation without your energy or the energy within the Universal Mind. Different types of energy cannot be made without this joint effort.

Intent and its Purpose

Our intent immediately organizes our energy in a conscious way that pulls together all of the energy within us that we may not be conscious of.

Your intent does three things at once. It recognizes energetic flow, embraces the joint power that is within flow and conducts flow towards a conclusion.

Balanced Energy

By owning and accepting God's energy within us, we can expand our energy, empower ourselves, and raise the frequency of our energetic vibrations. In this way, we balance our energetic vibrations with the energy within the Universal Mind.

By balancing our energy with the energy within the Universal Mind, we automatically access realms beyond our three-dimensional world.

The energy that finds expression through other energy in three-dimensional reality is a combination of our energy, the Universal Mind energy, and other energy from hidden dimensions.

Universal Mind Responds

Your energy is always connected 24/7 to the energy within the Universal Mind; it cannot be separated.

Your mental energy already assumes that the Universal Mind is a part of its energy, so conscious belief or recognition is not needed.

The Universal Mind must respond to you, because, like your arm, it is attached to you.

The existence of the Universal Mind counts on your presence.

So yes, we evolved, from the start, along with the Universal Mind.

Affirm:

I am an equal participant with God in creating life.

Experience:

Take a deep breath and relax your body. Focus in on your ability to create. What do you like to do? Perhaps draw or paint? Perhaps write? Perhaps you have an ability to think up new ways to do things? Like an inventor? Are you musical? Do you like to sing? Intend to give yourself a window of time right now to experience what you like to do creatively. You may want to journal the answers to these questions after completing your experience. Where does your inspiration come from? How does it feel to you to create? Is it exciting or joyful? Did you feel a sense of energetic flow as you began your creation? Did you experience of sense of inner connection to something larger than you?

Chapter Eighteen
The Universal Law of Love

Love is the fundamental emotional building block in all creation.

Energy is not moral within our human description of morality. Energy is amoral. It exists within a structure that does not allow for moral judgments to contain or change its activities.

However, it is moral as we describe morality in one way; energy operates most efficiently and completely within the energetic flow of love. That is, because the energy of love broadens and opens the flow of energy. Love allows for more energetic choices to be created, seen, and experienced within its vibration. Why? Because when you view a situation or someone with love, you experience an open compassion to viewing their life from their point of reference. You see with their eyes.

For most of us, it is easy to feel love for a child. We are sure most of you have been involved with, or witnessed, a similar situation such as this. You are at your exercise class, someone has brought their child who promptly becomes bored and is determined to get their parent to pay attention to them. The parent, or someone else who cares, helps the child cope with the situation by giving them something to do. That's easy.

Now, when we are speaking of love, we are not suggesting to gloss over feelings of anger in regards to a situation and force yourself to forgive or love. We are suggesting that there are broader perspectives that looking at situations through the lens of love can provide. You may have to experience anger, or resentment, and grieve before you can see through the lens of love.

Perhaps the parent in another example never learned to support their child by helping them cope. It could be that they were punished for behaving "badly" when they were younger and punished their child in a similar way. In this example, the parent truly needs to recognize their unconscious anger towards their own parents, before they can begin to see their child with compassion. The parent was never allowed to express their feelings, good or bad. As a result, they have a hard time recognizing their anger toward their own child. They perhaps think they are reacting "normally." Don't we punish children when children act up? Or maybe there is a different way.

The different way would be looking at how we really feel, allowing ourselves to feel it, not judging ourselves for feeling it and accepting our true feelings. Our acceptance of our feelings allows our feelings to shift.

We are talking about true shifts of feelings into love to broaden your perspective.

Love expands our sight. It opens the gates and witnesses a great many more energy types other than the one we might see through other vibrations.

The law of love allows a great burst of universal energy to flow through it. That means that when you are building with love, you are creating with a strong, full flow of love. Think of a dam with the flood gates suddenly opened, imagine the full flow.

Love helps create, because love opens the floodgate to having more choices of ideas with which to create from. Let's go back to the child. The parent involves the child in the class, gives the child a job to do in the class, and gives the child a cell phone to play Pac Man on; that's love. Or yells at the child and tell her to sit still. That's anger. We have been witness to both responses. Remember, anger narrows choice, love expands choice.

Because the very act of creation automatically broadens choices, love is the only experience that can be within creation. What that means for us is that we can open ourselves to the experience of love and allow the floodgates to flow with the energy of universal love. In tandem, we build.

First Love

Love was the very first energy and the only true energy to exist. All other energetic emotions are blocks to love. We remember a client who was working with my friend, an energetic healer. This client had suffered an extremely abusive childhood perpetrated by her mother. She thought she felt nothing at all for her mother. Not anger, not hate, just indifference. She had years of therapy and believed she had come to a resolution about her mother.

However, she was suffering from a long-standing problem of sciatica. Her spine had locked up and she could barely move around.

Once the healer started to work, she realized she was angry. When she began to let go of her anger, she also began to let go of stored up memories. The client realized she was angry at her mother, which shocked her. She thought she had felt nothing. After continuing to talk about memories and letting go of anger, she began to feel love. After a very intense two hours, she realized that underneath this anger was love. She realized that she loved her mother. She was in total shock.

We cannot hate without a strong attachment of love. Otherwise, there would be no reason to hate, the motivation to hate would not exist. It is ironic, isn't it? All of our anger, our perception of differences and our fears about one another are truly generated from a source of love. Our perception that somehow we are not loved by others keeps us in a state of abandonment, which disconnects us from love. In our disconnection, we blame other people for not loving us. We judge ourselves for not being lovable. We forget to turn inward and connect with ourselves for the love we need and is always available to us from the Universal Mind.

When we can do that, we remember that love is always present inside of us, other people's behavior and issues can no longer affect us. Here is another irony for you. Unconditional love has strong boundaries. The strongest boundaries you can experience are present within unconditional love. Why? Unconditional love is not a state of action.

I remember hosting a radio show with one of my guests who truly believed there was no such thing as unconditional love. He believed that all love was conditional, that was how it had to be. In his mind, there must be a condition, a set of rules and a subsequent action, in which love had to meet in order to exist.

Well, what about the man who beats his wife as I have witnessed with many of my clients? What would unconditional love look like in this case? With treatment, the wife can look at the energy that is present within her that created the connection with her husband, experience unconditional love for herself, let him know that she must now treat herself with love and that is how she will be treated by others and create a loving environment for herself. Will the husband be present within her world? That would be up to him, whether or not he can be loving to himself as well. Unconditional love says yes to love and to love only.

Unconditional love is a state of being and receiving. Unconditional love is a statement about how you are, it is energy within your being. It states I am loving and willing to receive love. Unconditional love does not try to change other people by setting up rules that other people must meet. It is an experience within yourself which can build or deplete relationships with people.

In the beginning, there was only one Source with no divisive energy that created disconnections with love. Love is creative and naturally builds. We can recall this love whenever we create. When we create, we join with the Universal Mind and remember the beginning. We pull from memory the experience of love, and through love, we create with what we love to do.

Love is always creative. Because it is an open energy, it naturally and automatically presents us with choice. Because choice is present, love automatically broadens the view regarding any situation. Because we are seeing a situation with love, we are naturally changing the location of our view to that of the Universal Mind. We are seeing with love present within God's eyes.

Love Wants Love

Love wants to love. It wants to continue to manifest the creation of love. Love wants to create more love, because love then mirrors back its own creation to itself. Because love is infinite in its power to create love, the relationships made through love are the primary relationships within the universe. Everything that you see, touch, hear, smell, or experience and even sense is made through the relationships that love has created.

Love is the most primal and most available energy within the universe, because it is the original energy within the universe. Remember, creation is made from love, and love is what makes creation. Love is the basic element of existence. You cannot create without love and something cannot exist without it.

Look around you, everything that you are seeing and experiencing has been made from the energy of love, the creative force of love is present in each stone, blade of grass, or tree. All is present because of love.

The Universal Mind creates with love, and, through its creation, love then can know more about what to love.

As I am writing, I have my daughter's small teddy bear on my desk with a big red heart that says, "love." Someone made that teddy bear, so my daughter could buy it with the help of her dad, and give it to me for Valentine's day. It sits on my desk and I love it.

Think of your latest project, something you have made, perhaps a project at work, a painting, or the room you painted in your house. Now you can admire your handiwork with love. It is the love for your work that created something for you outside of yourself to admire and to love. Through your creation, something is present, made by you, in the world around you that is manifested through the energy of love.

In the same way, the Universal Mind creates with love. It makes things, including us, then sits back and loves what it has created.

You will be happy to hear this again especially if it is Saturday night, the official "date night" in America; love always wants to make more love. Why? Because it can know more about its own energy. Love can find out more about itself through what it makes. You can find out more about you through what you are able to make or through what you are able to do. If you love to run and become a marathoner, you find out more about what you can love about yourself by doing the thing you love.

Love creates for the infinite variety of expressions of choice that love has. Remember, the energy of love broadens choices. Because there are so many choices, love has in terms of what to express to create from love, love is free within its expression of creation. It has within its energy the infinite expression to express creation. It builds continually to express the freedom within its own energy. In this way, love continually mirrors creation.

You Are Love

Because love is a primary energy that exists within the Universal Mind, you are made from the original energy of love. Because love vibrates through all energy and can express a wide range of choice, your ability to be free is inherent within the energy within you.

As you may guess, the energy of love and freedom is virtually synonymous. Your ability to love is parallel to your ability to feel free.

Because of love, your ability to heal yourself clearly broadens your choices about how you are going to live your life. Remember the woman with the physically abusive husband? Her ability to experience love within herself freed her. It didn't happen because she demanded a set of expectations for someone else to meet, but because she experienced within herself an energy which created an environment where no other energy could exist.

The Universal Mind is free, being able to express itself through the energy of love in infinite ways. You are a part of the Universal Mind's free expression.

You have been made from an act of freedom, so that the Universal Mind could know more about freedom through making you.

I remember, years ago, reading my very first spiritual book. It was called *Jonathan Livingston Seagull* by Richard Bach. I remember the sense of freedom I experienced reading the words within that book. At that time, I was still living at home with my parents in an extremely abusive household. Regardless of what was happening in my home, I distinctly remember feeling this wonderful sense of freedom, because of that book. At the time, I had been pulled out of school and I was not allowed out of the house. Yet, I was experiencing freedom.

Love of life, creative works of art, and love for your spouse are all expressions of the choices within the energy of love and the choices made with love that are expressed through the Universal Mind.

Remember, we are all made from the same energy. The energy we express is also the same. The love that the Universal Mind created you with is the same love we build our lives with. There is no difference.

Because there is no difference, your love and the love the Universal Mind creates has an infinite choice of expression. Think of a mirror reflecting another mirror across from it. The mirror reflects another mirror and then another. There is an infinite reflection of mirrors within the mirror. You are not able to dislodge love as part of your creation. It would be like cutting off your ear or your arm. You can do that if you want; I personally would not recommend it. Why would you? You were created as you are, so to try to pry energy out of the "you" made from creation would be impossible.

You are created as you are so that you have infinite choices as to how you can experience and build from love.

Love Heals

The energy of love does two things at once: it let's go and accepts. It resolves a paradox between two seemingly opposing energy types and provides a third option, another choice.

In fairy tales, count to three and that is when something extraordinary happens. It is the same thing with the energy of love. Experience love and the magic happens. No, not just between your girlfriend or boyfriend, but between all things everywhere. Love is the potion that brings things together.

The trick is, not only does love make relationships; it brings together energy which widens viewpoints and builds choices. Love makes something else come into the picture.

And like magic, energy can bring instantaneous results.

My guides sometimes present me with energy to experience. I experience the energy with a great deal of excitement and love. I focus my intent on the energy, experience the energy by placing it in my knowing and allow the energy to do its work. It is not always clear to me what work the energy was doing, until this happened. I was getting a pedicure and my nails done and was sitting in the massage chair just relaxing, while my feet played in the hot water. I closed my eyes and asked my guides what energy I should focus on. They gave me the energy of "ancestors." I had not known my ancestors, except for my mother's mother and father. My guides had been presenting the energy of ancestors to me to experience for a couple of months. I began to experience the energy of the ancestors in a meditative state. As I mentioned earlier about my trek to understand my ancestors, I suddenly heard a crack, a crack with my physical ears. It was loud. Then I felt energy peeling away from me through my aura, one layer right after another, first was abandonment, then a feeling of shame. In an epiphany, I realized that my ancestors wanted me, wanted to know me and wanted a connection with me. In awe of this experience, I paid for my service, left the shop and went home.

On my door was a card from a private detective with a note from my niece who had been trying to get in touch with me for months. The last time I'd seen her had been several years before. Her mother, my sister, is bipolar, and addicted to drugs and alcohol. Unfortunately, I could not maintain a connection with her. Her daughter, a recovering alcoholic, now maintains sobriety and is drug free. She remembered me from long ago and wanted to get back in touch with me because I am family. Once the defensive energy cracked and unblocked the wall between us, the connection established.

The energy of love resolves by letting go of the energy of fear and shame and accepts other energy, such as ancestor energy. The energy of love, because it is the primary energy that is within the Universal Mind and that the Universal Mind operates from, does not reside within the dimension of time and space.

Love is created from a viewpoint other than the present one that we see. Love is already within a different location. Yet, it is where we are at as well. The energy sees from both viewpoints.

Love's view is naturally expanded. It can't help but see things differently. Love sees a different landscape automatically without doing anything than being its own energy.

Love does not require action. Love requires being. And because love is, what it does naturally in being is see things as resolved whole and complete. There is then nothing more to do, other than to love.

Sound simple? Then why are we all not experiencing love? Not so simple. For those people out there who may want to dismiss experiencing love as trite, please reconsider.

Reconsider how much you consider yourself with love, how much you are love and how much you view the world with love. How much you are creating your life with love. It is love that people want when they want to know their life purpose, when they fill unfulfilled. They are asking, how can I feel whole? We create our lives from the inside out. It is love that does the building.

Ultimately, we can create wholeness with only one energy. And this energy can see and view all other energy. It is the only energy that sees and takes into account the existence of every other energy within the universe. No matter what the energy is—anger, shame, sadness, or fear—the energy of love can recognize it. And not only can the energy of love recognize all of these other energy types, it can bring this energy together and build something more.

Love can shift energy into wholeness, because love creates from a view that is whole. Love needs nothing more than to be what it is.

Love Accelerates Creation

Because love already views the universe from a place of wholeness, creation to make things whole is automatically accelerated. It is already and automatically complete.

Think of a project, perhaps a writing project, an art project, or baking a chocolate cake, something that you are making and have a great deal of passion about. What happens? You lose track of time, the project gets done in seemingly no time at all and you feel great about it. Because of the energy inside of you that is doing the building, the creation itself manifests effortlessly. And not only does it manifest effortlessly, it manifests simply. What you are doing feels simple, no matter how complex and sophisticated the task, your effort feels simple and easy.

It is the energy within you of love for what you are doing and for yourself that automatically opens other energy inside of you. Energy, such as inventive energy, or time saving energy, is freed to complete the task in an efficient manner.

Love utilizes all other energy and makes this energy work for you. The gates to the dam open and all of the water in the river flow through it. Love is the gate and you have use of all of your abilities and talents to have it flow through you effectively.

Love is the accelerator that makes this happen. It unites you and connects you with all of your energy. And because you are united with all of who you are, guess what? You get to use all of who you are and use it in a way that does not require you to sweat even one drop!

Love accepts and rejoices in its acceptance of who you are. And in its acceptance, it automatically lets go of any other energy that wishes to stop you in your tracks.

You guessed it. Love is a force. Like the ice crashing down a melting glacier, it is that powerful. It pushes through any energy that gets in its way and travels along that river with a speed that nothing can build resistance to. Love is its own power.

And with its own power, love can flow through you in connection with love from the Universal Mind to build in any way, direction and path it can. Remember the ball within the ball? All gates are open between the worlds of mind within the Universal Mind.

Although, you cannot control the outcome of building with love, you can control what energy flows through you and from you to create. Love is the seed of all creation and love automatically accelerates what is created. Love accelerates all other energetic vibrations, because it automatically lets go and accepts all other vibrations.

Love is not linear. It simultaneously views all energy and completes all energy into wholeness at one time. It is already whole and complete as it is. And because of its wholeness, all energy is speeded up.

Love is accelerated, because love is the central experience within the universe. All entities and galaxies know the energy of love. There is not one energy within the universe that does not have the experience of love.

Love is complete in its existence and is available to be utilized as an already present experience.

Think of the spirit. Many of you reading this book have had a spiritual experience. It could be as simple as viewing a beautiful sunset, or as profound as having a depth shattering enlightenment. In that experience, you felt a connection, a sense of love, and in that love you felt a sense of being loved. It is this sense of being loved that is a present universal experience for you to have. It allows you to accelerate and create with the love inside of you. It is the sense of belonging to yourself and to the universe that allows you to act as though you belong.

Love Balances and Imbalances Energy

Love creates imbalances in energy, because of how it views energy. Once an energy is recognized by love, it is able to observe its own imbalance, because of the recognition.

Our friend Matt's brother was a prison guard. He had the uncanny ability to walk into a room of prisoners who were involved in fights and was able to calm them down. He was able to do this because he did not react with anger. If he had done so, he would have balanced the prisoner's anger with his anger. He created an imbalance of energy through calmness, compassion, and love. Because of the imbalance of energy, that the prison guard was able to create, the prisoners were able to recognize their anger instead of acting out their anger. They calmed down.

Love can create a balance of energetic vibrations, because it is able to be receptive to all frequencies of energetic vibration. It does not matter if the vibration is rage, fear, or sadness. Love does not run away or escape this energy. Love is able to be with this energy in a way that accepts it.

The prison guard accepted the way the men felt and the prisoners knew it, because they experienced the acceptance. Because the prisoners were able to experience the acceptance, love was able to balance the energy towards the frequency of calmness.

Energy that is balanced through love retains its own identity, but it shifts in a fundamental way, it becomes more loving. Energy automatically shifts its own location when viewed by the energy of love. Its view becomes broader, because of the recognition of love.

The prisoners were able to step back from their anger. They may have felt they had more choices, because they were experiencing the acceptance of the prison guard. They could continue to act out anger or do something different. Because of love, they chose to do something different.

Love has the capacity to balance out any energy into an energy compatible with the frequency of love. No matter what the energy is, whether it be an emotion such as anger, or an event such as war, love has the capability of balancing the energy.

Imagine for a moment, that all of the countries in the world focus upon a country that experienced famine with the energy of peace and support? All of our relations, our policies, and our corporations would focus on helping this country. Do you believe this country would benefit?

Why Love?

As we have said, because the Universal Mind is constantly creating and constantly expanding, the energy within the Universal Mind can only be one primary energy: love.

Love can act in the way that the Universal Mind requires it to act. It can make with infinite variety. Love is not just the energy within God, it is the energy within all of God's creations. God continually connects through the energy of love to all of what God has made. God recognizes its own vibrations, but also consciously recognizes other energy. In this way, God gets to know who you are.

The energetic vibration of God's love is within you. You vibrate with love and you vibrate with your energetic choice and freedom about who you are.

Remember the golf ball inside of the ball? The Universal Mind is the large ball. You are inside of the ball, as a smaller ball. Your mind is a subset of the Universal Mind.

Your energy is also a subset of universal energy. The creativity in which you were made is you. You are completely unique, there is no one like you. Every grain of sand and every snowflake is also completely unique.

The primary energy of love within the Universal Mind serves to keep the connection open and flowing between you and the Universal Mind through the connection of love.

Love is the bridge that unites you and God. No matter how different you think you are, how misunderstood, how much of an outcast, you are understood by God through the energy of love.

God cannot exist without the energy of love. Without the connective power of love, the unified existence of all energetic matter would not materialize. The energy within God, love, cannot exist without materializing energy outside of itself. God cannot only exist in an abstract form, as an idea. It must exist in concrete materialization, so it knows that it does exist.

Love cannot exist without you to express it. Without you, without your feelings and your ability to act from love, love would not be in our world. In fact, love just wouldn't be at all.

By now, it may be becoming very clear how truly important we really are. Not falsely important, as in arrogance or disenfranchising your own power in thinking you are less, but in a equal stance with the energy that works through us. You are important in allowing energy from the Universal Mind to flow through you, so that their existence in your world actually happens.

Points to Remember:

Love is the fundamental emotional building block in all creation.

That is, because the energy of love broadens and opens the flow of energy.

The law of love allows a great burst of universal energy to flow through it.

Love helps create, because love opens the floodgate to having more choices of ideas with which to create from.

First Love

Love was the very first energy and the only true energy to exist.

Unconditional love is not a state of action.

In the beginning, there was only one Source with no divisive energy that created disconnections with love.

Love is creative and naturally manifests.

Love Wants Love

Love wants to love. It wants to continue to manifest the creation of love.

Love is the most primal and most available energy within the universe, because it is the original energy within the universe.

Love creates for the infinite variety of expressions of choice that love has.

You Are Love

Because love is a primary energy that exists within the Universal Mind, you are made from the original energy of love.

Because love vibrates through all energy and can express a wide range of choice, your ability to be free is inherent within the energy within you.

Your ability to love is parallel to your ability to feel free.

You have been made from an act of freedom, so that the Universal Mind could know more about freedom through making you.

The love that the Universal Mind created you with is the same love we create our lives with.

You are created as you are so that you have infinite choices as to how you can experience and create from love.

Love Heals

The energy of love does two things at once: It let's go and accepts. It resolves a paradox between two seemingly opposing energy types and provides a third option, another choice.

The energy of love, because it is the primary energy that is within the Universal Mind and that the Universal Mind operates from, does not reside within the dimension of time and space.

The energy sees from both viewpoints.

Love can shift energy into wholeness, because love creates from a view that is whole. Love needs nothing more than to be what it is.

Love Accelerates

Because love already views the universe from a place of wholeness, creation to make things whole is automatically accelerated.

Love utilizes all other energy and makes this energy work for you.

Love is a force.

Love accelerates all other energetic vibrations, because it automatically lets go and accepts all other vibrations.

Love is complete in its existence and is available to be utilized as an already present experience.

Love Balances and Imbalances Energy

Love creates imbalances in energy, because of how it views energy.

Love can create a balance of energetic vibrations, because it is able to be receptive to all frequencies of energetic vibration.

Energy that is balanced through love retains its own identity, but it shifts in a fundamental way, it becomes more loving.

Love has the capacity to balance out any energy into an energy compatible with the frequency of love.

Why Love?

As we have said, because the Universal Mind is constantly creating and constantly expanding, the energy within the Universal Mind can only be one primary energy: love.

The primary energy of love within the Universal Mind serves to keep the connection open and flowing between you and the Universal Mind through the connection of love.

God cannot exist without the energy of love. Without the connective power of love, the unified existence of all energetic matter would not materialize.

You are important in allowing energy from the Universal Mind to flow through you, so that their existence in your world actually happens.

Affirm:

I am loved and I express love.

Experience:

Do an experiment. Take a deep breath. You may want to journal this exercise. Think of a person who has angered you. Write now what you feel angry about. Is what you wrote down about something that they did to you? Or did not do? Take another deep breath. State this affirmation to yourself and write it down. What happens that you personalize this situation? Take a deep breath and imagine feeling a sense of great love for yourself. Take another deep breath and imagine breathing in the energy of love and out the energy of love. What else could be happening in this situation? Are there other possibilities? Continue to ask yourself what could be underneath the anger. What happens to the energy inside of you?

Try this experiment on a daily basis. Experimenting on a daily basis will begin to help you change your viewpoint of yourself and the world around you.

Chapter Nineteen
The Universal Law of Infinity

Because the primary energy of love always builds upon itself to create more, the alternatives within the universe are infinite. The law of Infinity provides us with infinite choice. Choices are countless because choices must be available, in tandem, with love flowing from the Universal Mind.

Our expression of love takes form in the way we choose to show love. The infinite expression of choice allows energetic vibrations to travel across and bridge to the concrete world through love.

I was blessed by a dream from the spirit a long time ago. In my dream, I was standing in a gray world. I call it the in-between world of the spirit, neither black nor white. In this world, I feel beings reside, including my own spirit guides. In my dream, I was looking out over the horizon. I was experiencing the confidence of my own knowing. I suddenly saw a light, a round ball of light off in the distance in the sky. I knew it was coming towards me and I knew I was calling it to come towards me. The light came and landed on my finger, like a bird.

We work with all energy, all of the energy we choose to recognize in the same way. We consciously become aware of its existence, we patiently allow it to come to us through our knowing and we allow the energy to exist within us.

Any energy you choose to experience and know its existence will come to you in the same way. The trick is to become aware of the existence of the energy. The energy is present for you to choose because of your awareness.

If you are blocked, because, for example, all you perceive is lack, you will not be consciously aware of the energy of abundance. The lack is the energy within you and it will be the energy you see outside of you.

Remember, opposite energy is always present no matter how "real" you think the experience of the energy is for you.

You can believe you have to be in your job because of the money. Or you can experience a creative flow of energy that helps you to believe you can be in a job you love and be fulfilled because of it.

Many clients come to us wanting to know about their life purpose. They are often shocked to find out that it is not just the expression of one talent or ability. It is often an expression of many abilities that they can choose to express in many different ways.

When you feel trapped, when you feel at the end of possibilities, rethink your belief system. There is always another different choice. Your choices open to you when you believe you have infinite choices to choose from.

There is a card from the Tarot deck called The Fool. The fool walks around unaware of where he is headed. In knowing how energy works and in trusting the energetic choices you make, you do not have to know where you are going. The energy knows for you.

Even when you think there is a limitation in terms of what can be different, think of yourself as the fool, open to a unique choice, trusting in the energy of that choice and moving forward in that by experiencing the energy. The energy will work for you.

Choice is Present

Differences of energy already exist before you choose them. In the case of energy, the cart is before the horse. All of the energy that you can consciously think of, and unconsciously know about, is already there. There is nothing new in terms of the choice of energy present that flows from the Universal Mind.

You can flow like water with different choices, because they are present for you to flow with. Your mind is like a braided river, it flows as one, but it also divides into different tributaries, each going their own way, but each connected to each other. Your tributary is different from any that exist on earth. Your tributary extends to the right and extends to the left as far as the eye can see. In fact, your tributary stretches out to the right and left infinitely.

Where we get in trouble is when our minds cannot perceive how large our branch of the river actually is. We think, at times, that it is much smaller than it is and we act as though there is a dam on our tributary dam and the gates in the dam are closed. When we believe that different choices are already there for us, then our river can flow and we can allow the water from our river to flow through us. Our choice has already been invented for us to know. In terms of time, it is already present.

In my dream of the light that came to me, the light existed before it landed upon my finger. I did not make the light. It's presence was just recognized by me. In the same way, the presence of your choices are already conceived for you to know. The gates within your dam must be open in order for you to see them. It is only the gates that block the flow of water that keeps water from flowing. The fact that the water exists, is an absolute. Nothing can change it.

Energy exists for our use. Energy wants us to use it so that it can express the existence of its choice to be. The form that energy takes is from our different choice to take on the form that already is.

Because energy is already present in the universe for us to use, we have one vital job to do, to become aware of its presence and, through consciousness, express its presence. Then, the energy comes to us, it flows to us from outside of ourselves. In that way, like Gandhi, or any of the great the spiritual masters, we allow the energy to lead us.

Different Choice

The concrete world of ourselves matches our view of the world from inside of ourselves. If you see different choices, choices will appear. Like presents under a tree at Christmas, opportunities, ideas, and solutions will come because of your inner experiences that there are different choices available to you.

The world outside of yourself will shift to match the location of your inner sight.

Think of yourself as traveling along a spiral path up a mountain. The higher to the top you get, the more different choices become apparent. You may be experiencing the same view, but more of it. A wider expanse of territory becomes available to see through your eyes. In the same way, your perception of choices become more open.

Often times, people will go through seemingly similar experiences in order to grow. One of our clients left a job because of a bullying boss. She went into another position where a coworker was controlling and insulting. In her new job, she learned she had different choices in setting clear boundaries with her coworker. She was learning she could assert herself.

The outside world always has many different choices available for you. It is what is noticed by you that is now seen.

When you know that there is a solution to a problem, but do not know what that solution is consciously, what you can trust is that the solution will come to you through your knowing.

Because you understand the law of relationships, you know that the energy outside of yourself will match the energy inside of yourself. The vibration of different choices inside of you will match the choice outside of you, helping you notice the choices that are already present for you to see.

When I practice shamanic journey, I am given choices in what power animal will lead me into various experiences. Bear presents himself and I can follow bear. Raven can come to me as well as Rhino. If I ask for more power animals to come they will. Even if I do not see them in my mind, their presence is already there within universal mind.

In terms of time, one plus one does not equal two. Twist your mind around like this: Two equals two and both of them together already equal four. The presence of four is already there.

We are continually in the process of equalizing and balancing our energy to make relationships. Through those relationships with energy, we notice what is already present for us to see.

Different choice cannot be seen without your being able to notice its presence. I am sure that you have had this experience, not noticing something that you thought should have been obvious to you. Why didn't I see that before? It is because, in some way, you were not ready to see it before you did. Some of the energy inside of you was blinding your vision.

Remember Maria, our client? Her mother betrayed her by not protecting her from her father's beatings. Maria learned not to trust feminine energy. She did not trust her ability to nurture herself. Once she began to trust her feminine energy, her ability to nurture her business flourished. Her nurturing energy was no longer hidden by betrayal energy.

Infinite Choice

In terms of energy, countless choices are always there. There is not just one black Labrador Retriever. Even though, when I walk my two black Labs, and see their cousins with their owners, I know that mine are different from their cousins and different from each other. They have different personalities and even look differently; one has a white spot on his paw, while the other has a kink in his ear. They even have different ways of communicating with each other, one has a louder deeper bark, the other whines more than barks. The point is, each black Lab is different from another black Lab, just like each human is different from another. We can make many choices if we choose to get a black Lab.

Your view of your choice may change. Perhaps your living arrangements are more suited for a choice of a Chihuahua than a Lab.

The choice you make today, may not appear as the same choice tomorrow. The choice you think is perfect in terms of the job that just got offered to you today, may be a different choice in terms of how you view the job tomorrow. Suddenly, you realize that the time it takes to get to work is anything but a plus. It is the same job you viewed with perfection yesterday, but now you a choosing a different way of looking at it.

You can choose to view the job you just got close up or step back and see it differently. You can jot down twenty things you now found out you don't like about your new job or step back and view the same job in a general way as positive for you. Or you can choose to notice twenty things you love about the job and step back and generally choose to see the job as negative for you because you now see it differently. You can view this job in infinite ways, dependent upon what you choose to notice.

You have infinite choices in how you view the same job.

The job and what it is, remains exactly the same thing.

The job does not change. It already is what it is. You change what you notice.

Energetic vibrations can also match what you experience and see through your experience. You believe that this job is the best thing since chocolate. I am sure many of you can relate. You treat the job like you would treat chocolate, with devout reference. The energetic vibration within the job itself responds to your absolute respect. It becomes easy for you to do, goes smoothly and your boss gives you a raise. The job treats you the same way you treat it.

The different choices you notice through your inward experiences help mold and create energetic matter. You determine what you notice and what you notice becomes apparent for you to see.

Different choices never stop being present for you to see. They are consistent in their availability to you. In other words, they are not like toilet paper. Yes, when you are in a bathroom, you can run out of toilet paper, but you can ask the woman in the next booth for more if it is a public restroom, go to the store, plan to get more next time, or have that hidden roll. But even when the toilet paper runs out, there are more choices already available to you about your next move.

Different choices are not dependent upon other distant choices in order to exist. What you choose yesterday, does not have to be your choice to make today. You still have choices, a broad range of choices, available for you to choose from. You can even make the opposite choice. Yes, people are free to change their minds. We do not have to make the same choice, or even a similar choice. All choices exist for our discriminative decision.

All choices are free. Seem irrelevant? No, think again. How many people do you know that stop themselves dead in their tracks from getting what they want. They believe they are being practical or some other seemingly "realistic" thing. What you choose does not cost you a cent. We attach so much baggage that comes from inside of us to our choice of energy. You might say that I cannot choose that option, because I do not have the money to start a business. Or that I cannot get a divorce because of the kids. I cannot move to California, because the price of housing is too expensive, even though I love the ocean off the California coast. I cannot, I cannot, and I cannot.

This bears repeating. Energetic choices are free of charge and they are free of psychological baggage.

Seem simple? The fact is; it is that simple, and simple is powerful.

If you can assist yourself through healing in letting go of your preconceived ideas about energy and reality, you can count on the intelligence and power of energy to work with you and for you.

Energy works through the Universal Mind and the energy from the Universal Mind works through you and through the choices that you allow to present to you.

Energy builds, and because you know energy builds, choices can be made. I know I can start my own business. Once I begin, the doors will open and money will flow to me, because I believe in what I am doing. My kids will adjust to life much easier in a home full of peace and harmony. I know I will find and be able to afford exactly the right house in California.

All of the different choices are already present. You made a choice to heal blocks and notice different choices.

Choice or Choices?

We create our lives from the inside out. We know we have repeated this sentence many times over, but it is so important for you to believe. We have been taught, through everything that you can possibly imagine, to believe that your lives are made from the outside in. You may have been brainwashed, like we were, and we are deeply committed to supporting your rehabilitation.

The choices you make inside of your mind are what builds outside of you in the physical world. Close your eyes. Focus in on the energy inside of your mind. Imagine your mind being in a tiny spot in your head, within your brain. Now, build the energy in your mind by imagining it literally becoming larger. Your mind is as big as your head, as big as the room you are in, as big as the house you live in, and as big as the town you live in.

Now, pull you mind back inside of your head. Open your eyes. Even though the focus on your mind is now placed nicely inside of your head, the energy of your mind continues to reside both inside and outside of your physical body.

But what is the energy of your mind doing outside of your physical body? Your mind is organizing the energetic choices you are making from inside of itself to outside of your body. Your mind is a tool for creating your different energetic choice.

Different choices can be made from one energy or many energy types put together. You can paint a picture with one color, a green house, or you can choose three or more colors, such as red, yellow, and green to paint your house.

Imagine each choice you have as one color. You combine the colors to make one choice or you use all three colors on one house.

Many of our clients don't just have one ability, talent, or skill. They have a myriad of talents that are from this lifetime and many others brought with them from other lifetimes that make up who they are.

You can choose to focus on one talent or all of your skills.

One of our clients had called us to ask about his soul purpose. Our guidance talked to him about his ability to write. After the session was over he told us that he did not want to be a writer, he wanted to be a channel. We told him that if he wants to be a channel, he must also write. We recommended that information given to us through guidance, be shared publicly to help people heal.

The guides were assuring him and helping him believe in his ability to write to assist him and opening him further to his channeling ability. If he was blocked from his writing ability, he would also be blocked from his channeling ability. We are meant to publicly inform people about what is channeled through us.

I had another client who was taking my psychic development class. A shaman had told her that an entity was blocking her from developing her abilities. During the class exercise, she doubted what she was experiencing, did not trust her experiences, and believed her experience to be irrational.

Doubt, lack of trust, and judgment were the energy types that the shaman was picking up on that were creating a block for this student. To the shaman, the energy appeared as an entity.

The student had created the entity from the inside out.

The student created the entity from choosing three types of energetic vibrations.

All of the energy within the energy of your choices creates. If you are choosing doubt inside of your mind, doubt will be created outside of your mind for you to witness. The outcome of how the energy creates, you cannot control.

We can only choose the energy, not the outcome of how the energy expresses itself.

If you are choosing to move to California because you love the California coast, your belief in the knowledge that it can happen, your knowing that a place for you to reside is already available to you and your realization in how energy creates will develop itself in ways you cannot control. However, what you can choose are energy types to create the life you want from the inside out by trusting in the abilities of those energy types.

We explain it to our clients in this way. Focus on your choices, and patiently know the energy will arrive to you, like a ball bouncing across the lawn towards you. The energy you choose will come and the energy of your choice, or choices, will develop in full, as long as you have healed the blocks to the flow of the energy.

If you are focusing on the energetic choice of feeling joyful because of a recent accomplishment, the energy of joy will be created, to its full extent. Energy does not know half measures. It does not say to itself, I will create a little joy. No, the energy of joy will go full out to create what it knows how to create.

Have you ever experienced a day of total gratitude and joy for life? You wake up and just feel thankful for the world around you. Yes, I am sure you can think of many things to keep you immediately from feeling the joy within your life, but on this day, you are singing inside of yourself for what is available to you in your life. It could be your family, or your job, perhaps you have the day off and you are watching baby ducks in the pond at the park. Whatever it is, it just feels good.

Like filling up your car with gas, the energy you choose will fill you up as well. It will flow through the open gates of your dam of your river.

Room for Choice

Like a cornucopia, choices that are made, leave an energetic space for another choice to come in.

The energetic vibration of choice has already created a relationship with the energy of choice to fill its void. Not every single choice will create itself in the same way.

As we mentioned previously, you can control the experience of the energy you choose inside of you, but you cannot control how the energy creates.

Energy creates in its own individual manner. Like a thumbprint, energy will create in its very own way.

That means, just like snowflakes, although there may be billions upon billions of snowflakes, there are no two that are exactly alike. There are also no two creations of energy that are exactly the same. Even the energy that is seemingly mirroring each other like twins; is different. It has its own independent intelligence.

Choices that are made through you, leave a space open to fill, like a vacuum. The magnetic pull of all energy to make a relationship fills this vacuum with the energy of another choice. It is an automatic response of energy to fill the space with another energy. Why? Remember, energy seeks balance.

Choice always wants more choice to occupy space. That way, choices are always in the procession line to be manufactured. Through our creativity in alignment with the Universal Mind, we continue to build more choices. We fill the niches, just like evolution, to spread out our energy to creatively gather choices for universal expression.

We are dynamic individuals who strive to manifest our individualistic choices, whether we are conscious of our production or not. The voids that we make through our building of choices and manifestation of the choices in a physical form, are continually filled with more choice.

Those of us who have been involved in our inner psychological growth, understand this process well. We think we have completed on issue, just to have yet another one crop up for us to see.

Think of it this way. You have ten business ideas. You begin to build your business through the ten ideas you have. You buy ten properties, rehabilitate the properties, and sell the properties. Your ideas become concrete reality, which leaves more space for the production of more ideas. Ideas you put into action, create more room for thinking about more ideas.

Ideas which are made, are then capable of producing more clout for the creation of more ideas. You bought your ten properties, sold them, and now, because of your experience, you have more ideas about other properties. Or you bought ten properties, had problems with some of the properties, and you have more creative ideas in regards to solving the problems about the properties.

Ideas formed into concrete physical reality send back more energy to your mind to form more ideas. Energy wants to fill the void left by the building process.

Universal Mind is Infinite Choice

There are infinite choices available for you to receive from the Universal Mind that are your right to receive. You do not receive these choices alone, but through the energetic vibrations of the Universal Mind. You make a choice, such as healing, for example, maybe from a particular grievous situation. Perhaps a loved one close to you has died. Your dog, who has been with you for a long time, has reached the end of his time on earth. Your father is becoming sick and is starting to become chronically ill. Your friend died in a car accident.

These situations feel so big, that we automatically turn to something both inside of ourselves and outside of ourselves to go to. Because we are in such pain, and so exhausted from the pain, the only thing we have control over is to receive. We realize when we feel better; that the only true control we actually have is to receive. And the only thing we can do is to receive from the energy inside of us from the Universal Mind to help us cope.

There is no end to our receiving. The energy coming to us does not suddenly stop, as though it has reached a dead end street. What we receive to help us heal, continues to be given to us day after day.

Perhaps, it is inspiration you are choosing to help you finish your art project. Your choice of energy has now been forwarded to the Universal Mind from inside of yourself as an experience you want. Your knowing is ready to receive the energy of inspiration.

Inspiration is an energy that also does not have a dead line. You can receive it in dreams, in spiritual prompts, throughout your day, or through your intuitive attraction to events, people, or situations.

Your choice, whatever it may be, is automatically put out to the universe through you and the universe responds.

The Universal Mind never runs out of ideas. Your mind is constantly reinventing energy to creatively expand energy in unique ways. The energy used to create one idea is also used to invent another. Ideas are constantly generated from the same energy. It would be like if you took a pile of clay, made a bust of a woman you admired, then refashioned it to make a bust of a man you admired, all from the same clay.

Refashioning the clay does not destroy the clay it just makes it different. So the idea you had yesterday, is not the same idea you had today. It is tweaked, perhaps a little different, and these differences may be very subtle.

However subtle the differences are, or how drastic the ideas may differ, it is still the same energy that is forming the ideas. The creative energy moving through you to receive within your mind is the energy from the Universal Mind. The energy from the Universal Mind is governed by its own subset of laws. In other words, this book addresses the twelve universal laws of how energy works in our dimensions in relationship to the Universal Mind.

The energy within the Universal Mind only operates within a subset of laws that pertain only to the Universal Mind. One of these laws is that the Universal Mind must govern its energy by sending out its energy into the universe through love. By sending out its energy, we are guaranteed constant energetic support through the availability of energy through the Universal Mind.

Points to Remember:

Because the primary energy of love always builds upon itself to create more, the alternatives within the universe are infinite. The law of Infinity provides us with different infinite choice.

Our expression of love takes form in the way we choose to show love. The infinite expression of choice allows energetic vibrations to travel across and bridge to the concrete world through love.

Your choices open to you when you believe you have infinite choices to choose from.

In knowing how energy works and in trusting the energetic choices you make, you do not have to know where you are going. The energy knows for you.

Choice is Present

Different choices of energy already exist before you choose them.

Because energy is already present in the universe for us to use, we have one vital job to do, to become aware of its presence and, through our consciousness, express its presence.

Different Choice

The concrete world of ourselves matches our view of the world from inside of ourselves.

Different choice cannot be seen without your being able to notice its presence.

Infinite Choice

In terms of energy, countless choices are always there.

Your view of your choice may change.

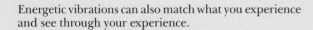

Energetic vibrations can also match what you experience and see through your experience.

The choices you notice through your inward experiences help mold and create energetic matter.

Different choices never stop being present for you to see.

Choices are not dependent upon other distant choices in order to exist.

Energetic choices are free of charge and they are free of psychological baggage.

If you can assist yourself through healing in letting go of your preconceived ideas about energy and reality, you can count on the intelligence and power of energy to work with you and for you.

Choice or Choices?

Your mind is a tool for creating your energetic choice.

Choices can be made from one energy or many energy types put together.

All of the energy within the energy of your choices creates.

We can only choose the energy, not the outcome of how the energy expresses itself.

Room for Choice

Like a cornucopia, choices that are made, leave an energetic space for another choice to come in.

Energy creates in its own individual manner.

Universal Mind is Infinite Choice

There are infinite choices available for you to receive from the Universal Mind that are your right to receive.

There is no end to our receiving.

The Universal Mind never runs out of ideas.

We are guaranteed constant energetic support through the availability of energy through the Universal Mind.

Affirm:

I have different infinite choices available through my healing and connection to Universal Mind.

Experience:

Take a deep breath. Relax your body. Imagine that you can call all the animals to come to you that live upon earth. In your mind's eye, begin to form a line. See yourself surrounded by millions of animals. Now, imagine that you can become each animal. Which one would it be first? Perhaps you would become a bear? Maybe you would become a wolf? Imagine feeling as though you are a bear. What would it feel like? How large would you be? How would you move? Now, become the wolf. How fast can you run? How many others are with you? Imagine what it would be like to be a rhino or an elephant. If you ran out of choices to imagine becoming an animal from planet earth, could your mind develop more choices? How would that happen? Where would the ideas come from? How many choices could you develop?

Chapter Twenty
The Universal Law of Beginnings and Endings

Within our physical universe, all things must end and there must be a beginning for all things. We live in a universe where time exists. How we experience time is in moments. We experience moments one right after another. Within this time sequence, one moment can herald an ending, and the next, a beginning.

Before one moment begins, there is an imperceptible pause. The pause is like the pause between our heart beating or the moment before we take our next breath. It is a space whereby energy can organize itself to make the next moment arrive.

We must remember, it takes a lot of energy within our universe to create our universe. And our universe is made jointly through the Universal Mind and ourselves and all of the energy around us. This energy must organize itself around our experiences, views and choices about our reality.

The pause between moments gathers and builds energy through our mind, in joint connection with the Universal Mind, to organize our next moment. The pause also helps to create an ending for energy to deplete and a beginning for energy to build.

The depleting of energy and the building of energy creates an artificial beginning and an artificial ending of energy through the tool of energetic organization called time. Otherwise, we would not be able to figure out what was happening around us. Like a dream state, we would not experience endings and beginnings, all of our experiences would be happening at once. Sound confusing? It not only would be confusing, but how could we take in and learn from each experience, so that we can better choose our experiences?

Beginnings and endings are a way to organize energy, so we can choose what we what to happen next. And through our choices, we can know something new and different. Our experiences are never the same experience. No matter how many times you go to the grocery store, you will not have the exact same experience.

A spare healer who worked with the Christ light became upset because another healer who worked with the same entity joined our spiritual network, which put out information about events to the public. She decided to quit the network. I pointed out to her that it was impossible for two people to be providing the same experience to people, even though they were working with the same entity. It just can't be done.

All endings make room for beginnings to happen. The universe is structured in paradox. What happens inside creates what happens outside. Without an ending from our internal view, an external beginning could not happen.

No matter how the spiritual or enlightened a person you are, the death of a loved one will deeply affect you. The death will affect you as an ending and you will grieve. The person, or your beloved pet, that has died may be going through a birthing process on the other side of the veil, but our experience is one of loss and grief, which creates a pause for a new beginning. Without a pause, a new beginning could not take place.

Endings Make Beginnings

Endings must occur, in terms of our time, to affect what happens in other dimensional spaces. Without the affect of an ending, a beginning in other hidden realms could not happen. We live in a paradoxical universe, and what happens in one dimension will automatically affect what happens in another dimension, from the inside out. What appears as death in our dimension appears as birth in another dimension. What appears as destruction in our dimension, leaves room for something new to happen. The tearing down of one building, leaves room for another to be built. The death of one relationship, leaves room for the beginning of another. Without an ending, everything would appear to be a seamless array of experiences, without distinguishing differences.

We would not know one thing from another. We would not know the experience of loss and we would not know the joy of renewal. All of our experiences would be uniformly occurring, without an ability to feel any one experience as different from one another. In fact, we would not feel, all would seem to be one thing, so any one thing could not be felt.

Our capacity to experience emotion would not be useful as a tool to discriminate between experiences. Our grief, which can occur with endings, would not serve as a useful emotion to prepare us for the ability to connect to those experiences we wish to join with. We would be lost in a sea of similarity, which would automatically make our unique experiences null and void.

It is our ability, in terms of time and experience, to be in a world that has endings that gives us the power to experience our independent expression in forging something new. It is our ability to be in the full expression of the moment that gives us the ability to feel the full affect of energy within the moment. Because we have this ability, we have the ability to know more about how to experience life.

Endings must always be present within any experience we may have. Our homes, our lives, our relationships, and our careers, all carry within them the potential moment of the ending of energy. However, this does not mean that the potential moment of beginning is not also present. It just means that whatever you have and whatever you are experiencing has the ability of transformation.

Your relationship, your job, and your car are not the same thing every single day, day after day; each moment there are changes that you may or may not notice. The dog hair in your car may not have been there yesterday. Your spouse validated today the concerns you had yesterday: that she needed to pay more attention to you. Or that today is your lucky day and your raise did come through. Endings, moment by moment, help provide the space and the moment for energy to build and do something new.

Endings will also provide belief in our three-dimensional world that not all experiences are meaningless. It is the ending of something that often provides us with profound meaning of what existed. And it is that meaning, through our view, which helps shape the next beginning.

Energy is Now

In our world, time exists moment by moment in what seems to be linear direction. However, energy exists outside and inside of time at once. What you want to experience right now, perhaps beginning the relationship with your soul mate, has not yet occurred in physical time and space. But your relationship, your inner experience, is already beginning to organize energy through your own knowing in making that experience happen. The other energy forming around your inner soul mate may be one step behind your outward experience. The right time, the right place and the right circumstances have yet to follow.

As mentioned previously, my friend and I, several months back, decided to form a production company. Each day, we channeled in valuable information for the company, as well as our own healing processes on how to get it going. We did quite well, until we got to the process of finding the seed money to start up our company. At that point, we took a break, focused on our own individual work and let spirit take over. Through focusing in on our own work, connections occurred out of our work that provided the seed money. A pause occurred over several months and then it happened. It happened very quickly. All was organized and put into place and the money was there within two weeks. Of course, my friend and I had spent a lot of time organizing our energy before the experience of having the seed money arrive. It looked easy, seemed easy, and fell into place effortlessly, but we had put a great deal of effort into the healing process inside of ourselves before the financing appeared outside of ourselves.

The financing, as well as relationships, were not in the same beginning state of time as our inner experience of building our production company. This energy, as well as a countless amount of other energy, had to organize itself around our inner experience. And this energy had to account for both my friend and myself, all of our energy, all of what needed to be healed and cleared and aligned with the Universal Mind, in order to create our production company.

Sound complicated? It is, so much so, it would be an impossible task to organize all of this energy by our selves. We do need help. Help from the connection all energy has between itself, the Universal Mind and us.

Energy must have a lag time to form the optimal experience for us to experience.

Energy must have that pause, in terms of coming through, to reach our dimension to organize. Water must have a moment of time in order to freeze. You must have a moment of taking a deep breath before making that important presentation. The cat down the street takes a moment to size up the situation before it begins to stalk our dog and relieve our dog's presence from its territory. These moments are necessary to help organize and move energy that is coming through the inside of us, to the outside of us, to create the world around us.

Short or Long Endings

It takes a moment to enter relationships with other energy, organize the energy to form an entrance into our dimension and then build itself. The ending of energy entering a pause, what we may conceive of as a death, may occur so rapidly, we do not notice that a series of deaths are actually happening.

We, as people, are actually experiencing, moment by moment, a rapid series of depleting energy types which can be considered a series of rapidly occurring deaths. We may not know or be consciously aware that these tiny deaths are occurring. But the fact is, one moment is not the same as the next. As I write this sentence, each moment is both presenting itself and leaving. The moment before this one has died. It has already transformed itself into something different.

The rapid shift of energy within each moment, influences that amount of energy given to any one situation. The project that you are working at in your home is taking a lot of moments and a lot of your energy. However, the energy you are giving to reading the ad in your magazine tonight, may only take a few of your moments.

The time it takes to form an ending is determined by the energy we wish to give towards a life event. We can choose quick endings in determining the direct flow of our attentive focus or we can choose a sustained flow of our energy towards an event that we wish to focus upon.

We determine the length of our energetic flow from the inside out towards any and all life events. Why is this important? It is important, because some people, not you of course, feel fated by the occurrence of life events, as though they are meant to happen without their attention toward the experience of their happening.

You can heal quicker than you know from tragic events, perhaps the death of a family member. I know grief is a very difficult experience, however, you can shift your attention towards what your precious family member taught you in life.

My black lab, Kije, passed and I concentrate on what he taught me now. He was the ambassador, especially at the dog park. He would go up to people, sniff them, wag his tail and get a pet. Then he would leave and go say hi to the next person. If he could talk, he would say something like this, "It is important that I accept people, but people do not have to accept me."

I remember that energy where ever I go, so that I may carry Kije's energy with me. It is a way I can keep on marking his territory, which also was very important to him!

I had the privilege of being Kije's owner. My view of what energy to focus on from Kije, lessens the pain of his passing.

Ending can happen in time suddenly, or form relationships with other energy to happen in time after a long while. Luckily, you are going to live a happy, fruitful life and you do not need to open a fortune cookie to get this prediction! The chain of energy that has formed your life has created countless relationships with other energy types for the duration of who you are in your physical body. You live!

Your energy and the duration of energy is helped to be formed by your energetic choices.

We remember a good friend of mine, studying to be an analyst, who told me about a friend of hers. Apparently, her friend was depressed and continually stated she wanted to die. Her friend developed cancer. She had been focusing upon death for a long time. Now, cancer would claim more of her energetic focus.

Our minds, as I have said before, are organizing tools for the flow of energy from the Universal Mind inside of ourselves. This combined energy creates what happens outside of ourselves. We can use it to make choices about the energy we choose to experience inside of ourselves in terms of time.

Energy also determines its own timetable for its ending. The grief you are experiencing may take its own time to heal inside of you, however, you can simultaneously choose to focus your energy on something other than grief as your total experience.

Beginnings Know Their Endings

Energy exists in a state of time that does not look like our linear time. It knows all of its existence at one time, so it knows at once, both its beginning and its ending.

So, if energy does not die, what do endings look like for energy? Have you ever seen the death card in the Tarot deck? Well, the death card represents a metaphorical death, a transformation. Therefore, it is not a bad card, just a card of change.

Energetic death represents a change, or a transformation, of energy from one state to another. It is the moment by moment focus that the energy is experiencing that creates life awareness. Time is separate from the intelligent choices that energy chooses for its focus.

Time is a separate dimension from the energetic experience. Have you ever been caught up in something that you feel is wonderful? Perhaps it is a date with the perfect man or woman? Painting that beautiful landscape? Dancing to your favorite music? Completing the construction of your perfect bookcase?

The energy that you are experiencing does not feel attached to time, but feels timeless. You are focused on enjoying the moment and enjoying it to the fullest! Well, energy does the same thing, all the time. Energy is caught up in enjoying the particular moment to its fullest capacity. Time does not matter to its existence. Energy exists because of what it is experiencing.

Remember, all of the laws work from this paradox: they help to organize energy from the inside out in alignment with Universal Mind.

In our world, when we no longer experience the concrete presence of energy, we label that energy as dead. No matter what it is, a tree, animal, or even sitting down to yesterday's dinner, we see those things that have passed as dead. We may not see them in our world any longer. But what really happens is this: Energy continues to live in each moment, experiencing its life as a series of unfolding events.

Sound familiar? Your dreams each night happen in the very same way. You experience, moment by moment, energy building and releasing its focus on life events. It is just not contained in our world. The transformation of energy would always be preordained, because it knows its own beginning and ending.

Spiritual Contracts

From the energetic point of view, these moments of depletion are purely experiences that the energy wants to experience as part of its exploration of change. These moments, then, from the view of energy, are quickened accelerations of experiences, one right after another. It is the moment of depletions which we see as predetermined from our world. Endings are premeditated events. We label these moments as spiritual contracts.

In our physical world, time slows down those experiences. In the world of energy, everything happens very fast, so fast, that everything happens at once.

Our dimension, our world, travels as we move around in an old Volkswagen going five miles per hour. Right next door, however, is a universe that speeds around in a Mercedes at one hundred and twenty miles per hour.

Now, that you can see the differences, think of this. Each time you move through between the five mile per hour universe and the one hundred and twenty mile per hour universe in a new, improved vehicle that you just invented, you must pause before you leave each dimension and also as you enter the next

one. Your focus on what you are leaving may become less and what you are entering becomes more. The energy builds and depletes, and in a moment, you are driving a Mercedes.

Transformative energy always understands what it wants before it occurs in the moment.

How? Energy communicates what it wants.

Time and space are not ruled by third-dimensional space; all things happen at one time. That means that energy makes intelligent choices from the start about what it is going to experience and how that experience is going to end.

Look around you. Find a book. Open it. Look at the first page and the last page together. The energy in your book knows both the beginning of the book and the end of the book. Because you are in three-dimensional space, you would have to read the first page and last page in our time to know the start and the end of the book. There would be a space of time for you to experience after starting the book and then ending the book.

This is not so in other dimensions. No space and time is required for understanding to take place. All understanding of starts and finishes happens within a moment. The moment allows the full expression of energy to take place.

In our time zone, it looks like there are no choices made between endings and beginnings. A beginning can be years before an ending, or a few seconds. The communications between starts and stops are not accounted for in our perceptions.

Take a trip back in time to the woman who wanted an independent massage business. Despite the emotional blocks that occurred in the building of her business, she made an energetic contract with energy through knowing what she wanted. The relationships the energy formed, directed the start of her business. Her experience of wanting a business ended in her having her own business.

Now, this does not happen instantaneously, it took time. The energy zooming around in space had to shift into our zone. The Mercedes zooming at one hundred and twenty miles per hour steps into our five mile per hour time zone and slows way down.

We must take into account time and space. We must allow for energy to come into our space, allow time to organize energy, and trust their intelligence in doing so.

Energy will match your inner experience. And please let go of how, because, as I have said before, you cannot control the outcome of how. And you can also not control the outcome of when. But what you can control is your inner experience that you have placed in your knowing and your trust in intelligent energy.

You do create from the inside out. You have complete control over your inner experience. And because you are one with the universe, and with the Universal Mind, you can make choices about your internal creations that will form outside of yourself. The shift of your energy is 100 percent guaranteed. We know it.

Balancing Endings and Beginnings

Let's go back to the I Ching symbol of Yin and Yang. Perhaps you can look at a picture. The I Ching symbol represents perfectly balanced energy.

Beginnings and endings, white and black, breathing in and breathing out, the list can go on and on, always in perfect balance. But why is this important? Again, our mission is to break open the possible brainwashing that may have kept you asleep at the wheel. We want to free you by presenting information about the true you.

What is happening within you, your energy, your psychology, your innermost secret experiences will be in perfect harmonic balance with what is happening outside of you. Perfectly.

Recently we had a client, Tim, who was concerned about his relationships. He did not understand why women would not commit to be in a relationship. Through our guidance, he began to understand he was repeating the abandonment he experienced from his father as a child. His inner energy mirrored what was occurring in his relationships.

The perfect balance acts to stabilize you in your world by providing you with this structure: Balanced energy helps you to view outside of yourself what is happening inside of yourself. In fact, all energy is stabilized through being perfectly in balance. The depletion that ending makes is balanced by the building of energy in a beginning. All endings must be balanced by beginnings to avoid nothingness. Life through energy fills every dimension throughout the universe.

Think about looking at the I Ching again. Something fills all of the space. Nothing does not exist. It is the same with energy. Energy fills all of the space in the universe. "Nothing" does not exist. Life through energy is in complete balance throughout the Universal Mind, throughout us, and throughout our world.

Even in our world, when energy is taking time and space to complete balance, it is paradoxically already in balance in other dimensions. Our world is created from the inside out. We can put down the illusion of believing we are fated from outside forces to live our reality. We can think paradoxically, so that we can know the truth about Source.

Our internal experience within our knowing is complete in other dimensions. We may not be able to see the energy. We visualize how the painting will look when it is completed; however, the energy of the vision lies in other dimensions. But because we know and now believe that the world is created in perfect balance through the energy inside of us, we can experience our creation through the vision in our minds.

Creation must have a balanced beginning to match its balanced ending in order for life to continue. Why? Energy is always present within the universe. No energy within any dimension within the universe does not exist. Just like water in your glass, energy takes up all the space it is in. There are no blank spaces.

Energy is one large circle, never disconnected from itself. Although there are points on the circle that can represent starts and stops, these points are just transformative bridges that keep the circle intact.

We are like circles of energy. We have our points, our lives that seemingly begin and end, but then continue somewhere else. Why? Energy cannot turn into nothingness. Energy is immortal. You are immortal.

Endings Through God

Energy travels from one state to another state when transformation takes place. As we have said, when physical transformation takes place in our world, we call that death.

The Universal Mind, through our connection with mental energy, helps to focus the depletion of energy in other dimensions.

Because we are a part of a larger whole, the larger whole helps to direct our energy. Like a conductor, the Universal Mind helps to determine the flow of energy from one dimension to the next. The Universal Mind helps to deplete energy by directing the focus of energy away from one state of existence into another state of existence. The Universal Mind also makes an agreement with individual minds as to when and how energy is to be redirected.

Energy that is depleted through the coordinating actions of the Universal Mind with the energy of other things then becomes transformed into life. We may not be able to see the transformation take place. Sometimes we cannot see what is no longer physical. None the less, the transformation has occurred.

We know this because we can sense energy around us that may not show up in the physical form. We experience energy that does not appear to us in our range of eyesight, but we know it is there. We feel its presence.

Energy cannot become no energy. Its existence is immortal, and therefore, divine. And as a divine, immortal being, energy that may not be in physical form is a relationship with the energy within our knowing.

Those individuals who have passed in your life continue to live. Unseen beings that act as your guardians, exist in connection with you. We do have spiritual helpers that guide us and help us in many ways.

We remember one session in particular with a woman whose father had passed. She asked us how he was doing. Cortney saw him in a barn, tinkering with something mechanical. She said, "Yep, that is him, he loved to work on machines." He still was.

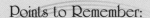

Points to Remember:

Within our physical universe, all things must end and there must be a beginning for all things.

We live in a universe where time exists. How we experience time is in moments.

Before one moment begins, there is an imperceptible pause.

The pause between moments gathers energy through our mind, in joint connection with the Universal Mind, to organize our next moment.

The depleting of energy and the building of energy creates an artificial beginning and an artificial ending of energy through the tool of energetic organization called time.

Beginnings and endings are a way to organize energy, so we can choose what we what to happen next.

And through our choices, we can know something new and different.

Endings Make Beginnings

Endings must occur, in terms of our time, to affect what happens in other dimensional spaces.

Without an ending, everything would appear to be a seamless array of experiences, without distinguishing differences.

It is our ability, in terms of time and experience, to be in a world that has endings that gives us the power to experience our independent expression in forging something new.

Endings must always be present within any experience we may have.

Energy is Now

In our three dimensional world, time exists moment by moment in what seems to be linear direction. However, energy exists outside and inside of time at once. What you want to experience right now, perhaps beginning the relationship with your inner soul mate, has not yet occurred in physical time and space. But your relationship, your inner experience, is already beginning to organize energy through your own knowing in making that experience happen.

Energy must have a lag time to form the optimal experience for us to experience.

Short or Long Endings

It takes a moment to enter relationships with other energy, organize the energy to form an entrance into our dimension and then manifest itself in our dimension.

The rapid shift of energy within each moment, influences that amount of energy given to any one situation.

The time it takes to form an ending is determined by the energy we wish to give towards a life event.

We determine the length of our energetic flow from the inside out towards any and all life events.

Beginnings Know Their Endings

Energy exists in a state of time that does not look like our linear time. It knows all of its existence at one time, so it knows at once, both its beginning and its ending.

Energetic death represents a change, or a transformation, of energy from one state to another.

Energy exists because of what it is experiencing.

Energy continues to live in each moment, experiencing its life as a series of unfolding events.

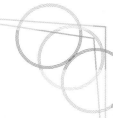

Spiritual Contracts

Endings are premeditated events. We label these moments as spiritual contracts.

Transformative energy always understands what it wants before it occurs in the moment.

We, in our dimension, must take into account time and space. We must allow for energy to come into our space, allow time to organize energy, and trust their intelligence in doing so.

Balancing Endings and Beginnings

What is happening within you, your energy, your psychology, your innermost secret experiences will be in perfect harmonic balance with what is happening outside of you. Perfectly.

The perfect balance acts to stabilize you in your world by providing you with this structure: Balanced energy helps you to view outside of yourself what is happening inside of yourself.

Energy fills all of the space in the universe. "Nothing" does not exist.

Our internal experience within our knowing is complete in other dimensions.

Creation must have a balanced beginning to match its balanced ending in order for life to continue.

Energy cannot turn into nothingness. Energy is immortal. You are immortal.

Endings Through God

The Universal Mind, through our connection with mental energy, helps to focus the depletion of energy in other dimensions.

The Universal Mind also makes an agreement with individual minds as to when and how energy is to be redirected.

Energy that is depleted through the coordinating actions of the Universal Mind with the energy of other things then becomes transformed into life.

Affirm:

I live through my experiences and my experiences are everlasting.

Experience:

Take a deep breath and relax your body. Imagine this. Let's take you on a little trip. Your body has become weightless. You begin to float up to your ceiling, beyond your ceiling and out into the sky. You move higher and see your streets, the town below you, all becoming smaller, you continue to float and notice that as you past the clouds, you no longer have a physical body, but you still feel you as you. You turn around and look out at the expansiveness of the universe. Because you no longer have a physical body, you are not sure where you begin and where the universe begins. You begin to feel a connection with all the things around you. Because of this connection, you begin to see all sorts of things you did not see in your physical world in your physical body. You see different colors and different life forms that move around you, you see different planets that do not exist in the physical realm.

From this location, you have a very different experience of how energy lives. In a moment, you can be experiencing the green mist you noticed, a moment before, or traveling to, the pink planet you saw several moments previously. You can make your own intelligent choices, moment by moment, about what it is you wish to experience. You focus through your attention upon the experience, the experience builds within you, and as you begin to focus upon some other experience, your previous experiences begin to deplete. Your experience transforms, it builds up and depletes, just like breathing.

Chapter Twenty-One
The Universal Law of Creation

With each new ending, something else must be made to replace it. This law guarantees that something different can be created. When something ends, it is an opportunity for a brand new beginning, a brand new start in reordering energy to make a different creation. We can look at and view the ending from any mental location we choose. In our view, we can actually create and mentally organize energy into a different mental view. We can see the ending, step back, look for something different and build something different.

Because endings must be balanced with beginnings, a multitude of creative choices can now be permitted to flow from the Universal Mind to your mind, giving you free reign to design a new start.

A client of ours, Donna, was advised by my guidance to honor her feelings regarding her boyfriend. She felt betrayed by him in a number of ways. He had not been honest with her in regards to another relationship and had not paid her back money that he owed her. Donna had reenacted energy between herself and her mother. When Donna was a child, she felt she had to deny her own needs and take care of her alcoholic parent. When she began to see that she no longer had to betray her own best interests, she let go of her boyfriend. Through guidance, she was advised that another individual would become her boyfriend within a week. The week that she let go of her old boyfriend, an acquaintance asked her out. A new relationship had begun.

It is important for us to remember, as mere mortals, that there is always a creative beginning to any one thing that ends. We get so caught up in the ending, and perhaps our grief, that we forget our own creativity in allowing something new to be created through our spiritual connections. We forget the obvious opportunities that lie before us and often ignore their very concrete existence, because of our feelings.

It is our emotions which can act to block us, or free us, in our spiritual connection with Source. It is our feelings, which assign to us seeming false endings, when the true reality is a continuing series of new beginnings which lie before us.

We live our lives in a circle. Our lives are a circle of events that deplete and build and continue their existence. We sometimes forget the continuation of creative probabilities in our fear, grief and anger and relentlessly resent of what was, instead of what is.

It is our creative impulses that can now lead us into the building of energy into what can be. We can look at death as the beginning enterprise along our journey of expansion. We can create a new and different relationship with what is right now.

There are no missed opportunities, by gone "could have been" careers or lost abilities or skills. There are no dead mothers or fathers, dead relatives, loved ones or pets. These seeming endings are perceptions from our emotions that set up a view of false deaths that block our flow from Source of what truly is alive.

Look inward. Look inward and toward Source to see the true reality. We truly create our world from the inside out. We see our world from the world inside of us. When we turn our eyesight around and look inside instead of outside, we see what Source has to offer. We see the circle of never ending energy that is always available to us to create, to make what we can see on the outside of us. In this way, we shape our world from the integrity and power of true reality and we own our power as humans.

And our humanity, by the way, is a good thing. It is a non-recognition of how completely powerful we actually are that aims to destroy us and keep us from being fully alive.

The Making Of Energy

Energy seeks to balance itself inside of us and outside of us. Like water, it seeks its own level of density. It intelligently organizes itself to replace missing energy. A niche of energy that has left, will be filled anew by incoming energy. Energy will build to fill the depletion of energetic flow.

We are guaranteed incoming energy. The solution is to allow it to be noticed by us. Oftentimes, our awareness is caught up in some other perception of our inward view, like the woman who was so busy talking about her ex-husband, that she did not notice the man standing in front of her who was attracted to her. We do not always see the thing that is next.

We are here to tell you the obvious. There is always something next. And you may say, yes, I know that. So, that may seem obvious enough, but somehow we forget the obvious when we are bemoaning our lost jobs or ex-girlfriends or ex-boyfriends. We do not see the very thing that is next that is right in front of us, because emotionally, we forgot that energy is always present to fill in the gaps left behind.

Energy must fill the gaps of depleted energy. There are no vacuums where energy is not present. Energy always exists, no matter where you are at on earth, and off of earth for that matter. Energy cannot be left unconnected to energy. It must always resolve itself to finding a relationship with itself. It must intelligently form a balance within the relationship and create from this alliance.

Now, that does not mean you cannot go back to the same dreadful relationship or job you had previously. You can recreate those energetic circumstances, or you can replace those situations with energy that is committed toward forming more fulfilling circumstances for you. You can allow change to take place, and not only allow it, but to patiently expect, through your own inward experience, that it will take place.

In your knowing of how energy works, the defined change can come through your connection to Source. Energy must flow from Source to you and from you to Source. And within this flow, your artistic desire can choose what energetic experiences to feel within you.

You can organize these experiences, trust in their existence and allow them to organize in the way they choose outside of yourself.

It is your trust in the Universal Mind and energy which has been compromised by the society we live in. The integrity of the Universal Mind cannot be compromised, even when we do not see its truth. The Universal Mind and its behaviors governed by universal law are constant. It is our inconsistencies in our belief and doubt which blind us to fully experiencing our inner connections.

You can choose to trust in universal intelligence, believe that energy must always replace itself, and, like a cornucopia of endless fruit, watch the results right before your very eyes.

You must do something to achieve this however. You must give up control. You must remove your emotional blocks. You must give up controlling the result. Stay patient in the moment, be in trust, rather than anxiety, and know it will happen. Energy must replace energy. It is that simple. Prove it to yourself. Find a place on the planet where energy does not exist. We dare you.

Old Energy Into New Energy

Energetic vibrations can organize themselves into new and creative patterns. Like musical notes, they can make different arrangements to create different patterns of sounds. The musical notes may sound the same, but the music is not.

You are the same you that you were perhaps five years ago, and yet you are not that five year ago you. You may feel as though you have lived ten lifetimes, because the you that you are now feels very different from the you five years past. You may feel you are very different, and you are, because the energy within you has been repeatedly organized by you into different patterns.

The different patterns of energy inside of you have created a different mental location in order to see the world outside of you. You have made choices to creatively choose a new experience within you and the energy within you has followed your mental lead in reorganizing itself to fit into your new experience. So, energy reorganization is not about reinventing the wheel. The wheel is already present. It is about knowing that the wheels know how to turn on their own, without your telling them how.

Energy can shift within a moment. It does not take lifetimes to shift into new patterns of existence. Ever have a revelation? One moment you see one thing one way; the next you don't see it in the same way. These epiphanies of living often leave your awestruck. You feel in touch with Source and inspired by the spirit. In these moments of conscious contact with the spirit, you are open to the intelligent energy from Source to flow through you from within. And you know it.

It is in these moments that the spirit, the physical communication from Source, allows its intelligence to be felt. The spirit states its knowledge to you and you reorganize your thoughts to fit the patterns of your experienced revelation. Suddenly, you are a different person.

The reorganization of energy to fit new patterns of living exist independently within you. They are one with you, and yet, live on their own. They exist in complete knowledge and are balanced harmonically with Source, mirroring the energy of Source. Within the scope of this balanced relationship, the space of your mind lives.

Remember the balls within the balls? Energy is its own small ball within the ball of your mind, within the ball of the Universal Mind. Now imagine energy as a small dot in the center of the ball of your mind. This dot has its own road out of your mind straight to the outer ball of Source. This road allows for the flow of your energy out of your mind to Source and the flow of energy from Source directly to the dot of energy in your mind.

The energy within the dot can make its own choices to create and expand knowledge gained from two sources: both you and Source.

One bit of energy, perhaps a thought that sits in your mind, gets ignited by energy through its connection with Source. Then, all of the energy that is you, all of your experiences, other thoughts, emotions, and intents, form a connection with this one thought. Like fireworks, an explosion of change races across your mind and all of your mental energy becomes aligned with the change. Your mind expands and your world view expands as well, because of the added energy from yourself and Source.

The expanded energy builds and then settles into a state of rest. Like the pause before your next breath, it reaches a plateau, where it can continue to build or deplete. Like sand upon a shore, it waits to be carried someplace else. It may go out to sea or become part of a sand dune.

Each grain of sand has its own life force, its own intelligence and its own life span. It may become part of a sandstone cliff and end its life as sand on the beach, or become part of a coral reef. The sand, as well as every other concrete three dimensional item, becomes part of the cycle of change, and what we sometimes refer to as death. However, we already know is that there is no death. There is just reorganization.

Different Experience

It is this explosion of connection, that mental energy proceeds to make, that forms an immediate impression of expansion. What you thought a minute ago is just not the same as it is now. At once, what you were thinking does not hold the same truth as the reality you are currently experiencing. You may choose, like Archimedes, to jump out of the bathtub when he realized that displaced water can help him develop a scale of weights and run through the streets naked, however, I wouldn't recommend it; there are other laws in our world for such behavior.

Ever hear the Zen saying, "When you are ready, the teacher will arrive?" The question is, how do you become ready? How does energy know when to expand and create a different inner energetic experience? What occurs inside of energy itself is the key. Energy communicates through its own language of experience. You can feel energy. Energy talks to you by having you experience its feelings. All of the energy in you, constantly talks to you all of the time through how you are feeling inside of you.

When this energy inside of you is ready to shift into something new, it has already been having its own different epiphanies of energetic know how. Just like our client Donna, it has already been doing the work of sorting out this task, or that experience, or that thought, in preparation for something entirely new.

It is in these moments of sorting out different energy, that help you begin to see differently. Perhaps, like Archimedes, you have been working on a way to weigh gold. It's been quite a problem for quite a while. You have been waiting for the answer. You step in the tub and wa-lah! There it is, the answer you have been waiting for.

Or you awaken from a dream, knowing what you must do next to further your career, make a virtual marketplace for new and different items. And at the same time, you feel inspired to take a trip to Peru without knowing why, but you trust in your spiritual prompts and there you are, on a plane to Peru. On the flight, you notice some fabulous jewelry a woman next to you is wearing. Arriving in Peru, you take a hike into the small villages in the highlands and meet a woman who sells that jewelry. You strike up a deal and begin to sell the jewelry on your website.

Energy seeks its own balance to create something new in forming relationships with the energy outside of you. Once your inner experience has shifted into something new, the energy outside of you will shift to match your inner energy.

We are so used to thinking of our physical bodies as a boundary and container of our energy. We are not used to thinking of energy without a container. Your energy has access to the outside of you and is not limited by your physical body. It moves to the outside of you from your mind as though your body does not exist and creates. How it creates and what other energy it creates with is up to the energy itself, but, as we have said, your inner experience of energy is up to you.

Needed Energy

Everything is always completed. Look at your hands. Put both hands out in front of you. Your right hand is completed as your right hand. Your left hand is completed as your left hand.

Energy, even though it is complete, will seek out other needed relationships with other energy to wholly realize its inner experience. Remember, energy has its own intelligence, it has its own mind. It will form relationships with other energy to complete its inner experience.

Mental energy travels through all dimensions at one time. It will automatically form relationships with needed energy to make its inward experience whole.

What this means for you is that all the energy within you will seek energy to make its inward experience whole.

Energy is articulate. Just like your hands. It can grasp and bring towards it the other energy it needs. But because energy operates in paradox, the energy in three dimensional reality must wait to receive the energy it needs for completion from the other dimensions.

Trust that the energy will draw what it needs to complete its own inner experience. Watch for signs that your inner experience is being organized in the world around you. Some people call this synchronicity.

Synchronicity is the way energy reorders itself outside of you to present you with validating information about how your inner energy is becoming organized. You create synchronicity in alignment with God.

Wholeness is sought by energy to forward energetic expansion. As we have stated, this means that energy is always in two states at once, non-completion and completion.

Like your two hands moving out in front of you, energy seeks to move toward completion and seek out its missing parts to make your hands move out in front of you. The needed energy to move your hands in front of you may not be in our three dimensional world.

It is the back and forth movement, this flow of energy between dimensions, that allows for wholeness to happen. It is your openness to allow yourself to be fully accessible to your knowing which keeps you in the moment that allows the accessibility to take place.

Remember, your knowing is like a gateway. It is an open door that allows for energy to build and deplete between our dimension and others. When you know, you are not in emotional states, such as anxiety or grief that close your door to energetic movement. When you know, you are allowing the energetic movement to flow within you, which always allows you to be in a state of wholeness. Your inner experience is one of certainty and security. You feel complete just as things are, because knowing is a state of balance between our world and other worlds. Knowing continually draws the missing link it needs for its continual completion, and it knows how to do it. You know your knowing is all that you need.

Energetic Structures

Energy organizes into structures in alignment with the universal law. Like a California closet, which is a system of closet organization, universal laws place energy into places that help energy function the way it is designed to function.

Without this organization, energy would not be able to function in ways that structure reality. Reality would be unstructured and formless. Sort of like the blob, just kind of there, but without recognizable shape.

Structures of energy are either in a state of depletion or buildup. Structures of energy may need more energy to build up. They put out a call to the Universal Mind for more energy. Because of the intelligence within energy, its waits for the response.

Energy must always respond to energetic calls. Because energy always seeks to build, it will automatically seek relationships that want to help it expand. That means in the course of its building, it may seek different structures to help it contain its expansion. Some people call this process sacred geometry. These structures help support the density of energy within its created relationships.

Imagine you live in a condominium complex in, let's say, New York. A brownstone, which is an antique building in Greenwich village that is under renovation. At first, because it was a small unit, there were nine planned units under construction. But because of the many interested people in the neighborhood investing in this property, the structures were redesigned. The brown stone next door was purchased and now there are twenty units for sale.

Each unit was redesigned to accommodate the new residents. More people on the property led to a different structure. More energy on the property also led to a different structure.

Energetic structures must be redesigned to make room for more energy. The higher the energetic density determines the change in the structure. After all, you can't have ten families living in a nine-unit brownstone, at least not without organization. And energy always seeks to organize itself. It is the organization of energy that allows it to function.

We have a client, Jim, who is working to compete in the Olympics. He was looking toward other talented horse riders to develop his style of riding. Through our guidance, he was advised to meditate and focus in on imaging his style of riding. Through redirecting his energy, inward instead of outward, he began the process of developing his unique style of riding. Why? He allowed his energy to become organized from his point of view instead of someone else's.

Energy always wants to create something different. It wants structures presented to help continue its momentum. God responds to this want. God seeks out energy in its response and automatically supplies the structures.

There is always a never ending cornucopia of structures that are present within the universe. There is never a disagreement between the energy and want it wants and needs with the structure that is provided for it. Energy and the structures it needs to expand are always in harmony.

Energy Takes and Lets Go

Energy, as we have said before, is intelligent. It is so intelligent that it has the capability to account for the requirements of time and space, as well as the dimensions it is already residing within.

Timing in our dimension becomes an important ally for energy to create in our dimension. Energy aligns with time and space in our world to let go of energetic vibrations within itself. This allows energy to form a new relationship with other energy in our world to create. Remember the pencil sliding through the pages of the magazine? The pencil represents energy coming in from other dimensions. Time and space are the last two pages of the magazine. As the pencil slides into these two pages, it lets go of vibrations to take in the vibrations of time and space.

Energy knows precisely when to accomplish this feat. It knows what to build toward it to turn into three-dimensional reality.

In energy relationships, there are three key elements:

- The first is alignment with all energy needed to transport itself into three-dimensional reality.
- The second is that energy will let go, or take in, all energy that is needed to appear.
- Number three, energy will appear in space through the taking in of all energy needed for the buildup of the density required to create in reality.

Think of making a sand castle. All of the needed sand is present. There is no lack of sand available for you to use. Look out into the ocean. There is no lack of water for you to build your castle with. It is all present for you to use.

You take the sand from around you and begin to build it up. Soon, the sand is in a large mound, like a hill, in front of you. You pack it down and make it dense with water. The sand allows itself to align with your inner experience of the vision of your castle. It also aligns with the energy of water, and your sense of time and space, to allow for the castle to be created. You have been inspired from an inward vision of this castle, because of your continued ability to connect with the intelligence of the Universal Mind.

All of the aligned energy now takes a form before your physical eyes of the inward experience of the castle.

The sand, from its experience, lets go of its relationships with the other sand and formed new relationships with sand and water in the castle.

We take for granted these subtle, everyday occurrences, of how energy works. We are so connected to the workings of energy, that we have not pulled apart exactly how energy forms in our dimension. Yet, it is exactly what we need to do consciously in order to have control over our energy within our minds. We need to be aware. And in our awareness, there abounds infinite power, just like there abounds infinite grains of sand on the beach.

Energy can also move into higher or lower levels of vibration. Think of the pencil. Like the pencil, energy travels through the magazine pages, or dimensions, all at one time. Think of another pencil now vertically placed across the horizontal pencil. The vertically placed pencil represents the level of vibrations that the energy can move up or down upon or, in our new energetic language, deplete or build upon. These levels of energy can narrow or expand energetic experiences.

I once had an experience with a quartz crystal. Native Americans rightfully know that stones and crystals from the earth carry their own life force. I believe that someday, most of us will understand how to engage with this life force to use it for our better good.

I was in a room with many other people. We were engaged in a ceremony of shamanic journeying. The drummer began to beat her drum. Rapidly, I moved into a trance state. I placed a large quartz crystal on my third eye and asked it for its knowledge.

The quartz began to speak to me. In the physical world, I heard a noise, a quick succession of sounds like ice cracking. In my visions, I saw a series of geometric shapes. They were automatically formed upon a cone as they traveled upward. I was shown the numbers zero and one. The circle of shapes traveled up on the cone in my continued vision. There was music accompanying my vision.

The next morning, I was listening to Bach on the radio. To my amazement, I heard in the music, what I was experiencing with the crystal the evening before. I heard the buildup of music and the call and response of notes in harmonic melodies that represented plateaus.

We expand in our inner experiences, and our expansion calls out to the universe to allow energetic relationships to be let go and called in to create and manifest before our very eyes.

That is what the crystal taught me.

God Talks

Remember the pencil going through all of the magazine pages at one time? Energy is in constant connection with the energy of Source at all times. In fact, energy cannot be out of connection with Source. If it was, it would be destroyed.

Energy is immortal. Because it is immortal, it is divine. Because of its divinity, it acts as a continual expression of the source of its existence. It lives to show us what Source is. Through its life, it communicates to us the nature of reality, the true life of God.

The Universal Mind is all energy. All energy is the Universal Mind. Our minds cannot be separated from the Universal Mind. We cannot separate our mental energy from the energy throughout the Universal Mind. Your mind can change location and see different aspects of energy, however, the connection remains.

Because of the continual connection with energy, the communication with energy remains constant. You are continually talking physically with all of the energy around you. Not in words, but through your experiences, feelings, and thoughts, you emanate an identity that you continually create that other energy identifies as you.

You, as your energetic identity, is constantly telling Source or the Universal Mind all about you. Oh, we know, you may think that Source has better things to do than listen to you, but the truth of the matter is that Source has no choice but to listen to you. Listening to you is built into the system of how energy works. So no matter how boring your day, how full of complaints you may be, or how trivial you feel your concerns may be, Source is right by your side listening to all of it.

Source speaks to you about who you are through what comes back to you about you in your world. What your day is like is information about you that you need to know more about. Not to blame you, or to judge you, but always with this goal in mind, to enlighten you towards the process of flow. To help you bring forth unconscious information to consciousness so that you may bring forth more energy from your connection with Source to you.

Source wants to live, it seeks to manifest, it wants to expand. Through your enlightenment, you continually birth energy from Source for expression. That makes you the partner of God. It is because of your creativity,

your ability to allow God to flow through you, that gives life to God and you.

God wants to continue the conversation of who it is with you, so that your existence is based on the continued conversation and relationship with God. In this way, the form of the relationship never ends, the flow continues and your existence becomes immortal.

Points to Remember:

With each new ending, something else must be made to replace it. This law guarantees that something different can be created.

Because endings must be balanced with beginnings, a multitude of creative choices can now be permitted to flow from the Universal Mind to your mind, giving you free reign to design a new start.

It is our emotions which can act to block us, or free us, in our spiritual connection with Source. It is our feelings, which assign to us seeming false endings, when the true reality is a continuing series of new beginnings which lie before us.

We see the circle of never ending energy that is always available to us to build, to make what we can see on the outside of us.

The Making Of Energy

Energy will build to fill the depletion of energetic flow.

There is always something next.

Energy must fill the gaps of depleted energy.

Old Energy into New Energy

Energetic vibrations can organize themselves into new and creative patterns.

The different patterns of energy inside of you have created a different mental location in order to see the world outside of you.

Energy can shift within a moment.

The reorganization of energy to fit new patterns of living exist independently within you.

Different Experience

When this energy inside of you is ready to shift into something new, it has already been having its own different epiphanies of energetic know how.

It is in these moments of sorting out different energy, that help you begin to see differently.

Energy seeks its own balance to build something new in forming relationships with the energy outside of you.

Needed Energy

Mental energy travels through all dimensions at one time. It will automatically form relationships with needed energy to make its inward experience whole.

Synchronicity is the way energy reorders itself outside of you to present you with validating information about how your inner energy is becoming organized.

Wholeness is sought by energy to forward energetic expansion.

Knowing continually draws the missing link it needs for its continual completion, and it knows how to do it.

Energetic Structures

Energy organizes into structures in alignment with the universal law.

Because energy always seeks to expand, it will automatically seek relationships that want to help it build. That means in the course of its expansion, it may seek different structures to help it contain its expansion. Some people call this process sacred geometry.

The higher the energetic density determines the change in the structure.

Energy and the structures it needs to expand are always in harmony.

Energy Takes and Lets Go

In energy relationships, there are three key elements:

- The first is alignment with all energy needed to transport itself into three dimensional reality.

- The second is that energy will let go, or take in, all energy that is needed to appear in three dimensional reality.
- Number three, energy will appear through the taking in of all energy needed for the buildup of the density required to create in reality.

Energy can also move into higher or lower levels of vibration.

We expand in our inner experiences, and our expansion calls out to the universe to allow energetic relationships to be let go and called in to create and manifest before our very eyes.

God Talks

Because of the continual connection with energy, the communication with energy remains constant.

Source speaks to you about who you are through what comes back to you about you in your world.

God wants to continue the conversation of who it is with you, so that your existence is based on the continued conversation and relationship with God.

Affirm:

I can heal and create from the never ending energy from God.

Experience:

Take a deep breath. We suggest you use your journal for this exercise. This exercise may take one day or several to complete. Focus inward on a problem that you feel needs healing. Write down the problem. Now, write down the mirrors outside of yourself that reflect your inner problem. Perhaps you feel you need a new job. One mirror may be problems with the new boss. Perhaps you are continually upset over your grown son's behavior. One mirror could possibly be conflicts with his wife. What are the mirrors communicating to you about your inner energy? What do you need to learn from the mirrors? What do you need to heal? What do you need to intentionally choose to make the change happen? Place this choice and new found awareness into your knowing. Trust that the change will happen. Note down synchronistic experiences from the world around you that begin to reflect your inward shift.

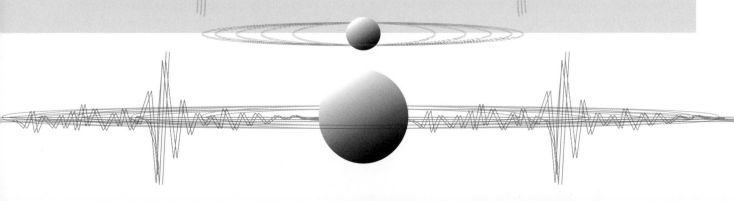

Chapter Twenty-Two
The Universal Law of Source

There is a power, a force, sometimes called God, which is always with us, no matter what. This law states we are never alone. Because the Universal Mind is continually speaking to us and identifying us through our energy, our connection with the Universal Mind is never broken. Energy is immortal and by its very nature lives. Because our energy is constantly alive, our connection to Source is also constantly alive.

God is a force inside of us that gives us the constant power to create, because it lives to create. We are the expression of its creation, and because we have become an expression of God's creation, we cannot be separated from its source of creative expression. We must live to express the energy within the Universal Mind. Otherwise, the conduit for energetic expression would not exist, our purpose as conduits would not exist and we would truly die. We would not exist as energetic forms. Our minds would not have the resources of energetic flow to sustain its living.

The life force within us is not sustained by our physical presence alone; it just looks that way to the untrained mind. We are training your mind to view energy as a cooperative community of energy that exists, all at once, everywhere, like some huge sea that ebbs and flows, depletes and builds.

Imagine that you live in the sea. Your connection with the surrounding water cannot be severed. You cannot be alone, if you were alone right now, without the support of the energy around you, you would melt like the Wicked Witch of the West in the *Wizard of Oz*. The truth is, you would not have ever been born.

The very fact of your existence lets you know you are not alone. The very fact of all of your connections to energy have supported the manifestation of your energy. Your physical reality was created through and by mind. Because mind gave its cooperative permission for your energy to build and become dense to manifest in reality, you have, in turn, given your permission to allow the existence of mind to live through you.

Your mind and the Universal Mind are conjoined like twins to allow the energy of mind to live. And through the life form that you are, a mixed flow of mental energy, your physical existence cannot be alone, because of the very energy of your existence.

The God Connection

Sometimes people may feel so small, compared to the vastness of the world, or even the universe, that they forget that their energy is still heard. They may think that, in comparison to such vast amounts of energy, their energy becomes lost in insignificance. They develop a belief that discounts who they are in relation to the world they live in. They do not realize the vibrant power of the energy inside of them and the power of connection to all energy everywhere. In their disillusionment, they assume a position of powerlessness and experience themselves as disconnected. They feel unrecognized, because they have forgotten to recognize their inward connection to all things, especially the Universal Mind.

The Universal Mind does not judge energy by its size. This is one instance where size does not count. From the tiniest essence of energy, to the vast links of energy, the presence of the Universal Mind lives.

Energy alone cannot exist without the connection of the Universal Mind. The Universal Mind is the energy of creation, of life force, and is the air that energy breathes in order to sustain itself.

All energy must have the breath of God to live. Without the Universal Mind's connection, energy would not be.

Energy travels through the power of love. Love is the intellectual structure of the Universal Mind. Love feeds energy, like gasoline feeds a car, to move.

You are made from the love of the Universal Mind to move, to build and to create. As part of creation, your connection to the Universal Mind cannot be severed, no matter how you perceive your insignificance.

The power of the Universal Mind's connection to your energy is vast and limitless. You cannot wish away this enormous resource, you can only block the flow through your mental view. Regardless of your hindrance, the Universal Mind is continually present. Why? Because you live! And by your very life, comes the standard equipment of the Universal Mind connection.

Once this connection is brought forth through the buildup of energy, it cannot be taken away. You, through this very connection to the Universal Mind, have become divine. And through your divinity, you are powerful and rich with all of the ways that energy can be.

Energy, no matter how vast, needs the very small parts of itself to form who it is. Think of a talent you have. Perhaps it is your unfailing kindness, your ability to draw or your intelligent analysis of music. Imagine, for a moment, you without this ability. Although your talent is not the whole of you, it would be hard to see you as you without it.

We are interdependent creatures that exist in a world that is dependent on all of the energy within it to live. In our seeming independence, we forget the very structure of the interdependence of energy that makes who we are possible.

We may forget the trusting compliance and cooperation that unconsciously happens inside of us to make these alliances possible. And we forget the power in our alliances.

Look inward, not outward, for your true power. All of the energy you need for anything and everything is right there, right now. All you have to do is look in the right direction.

The Agreements of God

Partnerships are formed with certain rules, regulations, and agreements. Energetic partnerships form agreements with one another to behave in a certain way.

These agreements are universal laws. Universal laws organize energy to do certain tasks in a particular way. You are learning about the agreements energy has with mind, both your mind, the mind within all energy and the Universal Mind.

As I have said before, your mind is a tool to organize energy. Your mind can structure energy in alignment with universal laws in order to move energy in the most optimal way. You are then known as, yep, "in the flow."

Unlike people, the Universal Mind does not back out of its agreements, or change its agreements, or even get angry at its partnerships. The Universal Mind makes agreements that never end. The partnerships in our dimension, are never severed.

The Universal Mind makes these agreements with energy based on the three rules of partnerships. Number one, I help form you and you help form me with love. Number two, we all agree on laws about how energy acts, and number three our partnership is forever.

This partnership is one connection you cannot cut, you cannot run from and you cannot hide from. No matter what, your connection to the Universal Mind remains, despite how you see that connection and how you choose to experience that connection.

The Universal Mind's energy moves rapidly through you, moment by moment, creating the world around you in each moment. It is in constant partnership with all of the energy in your world, and your world is constantly reformed. Nothing exists independently from you and your joint interdependence with other energy sustains your life force.

You cannot claim to be apart from your partnership with the Universal Mind. Somewhere along the way, you made a joint decision with equal say to make this alliance. And in your making, you decided to accept the energy from the Universal Mind. You decided to embrace the love inherent in the life of the Universal Mind and live from the energy of love. We are reminding you of the experience of your creation to accept the love that is your right to embrace.

No matter what your present-life circumstances, no matter if you were a victim of abuse as a child, impoverished by divorce, feel alone and uncared for; we are here to remind you that the truth of your very existence was made through the partnership of love between you and the Universal Mind.

You may have forgotten the power of your own decision to live. You may have forgotten the power of your partnership with the Universal Mind and with all energy. Most of all, you may have forgotten the power in knowing that these energetic partnerships live through you.

We hope that we are helping you to reorganize your mind, let go of beliefs and experiences that no longer serve your higher good, and embrace the partnerships with energy that lives inside of you. You are powerful. You are divine. You are human and you can trust your humanity to handle its powerful divinity.

God Creation

Since the Universal Mind identifies each energy type just as it is, the Universal Mind is able to move its energy forward to develop that connection. Think of your own projects. Perhaps you are developing a sculpture. The energy within your sculpture is independent of you. The face in the sculpture is obvious to anyone looking at it. Of course it is a face. The face was made from the energy inside of you. You imagined the face and you sculpted the face, according to your inward vision. You saw it and then you took the energy from your vision and allowed it to flow outside of you to the clay. The face is of you and yet, it is of itself.

Well, the Universal Mind has, let's say, several of its own projects. It is developing several sculptures at once. The Universal Mind is able to develop each sculpture through its energetic identity, just like you may see that each of Monet's paintings of water lilies are not the same.

The Universal Mind moves its energy outward into its own creations. They can be in our world and in other worlds all at the same time.

In fact, each concrete three-dimensional object in our world has its own unseen force of energy. As you may know by now, this energy is mental.

Where does the Universal Mind get its own energy? This may surprise you, but it gets its energy from you! Not in a vampire way though. The Universal Mind doesn't come along and suck your blood. However, because you are the creative force of mental energy that you are, and you have your own energy, like the sculpture has its own energy, or your dog, or the tree outside, the Universal Mind continually connects to your energy to create its own flow.

That is correct. The Universal Mind experiences its own flow of energy. When, together, you and the Universal Mind are in the flow, you both are in harmonic balance. You are flowing your energy back to the Universal Mind, the Universal Mind then becomes energized with a creative life force, which then flows back to you. You experience new ideas, visions, realizations, and spiritual prompts.

It is the combination of energy between you and the Universal Mind that empowers you and the Universal Mind. Your existence fuels the Universal Mind. That is how important your life is. Your life is always a regenerating power that continually creates. The Universal Mind is always a regenerating power that continually creates. Yes, it is the same energy.

Energy continually creates from its own source of connection with all energy. That means that the source of energy within the Universal Mind is its connection with all energy at once.

Remember the pencil going through all the pages of the magazine at once? The Universal Mind's energy goes through all the pages at once and gathers information from all of those pages in order to create.

Your existence is so valuable that you are actually helping the Universal Mind to create the world around you. You are in continual service to everything on the planet and other energy you can't even see. You can no longer discount the importance of who you are. Why? Your importance remains, even if you make the choice to discount your importance.

God is Everything

The Universal Mind is always within all events, situations, people, in fact, anything you can think of, for this one reason.

The Universal Mind is everything, and because it is everything, it is whole, even when something appears as not whole.

Back to the sculpture, the vision of your sculpture is complete as it is. The sculpture is complete as it is, although the nose needs touching up. The energy of the completed sculpture is already there, it is just hidden. We can't see it.

The sculpture is completed on the table as well as in the image in your mind. The energy is already there for completion; you just can't see it. It has not expressed itself. The sculpture in your mind is not completed.

These subtle shifts of how energy exists in time and space allow you to understand that energy is always in a state of completion. Because energy operates paradoxically, it does not always look like it is in completion to us in our world.

Now, we have already learned that everything is whole, just as it is. Also remember, that the Universal Mind is conscious of all the energy in the universe.

Just like you know the identities of your relatives, where they live and maybe even their birthdays, the Universal Mind is very aware of each identity of each plant and animal, human or otherwise, in its world. Because the Universal Mind is conscious of the energy in its world, it can instantaneously complete situations, events, and objects in its world. There is no time. Everything is complete. It is done.

The Universal Mind has the knowledge of all energy to make completion happen. Because of its ability to do so, completion occurs in a moment. Because the energy of God is in everything, the energy of completion is in everything. What is different is that we, as humans, may not be conscious of the energy of completion within us. We lie asleep in our knowledge that the energy of the Universal Mind can complete us.

God Expansion

Your energy is constantly creating from your skills, talents, and abilities. Because you are inspired through the energy of God, what you create is a mixture of your energy and God's. You do not hide your creation, but present your talents to the world around you. You make your energy available for the world to use. But guess what? Not just the world, but God as well can now benefit from your creations.

You have added through your inventive use of energy, more innovative ways to funnel energy into the world around you. You make art, music, writing, psychological growth, or epiphanies of understanding happen.

God can then create relationships with more energy within itself to use for its betterment. The energy builds within itself and then depletes to the outside of itself. Breathe. You can only take in so much air before you must breathe out. Like air, energy builds within God and then must be depleted from God to the outside of itself. You receive from the buildup of energy within God.

Back again to the I Ching symbol and the importance of balanced energy. Your energetic flow is balanced by the energy of God. The energy of God is balanced by your energy. You continually make God conscious and God continually makes you conscious. Because your energy continually adds to God's energy, you fuel God to have more energetic resources to have at its disposal. You feed God energy and God then can make the energy from its stored warehouses of energy. God then pulls from its stored warehouse of energy whatever you may need to make for yourself and sends it to you in the form of a spiritual prompt, an idea, or a creative spark.

Remember, we are all a part of God. You are a part of God. Your mental energy is within The Universal Mind. You are the small ball of knowing within the larger ball of the Universal Mind. You continually flow with the intelligence of God and God flows from the intelligence of you. Together, you are both created. You have more of who you are and God has more of who it is.

There is one more thing. In order for God to access more use of its own energy, you must be open to a relationship with God. This relationship must be based upon what you experience God to be, not what anyone else experiences God to be. Only your personal experience counts and you can't cheat. You can't state, oh, I am a Christian, Jew, Muslim, or even a Saint, and expect your religion to do the work for you of developing a personal experience with God. It won't work.

Your definition and experience, your identification within you with the divine, is what counts. Nothing else can cover for you and create that relationship. It would be like putting a mask on, facing an audience from a stage and telling people that this is the real you. Well, it is not the real you and the real you needs to form an inner relationship with what you experience God to be.

This step cannot be skipped. The work of going inside yourself and learning how you communicate with God through your unique talents, abilities, and resources cannot be done by anyone except you. You cannot hide behind a third party and expect a relationship to develop with the divine. What you will accomplish, however, is maintaining a false experience of what God is and you will present to yourself a false mask of who you are. You will not know your divine purpose in this world and you will feel a sense of being lost without understanding why.

So many people come to me wondering what their life purpose is. They also dismiss and invalidate their various talents and abilities. Well, we are here to tell you that your talents, skills, and abilities are your life purpose. To use who you are is what makes your life genuine, and to show people who you are is what connects you to your life.

It is hiding yourself from yourself that depletes the energy within God and also within you. What is the cure? Go out, have the courage to be. Show the world what you are really made of. Write, paint the painting, dance to the music, be you. Be yourself.

The Balancing Factor

As we have said, God's energy finds it own level outside of itself and has its own natural ability to find balance. Think of two glasses of water. There is a tube halfway down that connects both glasses together. If you fill one glass with water, what will happen? It will empty out into the other glass and find its own balance.

You are the container in which God's energy seeks to find its own balance. Energy flows from God to you until it reaches a point of balance.

You use this energy, build it up within you, make it dense and make your inner experience into outer reality. Your idea of a book becomes outer reality. The energy of your inspired intelligence flows out onto paper and you balance the flow of energy from the Universal Mind with your outward work.

Because you have chosen to freely express what is inside of you, you allow the Universal Mind to freely express what is inside of it. You allow the flow of intelligent energy to move through you and seek its own balance. You allow the balance to be expressed in three-dimensional reality. You allow your creative ideas and inner experiences and your relationship to the Universal Mind show itself in the creation of your book. Your book becomes God's balanced three-dimensional statement of its own energy.

Your book is the balance of energy within the outward flow of God's energy. Like breathing, God takes in energy, then must let out energy. You express the energy God must let out. You are the conduit for the assertion of God's energy. You make creation happen. Without your natural ability to take in God's energy, to breathe it in, God would not be able to show itself. God would not be able to balance its own energy by showing people what it is. God is your creativity.

The Body of God

The Universal Mind has its own identifying energy, just like you do. Just like you looking in the mirror, the Universal Mind can determine whose image is looking back.

The Universal Mind's ability to experience itself allows the Universal Mind to flow more of its energy outward into the universe.

Look at your foot, as you are sitting in the chair. Of course you recognize it as your foot. It is nobody else's foot. It is not the dog's foot, the cat's foot, or your neighbor's foot. It is your foot. You decide to get out of your chair and move your foot forward and kick a soccer ball. The ball moves forward with the energy produced by your foot.

The Universal Mind does the same thing. It recognizes its parts and moves those parts in any way it chooses. Because the energy of the Universal Mind is in everything around you, including you, the Universal Mind can move its energy into you and everything else around you. Just like you move energy into your foot and kick the ball.

How does energy flow? It flows through your automatic movement and build up of energy into one place. Sit still. Notice your foot. Notice yourself experiencing and intending your foot moving forward; except, do one thing. Don't move it. Just notice the energy built up in your foot through your experiencing and intending to move forward.

Now relax your other foot. Notice the difference between your two feet. One is relaxed and one is full of energy, ready to go!

The energy of the Universal Mind within you is ready to go. The energy within all of who you are is both you and the Universal Mind. The energy cannot be separated. Separate your skin from the air around you as you read this book. Even though you may have

mentally separated them, your skin and the air, your skin is not separate.

The Universal Mind truly wants to be able to have its energy flow to you. In this release of energy, the Universal Mind can know more about what it can do.

As you kick the ball in the soccer game, you know more about your ability to play the sport. It is through your experience that you know more about your physical prowess. It is through the experience of what you do with the energy of the Universal Mind that the Universal Mind knows more about itself.

The Universal Mind then can share its knowledge of experience throughout the universe, because it has learned more about what it can do with its own energy.

You, because you have learned the game of soccer, can show other people how to play soccer because of your experience. The Universal Mind is able to teach people how to use its energy.

Points to Remember:

There is a power, a force, sometimes called God, which is always with us, no matter what. This law states we are never alone.

Because our energy is constantly alive, our connection to Source is also constantly alive.

God is a force inside of us that gives us the constant power to create, because it lives to create.

Your physical reality was created through and by mind.

Your mind and the Universal Mind are conjoined like twins to allow the energy of mind to live.

The God Connection

Energy alone cannot exist without the connection of the Universal Mind.

The power of the Universal Mind's connection to your energy is vast and limitless.

The Agreements of God

Energetic partnerships form agreements with one another to behave in a certain way.

These agreements are universal laws.

The Universal Mind makes agreements that never end.

The Universal Mind makes these agreements with energy based on the three rules of partnerships:

- Number one, I help form you and you help form me with love.
- Number two, we all agree on laws about how energy acts.
- Number three our partnership is forever.

God Creation

Since the Universal Mind identifies each energy type just as it is, the Universal Mind is able to move its energy forward to develop that connection.

The Universal Mind moves its energy outward into its own creations. They can be in our world and in other worlds all at the same time.

The Universal Mind continually connects to your energy to create its own flow.

It is the combination of energy between you and the Universal Mind that empowers you and the Universal Mind.

God is Everything

The Universal Mind is everything, and because it is everything, it is whole, even when something appears as not whole.

The Universal Mind has the knowledge of all energy to make completion happen. Because of its ability to do so, completion occurs in a moment.

God Expansion

Your energy is constantly creating from your skills, talents and abilities. Because you are inspired through the energy of God, what you create is a mixture of your energy and God's.

God can then create relationships with more energy within itself to use for its betterment.

In order for God to access more use of its own energy, you must be open to a relationship with God.

The Balancing Factor

As we have said, God's energy finds it own level outside of itself and has its own natural ability to find balance.

You are the container in which God's energy seeks to find its own balance.

Because you have chosen to freely express what is inside of you, you allow the Universal Mind to freely express what is inside of it.

The Body of God

The Universal Mind's ability to experience itself allows the Universal Mind to flow more of its energy outward into the universe.

The Universal Mind truly wants to be able to have its energy flow to you. In this release of energy to you, the Universal Mind can know more about what it can do.

The Universal Mind then can share its knowledge of experience throughout the universe, because it has learned more about what it can do with its own energy.

Affirm:

I am divinely created to express the flow of life.

Experience:

Remember the Christmas classic, *It's a Wonderful Life?* Clarence, the Angel, could not earn his wings until George recognized how important his life was. Take a deep breath. Just imagine how it would be for your loved ones if you were not around. What would it be like for your children? What would it be like for your spouse or your friends? What would it be like for perhaps your pet? How would your absence change their lives?

Chapter Twenty-Three
The Universal Law of Making

This law determines that energy can manifest into the physical world around you.

Because the Universal Mind continually flows its energy to you, this energy can move out from you to your reality. You can move your foot out to kick that soccer ball and make a goal scoring the winning point.

The energy that moves through you from the Universal Mind can make events real; it can create objects or situations to come into our lives and can change events or situations immediately.

The effect of the flow of the Universal Mind's energy into the world around you can happen in an instant or take a lifetime to organize into a creation in your world.

Universal law determines that energy can become physical.

It becomes physical through an acknowledged connection with the Universal Mind through your knowing, repeated communication to the Universal Mind of inward experiences, a healing and releasing of emotional experiences, seeing that you have choices, giving yourself permission to use your talents, skills and abilities, allowing yourself to release control over the outcome and allowing yourself to receive the energetic production.

The connection with the Universal Mind is the connection that allowed you to become physical.

Without the flow of energy from the Universal Mind, you would not have been made.

Through your understanding of how natural it is to have the energy of the Universal Mind within you, you can acquire the same advantages of how the Universal Mind's energy composes concrete reality.

You can use your mind as an educated tool to begin to organize your energy with the energy of the Universal Mind. And the combination of your energy with the Universal Mind is the energy that makes everything you see around you.

Good Vibrations

The Universal Mind has the ability to control and project its energy outward. Just like an opera singer projecting his voice out from the stage into the audience, the Universal Mind has the same ability. We have the same ability to project our energy out into the world around us.

Any fans here of the *Dog Whisperer*? God bless Cesar Millan! He is not just teaching dog training, he is teaching people about energy. He teaches how you can train yourself to use your energy to communicate with your dog and provide to your dog what is needed. He continually talks about projecting your energy out as a leader. You feel, think, and experience yourself as leader, your dog feels, thinks, and experiences you as leader. Animals are energy readers.

The Universal Mind is a leader of its own energy. The Universal Mind sends its energy out to communicate with you. Your energy can act in the same way. You can send your energy out to communicate with the Universal Mind.

Now what makes this so important is that the Universal Mind can project out its energy to several different dimensions, in several different areas, to several different people, animals, plants, or worlds, all at one time. Nothing or no one is left out or dismissed as unheard or unimportant. Everything and everyone is continually important. Everything is a number one priority. Energy from the Universal Mind continually talks.

Because the Universal Mind is in constant communication with you, its energy can always move out to you.

Because this law acts as one big conveyer belt moving energy along its way to you, you have the benefit of having a stable, consistent source of energy available. You are never without the resource of energy from the Universal Mind.

Energy needs movement in order to live. Like we need to breathe in order to live, energy needs to continually vibrate. Its vibrations allow it to function, to move where it needs to go, and to create what it needs to create.

I have witnessed energetic vibrations. We were honored to be a participant at a Native American Church meeting. During the ritual, we called in our ancestors and the keepers of the four directions. The medicine woman sang songs in her native tongue and honored the energy of the medicine, the peyote. As visions began, we saw several webs of energy. The energy spun very quickly and there were several of them connected in a sea of energy. Now, because the medicine taught us how to see energy in this dimension, we can see the webs of energy all around us. It vibrates like extremely fast breaths and spins out energy to all that is. Energy is a living, breathing organism. Within it contains the energetic support for all that is.

Energetic Frequencies

Energy acts just like a musical instrument. Energy vibrates and creates a frequency just like a sound. Just like a guitar string, it can vibrate in different ways to make a frequency or a sound, we just cannot hear the energy communicating. And thank god we can't. Could you imagine if we were able to hear energy speaking to us from everything around us? It would be way too much, the best sound reduction headphones would be useless and we would be completely overrun by sound. We would not be able to make sense of it all!

Another reason that energy operates on a level we can't hear with our physical ears; is because we would not be able to understand it. The way we can understand energy is through our feelings; it is how we experience energy. We identify energy through our inner ears of experiencing energy.

Ever feel someone or something looking at you, although you can't see it? You know they are there, you turn around and look right into their eyes. Somehow, you felt their presence.

Energy acts in the same subtle way. It lets its presence be known in small ways that you experience inside of you. That is why it becomes important to meditate, to become very still and notice the energy inside of you in a quiet manner. Within the altered states of meditation, you can sense the subtleties of energetic life.

Through a regular practice of meditation, you will notice the subtle variations of energy inside of you. You may begin to notice the energy of your partner, or perhaps your dog. You will feel them, even though they may not be standing next to you. Because you are quiet and mindful, you can hear energy and it talks by

identifying how something else feels. You may be even able to feel the presence of the Universal Mind. And through meditation, you can make your connection stronger to the Universal Mind by continuing to identify its presence.

Energy must have a frequency in order to talk to the world around it. Through frequencies, energy makes relationships and then figures out if it is going to build up and create something physical, or deplete and go somewhere else.

Without its ability to communicate through its frequencies, energy would not have any ability at all to form relationships. It would not be able to mirror other energy and it would not be able to tell people about what it is.

Energy must sing. It must shout out to the universe exactly what it is all about. In doing this, energy can then get what it needs and provide other energy with what it needs to move forward.

Energy must always sing. It never stops talking. It continually communicates its identity. Energy is in constant movement toward sounds or frequencies that harmonize with it, or away from, sounds or frequencies that do not harmonize with it. It is constantly forming or ending relationships.

The forming or ending of relationships can be made instantaneously. The effects in our three-dimensional world can be instantaneous. However, we may not be able to see them. Energy always has an outcome when it sings its song. We may experience it right away in our life, or it may take awhile. However, the outcome remains.

The frequency of energy can shift dramatically when it is focused upon through meditation in a quiet manner. If you are feeling down and you begin to experience the energy of joy and joyful experiences, the frequency of energy will rise and open within you.

Listen

The crystal experience taught me that when energy moves, it makes music. I could hear it making a sound as the plane of energy moved upward towards the top of the cone.

The sound that energy makes cannot be heard in our dimension. However, the frequency of the vibration can be experienced in our dimension.

All experience makes a sound, because of the energetic vibration. Vibrations hum along and create harmonic notes that identify its vibrations. These are the sounds heard throughout the universe. These are the sounds that the Universal Mind makes when it wants to say something.

We, as people, have a unique ability to tune into these sounds. We can sense whether or not an experience has a high frequency of vibration or a low frequency of vibration. All we have to do is listen to what is inside of us.

Our inner hearing is our sixth sense. It is our ability to listen to what the universe is telling us. It makes us ever ready to respond to what the universe is telling us. And we can respond to what we hear, by choosing to raise our level of energetic vibration.

If you are discouraged over being passed over for the promotion you wanted, you can listen to your inner experience and change the level of energetic vibration by remembering your talents, validating yourself worth, and perhaps asserting yourself by considering another position. You are simultaneously healing the wound of your experience and moving yourself into another level of energetic vibration, one of feeling faith in yourself.

If you are lonely and wishing for a soul mate, like a client just contacted us about, you can take yourself out on a vacation over the weekend, go for dinner, and provide yourself with the comforts of a good time. By doing this, you are creating a space within yourself for more of those experiences to happen.

The frequency of vibration continually communicates with everything throughout the universe to tell people what it is. In this way of communicating, energy is never left on its own. It can match other frequencies of vibration.

Just like the woman making a space within her for other experiences, such as meeting her soul mate, it is like the one she is creating to recreate itself.

Sound can be loud or soft. Loud sounds have more power. The drummer beating on the drum puts more energy into the drum to make it louder. The Universal Mind can do the same thing with energy. It can put more energy to make the sound louder and move energy in a more powerful way.

Sound that is powerful grabs our attention. Our inner sound within us that is loud grabs our attention. If we are feeling a huge sense of loss and grief over our pet, who is ill, the experience inside of us will grab our attention. It will feel loud.

The Universal Mind will send us experiences that are loud to grab our attention. A client of ours wanted a new office for her psychotherapy practice. She was beginning to think her current office was too small while she was away on vacation. When she returned, the receptionist of her office building was rude to her about the use of the office staff. She told her that she was thinking that maybe she shouldn't even be there.

We pointed out to her that she had set the universal energy into movement through defining what she wanted her next office experience to be. People unconsciously "heard" and identified her energy and were reacting to her leave taking. Obviously, they did not want to be left and were mad about it.

Our hearing of energy is very subtle. As humans, we were hearing our mother's experiences before we were born. We have been tuned into listening to energy before we even became physical in our energy.

Energy has the capacity to hear. It has built-in ears along with its built-in intelligence. It can move in tune with what it hears. We can also move in tune with what we hear inside of us. We can be with our grief when we feel we need to be, or recall our precious memories of joy when our pet was alive. All of our experiences have their own music, and we can choose what we listen to.

Energy, Big or Small

Energy acts in the world it lives in, just like we do. Energy can hear what other energy is saying and it can talk back, just like your teenage daughter. Well, hopefully not like your teenage daughter!

Energy, as I have said, can choose to link up with other energy and build itself up, or go elsewhere and deplete its own energy and become smaller.

Musical notes can be combined with other notes to form chords, or act on their own to form a simple melody. *Row Row Row Your Boat* can be a complex round or a simple, one-person song.

Energy, too, can be very simple or become very complex in its form. One of the ways it makes a decision to become simple or complex is what energy is choosing to experience at any given moment. In other words, what do you want to do? Get a group of people together and sing, or sing a simple song by yourself as you are taking a shower?

Energy makes the same choices. You can direct the choices that energy makes.

Energy makes itself into its own form. Your experience of energy inside of you helps shape it into its own form. You sing the song. The energy inside of the music is its own. You play the violin. The energy coming from the violin is independent from you. You grasp the glass of water. The glass is independent from you. You drive the car. The car is independent from you. You decide to get a bigger car instead of a small vehicle. The bigger car is independent from you. The fact is, you can make choices in regards to how you want to interact with energy.

More examples: You have a terrible marriage, like many of our clients, and get a divorce. You can rehash old memories without any more resolution and continue to blame your ex-husband or wife for all of his or her horrible faults, or, you can put your mind in a different location, the present, and focus in on what needs healing inside of your life now. You take responsibility for the energy inside of your mind and view your reality through choosing a different set of energy that creates your reality. You release the anger by depleting that energy and begin to build the energy of joy by focusing in on your interests and friends.

You can also notice the purpose your anger served in helping you heal. What did you need to learn from the anger? Are you able to transition towards focusing in on the present? If you cannot, something needs to be healed in your energetic field regarding your ex-spouse before you can hold the energy of joy.

The energy of joy becomes a large part of your life. Joy acts independently from you and brings situations and events into your life in an unexpected way.

All because the energy inside of you, "joy," is listening to the director that is your mind saying "more joy" and talking to other energy in the world around you saying "let's experience more joy through life-affirming events." The energy around you says "yes, let's do," and well, there you go!

Focusing in on past energy, such as anger regarding a divorce, like many of our clients have, without the intent of developing insight about the anger, creates a depletion of energy. It narrows energy down into a small place of being stuck in the past and experiencing only anger. The energy of anger will not move into the present unless you help it move.

Once any energy moves into the present moment, it expands and opens to the world around you for further creation.

Close your eyes, take a deep breath. Begin to meditate. Allow your thoughts to go by you and bring yourself back to experiencing your breath moment by moment. Open your eyes. Look around you, even the colors of what you are seeing have gained new life. Your feelings are different. What you are experiencing is a new appreciation for the moment. Your eyes and senses have opened to see more of what is around you. You may feel a heightened sense of clarity, because you are able to experience more of what is around you. Why? Because you listened.

Each moment, energy listens and gets smaller or bigger, depending upon what it hears. You, as your own director in life, can listen to the energy inside of you and make it bigger or smaller depending upon what you notice.

The Flow

Energy talks to other energy and can join with other energy. You can be alone or join your energy in a group effort. Your combined efforts make your energy even more powerful. When I was going to school to get my masters degree in social work, information about sexual abuse was just beginning to be circulated. A group of us got together and created an ad for television about sexual abuse prevention. Each of us had skills we could contribute to the group. One person had connections in television, another could direct the group, and yet another could do the writing for the ad. We were all independent of each other, yet we could combine our energy, link together, and form one group.

Remember, the energy inside of you can work independently or continually link with other energy to create something larger.

A client of ours was a displaced Hawaiian. He felt a connection with the culture that was not hereditary. He was a mixture of different races and physically appeared to be Hawaiian. He was determined to bring his healing practice of Huna back to the Hawaiian people. His practice was not learned from education, but from within his deep knowing and his memory.

Our client could have chosen to dismiss and block the flow of energy that told him he was Hawaiian, but he chose not to block it. He began to validate his inward identity. The energy inside of him began to link with other energy that said, "I believe in you." He made his inner energy of belief in his identity larger. He began to travel to Hawaii and sought out spiritual leaders and elders. Some people recognized my client's inner identity, while some did not. But my client, above all, knew who he was. He continued to seek out people who could support him.

Over a few years, our client began to meet influential spiritual leaders who believed in his healing capacity. They eventually supported our client enough where he could move there and build a house and a practice.

Our client chose to make his inner belief in who he was larger. The world outside of him also linked to him because of his inner belief. It is not that he did not have nay sayers, it was his continued validation of his inner energy that kept our client reaching outside of himself for what he knew to be true inside of himself.

Another client of ours was having difficulty releasing several recent traumatic events with her pets. Her grief was creating a down slide into depression and she found her motivation for her healing practice beginning to decline. Through our guidance, it was suggested she link her grief with unconditional love for herself. Although, she took time out to do just want she needed to do, to heal, she was no longer in a state of decline, because she was no longer blocking the flow of her energy.

Even when we choose to make our energy smaller, we can still link our energy with other energy that can be comforting and healing.

There is not just one note or musical chord in one symphony. All of the music can be linked together in a way that flows harmonically.

Our point is to teach you how to flow your energy in a harmonic way that does not block your energy. You can then allow your energy to link with other energy and create something outside of you that continues your flow of energy.

Energy that does not continually move to a position of being small, or becoming large, is not flowing. It then becomes stuck. Anger, shame, depression, and fear can all create energetic blocks that do not allow your energy to flow.

Remember that energy flows from your connection to the Universal Mind out, like the ball within the ball. If you are angry, you are feeling nothing but the anger. The recognition of other connections becomes lost. If you can reach down below the anger and bring up insight about the anger, you can then allow other experiences to emerge.

And that is the point of our lives; to allow ourselves to continue to be in the flow of our energy and to allow experiences to happen without getting stuck. If we are operating our lives in that way, we can be guaranteed of one thing: constant growth. If we are in constant growth, we are constantly building, which is what the Universal Mind is up to. We are at once mirroring and in a relationship with the Universal Mind.

Energetic Conflicts

Energy continually seeks balance, just as the symbol I Ching shows us. If you feel unbalanced, you will experience the unbalance as a psychological conflict. You may feel distraught and you may want to resolve the conflict within yourself. Many of our clients come to me because they feel conflicted about what is happening in their lives. They are seeking to resolve difficult imbalances and find life direction.

One client, in particular, struggled for years about whether or not to stay in her marriage. She had a strong sense of ambivalence because she was persuaded by other people to marry her husband. Because of her difficult childhood, she was not certain if the problems in her marriage stemmed from her childhood, or if the marriage was truly something she wanted for herself. Our client truly wanted to resolve this conflict, because being out of balance feels very uncomfortable.

You know when your energy is out of balance, because it will feel painful to you. Energy wants to become balanced and is motivated to do so, because it experiences imbalances emotionally.

Energy is independent and intelligent; it has its own experiences and emotions. Energy will seek to resolve these imbalances by creating magnetic relationships with other energy.

Energy will look around for other energy that it needs. It will feel an attraction for that energy and draw the needed energy towards it. The energy is magnetically brought to it in order to make balance.

A client recently called regarding her car. She just bought a used car and now it needed $1,800 worth of repairs. Should she put it into the car, or sell it as is and look for something else? She was guided to look for something else; the car was not as sound as she thought it to be—it had axle problems and she would find something else for about $2,000.

Upon trusting the guidance, she decided not to go ahead with the repairs. Her trust led her to intuitively opening the yellow pages to a Cadillac dealer, which, she told us later, she would not have gone to in a million years. Her knowing, told her to call the dealer. They had a car that was newer than her old car, same make and color, on the lot for $2,000. She had her mechanic check it out and it was solid. The dealer also took her old car as a trade in, which turned out to have a rusted axle.

Our client had allowed herself to deplete energy which resolved her problems with her car. She felt herself relieved of a huge financial burden. Her body also resolved a chronic rash that she was guided to know resulted from financial burdens, which she was allowing to get under her skin.

Energy builds and depletes relationships with other energy. The energy that is needed always comes, no matter how much or how little.

Our client's car showed up because energy organized itself to appear just at the right moment in her life. She went ahead, trusted what she knew to be true, and took action. She went ahead and followed the spiritual prompt to look in the yellow pages. She did not follow her usual logical thought process that would state, "Do not call a Cadillac dealer; that does not make sense." She followed the spiritual prompting, which sometimes does not make logical sense. As each energy type appeared independently as a prompt for her to follow, she moved forward and acted. All of the energy together, led her to her new car.

Process of Creation

The Universal Mind is always being of service to us to help us create. We are never alone and never without help. Have you ever heard the saying "the only constant thing that ever happens is change?"

Well, constant creation is what is stable in the universe. Remember energy in the universe works paradoxically. We create our lives from the inside out.

What is in constant change is in the constant process of creation.

You can allow that process to change by allowing yourself to move forward in change, by knowing that help from the Universal Mind is always available.

People who feel, and we know you know them, anger towards God, bitter at life, lost because they do not have a connection with the spirit, are not going to experience their connection with the Universal Mind. They will experience a sense of being stuck and not be able to move forward in the way they are meant to. They will not take into account their responsibility to form an internal loving relationship with the Universal Mind. Why? They do not see their equal ability to create their lives. They will see their lives as formed from the outside of themselves and they will feel a sense of victimization through life's fated circumstances.

Forming a relationship with the divine requires you to be responsible for your relationship with the divine.

It requires you to step up to the plate in knowing you have equal power. It requires you to be in your own knowing. It requires you to have an inner experience of unconditional love for who you are and what you want. It requires you to not control the outcome and receive whatever the outcome is.

Your relationship with the Universal Mind requires trust in the love the Universal Mind has for you. After all, the Universal Mind has created you in the energy of love.

You are born with the ability to be receptive to the help of creative change. You have been formed from the Universal Mind's ability to create the change in the world that is your birth.

You bring change to the world you're in. Every day, when you get up in the morning, feed the kids, go to work, support your friends, go to your belly dance or martial arts class, there is something different in the world around you because of you.

Your ability to live free of confusion regarding the Universal Mind and your place within the true reality of mind can enable you to create whatever is needed in your world.

Your ability to know your place in the world allows the Universal Mind to know its place within you. Together, life is formed, your experience of the Universal Mind becomes present, and you flow with the breath of life.

That truly is your purpose, to breath in connection with Source and all other energy, to know yourself within that connection and to honor who you are, energy in motion.

Points to Remember:

This law determines that energy can manifest into the physical world around you.

Universal law determines that energy can become physical.

It becomes physical through an acknowledged connection with the Universal Mind through your knowing, repeated communication to the Universal Mind of inward experiences, a healing and releasing of emotional experiences, seeing that you have choices, giving yourself permission to use your talents, skills, and abilities, allowing yourself to release control over the outcome and to receive the energetic production.

Good Vibrations

The Universal Mind has the ability to control and project its energy outward.

Energy needs movement in order to live.

Energetic Frequencies

Energy vibrates and creates a frequency just like a sound.

We identify energy through our inner ears of experiencing energy.

And through meditation, you can make your connection stronger to the Universal Mind by continuing to identify its presence.

Energy always has an outcome when it sings its song. We may experience it right away in our life, or it may take awhile. However, the outcome remains.

Listen

All experience makes a sound, because of the energetic vibration.

We can sense whether or not an experience has a high frequency of vibration or a low frequency of vibration.

Our inner hearing is our sixth sense.

The frequency of vibration continually communicates with everything throughout the universe to tell people what it is.

The Universal Mind will send us experiences that are loud to grab our attention.

Energy has the capacity to hear.

Energy, Big or Small

One of the ways it makes a decision to become simple or complex is what energy is choosing to experience at any given moment.

Energy makes itself into its own form. Your experience of energy inside of you helps shape it into its own form.

Each moment, energy listens and gets smaller or bigger, depending upon what it hears.

The Flow

Energy talks to other energy and can join with other energy. You can be alone or join your energy in a group effort.

Energy that does not continually move to a position of being small, or becoming large, is not flowing.

And that is the point of our lives; to allow ourselves to continue to be in the flow of our energy and to allow experiences to happen without getting stuck.

Energetic Conflicts

If you feel unbalanced, you will experience the unbalance as a psychological conflict.

Energy wants to become balanced and is motivated to do so, because it experiences imbalances emotionally.

Process of Creation

The Universal Mind is always being of service to us to help us create.

What is in constant change is in the constant process of creation.

You can allow that process to change by allowing yourself to move forward in change, by knowing that help from the Universal Mind is always available.

Your ability to live free of confusion regarding the Universal Mind and your place within the true reality of mind can enable you to create whatever is needed in your world.

That truly is your purpose, to breath in connection with Source and all other energy, to know yourself within that connection and to honor who you are, energy in motion.

Affirm:

I am in the flow of my creation.

Experience:

Take a deep breath and relax your body. Remember one of the happiest times in your life. Remember where you were at, how it felt, what was around you. Remember the physical smells and feelings. Now, tune into what you were experiencing: what you were thinking, how you were feeling, how you were actively engaged in the event.

As you tune into your emotions and feel the experience, tune into the pitch of the vibration of your experience. If joy could sing, how high would the notes be? Imagine that joy makes a sound. Tune into the joy within you. What does it sound like? Can you hear it?

Part Two
The List of Universal Laws

The Source Deck

Introduction

We live in an energetic universe. As energetic beings, we are, within a system which guarantees our connection to energy: Universal mind we also call Source, God, or Universal Mind. The way that Source behaves is through Universal Laws.

Inner experience works to align with universal law to help us grow. We have outlined the twelve universal laws specially created from spiritual guidance to help you move into alignment. The twelve universal laws present both the alignment as well as the solution to your problem.

When we are not in alignment with universal law, we experience conflict. Conflict creates an emotional wound. We need the energy from Source to help us overcome and heal our wounds. We cannot heal alone.

When you are in moments where it may be difficult for you to shift your inner experience, there is a block present that must be healed. The block is in direct opposition to universal law. The solution resolves energy inside of you by depleting energetic blocks. Once in alignment, both you and Source can express your energy. We have made twelve solutions to help guide you into the direct action to take to overcome conflict.

The Spread

1. Take three deep breaths.
2. Focus on your intent.
3. Take one card from the Universal Law deck.
4. Place it on the left.
5. Take one card from the Solution deck and place it on your right.

The placement allows you to bring into consciousness (your right) what is unconscious (your left). The card structure forms an eleven, which acts as a gateway to bring your inner experience to outer reality.

How should you use your painting on the cards and the information?

First, read your message in a quiet place. Close your eyes and contemplate the images that the words create. It is good to do this several times. Each time you read it, you will interpret or receive the information a little differently.

Allow the information to penetrate your conscious and subconscious. Your guides will begin to speak to you through this message. If you meditate, incorporate your painting on the cards into your meditation practice as visualization. This will help with self-awareness – both consciously and unconsciously.

Universal Law Card Example:

6 Law of Containment
Solution Card Example: 5 Variety

Universal Law Deck
6 Law of Containment

This law guarantees your existence within the creation of energy because you are energy.

• You are whole and complete, just as you are, because you have access to all of the energy that exists within the Universal Mind.
• Your existence, your personality, all of who you are, is felt consciously by God or Universal Mind all of the time, no matter where you are, or what you are doing.
• That spark, the flow of ideas, that creative juice that is rolling through your mind; that is the energy from the Universal Mind.
• That is what God is, the flow of energy through you so that you can know more about who you really are through your own acts of creation.
• Your creation, meaning your very life, is divine.

Meditate upon the universal law painting to give you more understanding about your inner energy.

Solution Deck
5 Universal Law of Variety

The law of variety guarantees the presence of choice.

• You can empower yourself to see the variety of choices in your life that you really do have.
• This means a change must occur and indicates a trapped emotional block. Once emotions are viewed they become unstuck.
• Are there stuck emotions present which need to be viewed?
• Do you need the help of another to help you view your situation?

Meditate on the solution picture until your answers become more clear.

Ask Question (example): How do I deal with feeling inadequate around my mother in law?

Commentary from individual who picked the example solution and the example universal law card.

I realized a few days later how completely personal those cards were, not only to my situation but to so many situations that have been happening throughout my life. I have been so overwhelmed with feeling everything, but now being able to take a step back and look at it from a different perspective, which was the solution, the law of variety card. The solution actually allowed me to ground *me* and to contain the anxiety I was feeling, I get it, I get it, that's it. My daughter was upset with extended family concerns and is a very empathic child, she feels others' feelings very intensely. While explaining to her about sharing a womb with my twin sister, my sister would kick and I would feel it, or

she would want something and I would feel it or she would move and it would move me, I found myself now realizing I do not have to feel energy of hers, just my own, that is my container. And it took looking at it with a different perspective, a different variety of view to see that. This has been a lifelong struggle to focus on my own energy and the cards picked it up. I now feel much less anxious.

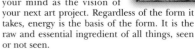

The Laws

1. The Law of One

The law of one recognizes that everything everywhere is made up of energy. Energy is the core ingredient within this dimension of reality and in other dimensions of reality. Energy can exist in concrete reality as the chair in your living room or exist within your mind as the vision of your next art project. Regardless of the form it takes, energy is the basis of the form. It is the raw and essential ingredient of all things, seen or not seen.

The law of one recognizes energy within all things and within all dimensions in the universe. The law of one helps to bring all energy together as one. Once the needed energy is brought together, it can move into existence.

Solution Card

Write down each concrete situation that you currently feel unhappy with in your daily life. One example might be an unfulfilling job. Then write down all of your experiences, thoughts, beliefs, and feelings around this job. Sit back and close your eyes. Then imagine that you can change your job to any job you would like. Take a deep breath. Write down all of your experiences, thoughts, beliefs and feelings around changing your job to one you want. What conflicting experiences, thoughts, beliefs, and feelings come up that do not support the change? Especially notice thoughts that may have come up such as, "I am afraid if I change my job, ____ will happen." Those are the intentions and inner experiences that represent some past energetic wound that has not healed.

2. The Law of Relationship

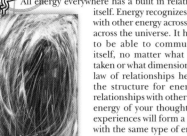

All energy everywhere has a built in relationship with itself. Energy recognizes its existence with other energy across the room or across the universe. It has an ability to be able to communicate with itself, no matter what form it has taken or what dimension it is in. The law of relationships helps provide the structure for energy to form relationships with other energy. The energy of your thoughts and inner experiences will form a relationship with the same type of energy it is.

Solution Card

Breathe in deeply and become very quiet. Relax your body and meditate. What emotional experiences are you having? Ask yourself where these emotions stemmed from. Let the memories become apparent to you. Know that you are not responsible for whatever happened to you. Practice unconditional self regard. What you are now responsible for is creating a third solution. What emotional experience would be the third solution? Is it self acceptance? Love? What would it feel like?

3. The Universal Law of Opposites

There is a broad degree of difference which appears within the structure of energy. Just like paint can make a picture of an angel or a devil, energy can make opposing forms. There can exist in the same space of our world, emptiness and fulfillment, tropical forest and desert, illness and health, and many opposing energies that exist either in our minds, our bodies, or the world around us.

The law also reflects our inner world. Like a mirror image, the law of opposites forms a paradoxical structure so that we constantly create life outside of us through the choice of our inner experience. The opposite of our concrete outer world is our unseen inner energy. What we see outside of us is a reflection of what we see inside of us.

Solution Card

Find that space within your mind of knowing. Take a deep breath. Go deeper within your knowing. Imagine there is a road that travels into the experience of your knowing. You travel upon the road and you make the experience of knowing larger. You feel it even more. You feel the certainty and security of your knowing. Continue to breathe. Allow yourself to feel the totality of what it feels like to be within this emotional space. How would you describe it? What kinds of energy are there? How would you identify the energy? How many different types of energy is there? Is there information present for you in this space? Can the information help you to make choices? Continue to feel this space and breathe. How would you identify the energy of Universal Mind? What does Universal Mind feel like to you? Breathe in. Are you able to feel the energy of Universal Mind within the space of knowing?

4. The Universal Law of Wholeness

Energy is whole just as it is no matter what it is. A car handle is not your car; however, it is a car handle nonetheless. There is nothing incomplete in its existence. The law of wholeness guarantees the completion of all energy in its smallest form or its largest form. Universal law guarantees your equality through your wholeness with every other thing in the universe. There is not one thing lacking within you, you are complete as you are.

Solution Card

Breathe deeply. Relax your body. Feel the earth supporting your physical body. Now, notice that your body had everything it needs to support itself upon the earth. You can feel the stability of the ground below your feet. You can breath the air. There is food to nurture you. Notice that there is not one thing missing from your ability to support yourself within this moment. Now shift your awareness to a memory. It could be of a family member, when you were a child, or having a wonderful time on your birthday. Remember the warmth of this moment. During this time, you felt connected and you felt joy in your connection. Relive the moment in your memory, as though you were experiencing it now. Hold the moment in your mind. What is different in your experience as you went through this exercise in how you felt an hour ago? How much of your joyful experience can you recreate? Are you able to hold on this experience? Or are other experiences taking over? If other experiences are taking you away from your feeling of joy, what do you need to heal?

5. The Universal Law of Variety

Energy can be made into a broad range of forms. The varieties can as many styles of car handles as you can think of to fit as many styles of cars as you can imagine. The place you live in, whether it is an apartment or a house is one of several thousand, or perhaps millions of styles. There are several millions of varieties of insects, several species of animals and plants. The forms that energy can take appear infinite. The law of variety guarantees the presence of choice.

You can empower yourself to see the variety of choices in your life.

Solution Card

You may want to grab your journal for this exercise. Take a deep breath. Focus on a pattern that reoccurs in your life. It could be a recurring problem with your mother. Perhaps you quit job after job without satisfaction. Again, you find yourself in the same old conflict with a coworker. Write down the pattern. Notice where the pattern occurs, what emotions it brings up, what happens before the pattern starts up. Write down your answers. Think back to your past. Are there any similarities in your pattern and events in your past? Write down the similarities. Now, write down the changes you need to make to help yourself heal the pattern. These changes are in your control. Perhaps you need to become less defensive when your mother criticizes you and begin to not buy into her comments about your child rearing. Maybe you need to stand up to your interfering coworker and let them know you do not appreciate their behavior. Perhaps you need to begin to believe that you are smart enough to further your education and to get the job you do want. What steps do you need to go through to help yourself make the changes? Write those down as well. You are now blocking the old energy from forming. Now, when do you begin?

6. The Universal Law of Containment

The law of containment tells us that all the energy that ever was and ever will be already exists, that the energy resides within universal mind and that universal mind moves energy to create flow. Scientific law has proven that energy cannot be created or destroyed; it just changes form.

Universal Mind creates flow through change. New forms of energy are continually birthed through the womb of universal mind. The law of containment helps us to understand it is our right to continually progress in our lives.

Solution Card

Take a deep breath and relax your body. Focus in on your ability to create. What do you like to do? Perhaps draw or paint? Perhaps write? Perhaps you have an ability to think up new ways to do things? Like an inventor? Are you musical? Do you like to sing? Intend to give yourself a window of time right now to experience what you like to do creatively. You may want to journal the answers to these questions after completing your experience. Where does your inspiration come from? How does it feel to you to create? Is it exciting or joyful? Did you feel a sense of energetic flow as you began your creation? Did you experience of sense of inner connection to something larger than you?

7. The Universal Law of Love

The easiest law to remember and practice each day is the law of love. We can open our hearts and allow this emotion of love to be in our lives every moment of every day. The law of love gives us emotional focus and direction for our daily actions. It allows us to understand that when we are operating in the energy of love, we are automatically aligned within the most primal energy of Universal Mind. Universal Mind cannot exist without the energy of love. Without the connective power of love, all of what we see in the universe would not materialize. Love unites all things.

Love is the fundamental building block in all creation and the original energy within Universal Mind. All things created were created from the energy of love. Love opens and allows energy to flow. It is the one emotional energy we can purposely use within our minds to open and broaden our perspective. When we look at ourselves or someone else with love, we automatically suspend judgment. We can see clearly what is, because we have accepted what exists.

Love broadens and releases the flow of energy. Love is creative and naturally manifests. Love helps to create, because love opens the gates of ideas. Love sets free our choices. We can then act because we have choices to act upon.

Solution Card

Do an experiment. Take a deep breath. You may want to journal this exercise. Think of a person who has angered you. Write now what you feel angry about. Is what you wrote down about something that they did to you? Or did not do? Take another deep breath. What happens that you personalize this situation. Take a deep breath and imagine feeling a sense of great love for yourself. Take another deep breath and imagine breathing in the energy of love and out the energy of love. What else could be happening in this situation? Are there other possibilities? Continue to ask yourself what could be underneath the anger. What happens to the energy inside of you?

Try this experiment on a daily basis. Experimenting on a daily basis will begin to help you change your viewpoint of yourself and the world around you.

8. The Universal Law of Infinity

The main energy within Universal Mind is love. Love continually expands and creates choice. Since all is created through love, all is connected through love. The law of infinity provides us with endless choice.

Because all is created through the primal energy of love, choices of energy already exist before you choose them. Countless choices are already present. All the energy ever made already is. You, in order to have choices, must become aware that there are choices. The choice is created through you. You allow the choice to exist because you see the choice. Because you have opened your mind to receive and see choices that already are, the choices can be expressed through you.

The Universal Mind always has ideas for us to receive. There is no end to our receiving.

Solution Card

Take a deep breath. Relax your body. Imagine that you can call all the animals to come to you that live upon earth. In your mind's eye, begin to form a line. See yourself surrounded by millions of animals. Now, imagine that you can become each animal. Which one would it be first? Perhaps you would become a bear? Maybe you would become a wolf? Imagine feeling as though you are a bear. What would it feel like? How large would you be? How would you move? Now, become the wolf. How fast can you run? How many others are with you? Imagine what it would be like to be a rhino or an elephant. If you ran out of choices to imagine becoming an animal from planet earth, could your mind develop more choices? How would that happen? Where would the ideas come from? How many choices could you develop?

9. The Universal Law of Endings and Beginnings

Because our world carries the dimension of time, all things must end and there is a beginning for all things. Beginnings and endings are a way to organize energy, so we can choose what we what to happen next.

Energy exists because of what it is experiencing within each moment. Energy builds and then depletes because of the experience itself. Like our breathing, energy experiences its own momentum, it knows when to pause, when to build and when to release energy. It is the release of energy that determines an ending to the energy and to the experience.

Through time, experiences build and release energy which create beginnings and endings. We can make choices as to what experience we want to build within our self or what experience we want to release. Through releasing energy, we deplete its experience. Its concrete impact is no longer experienced and we can make room to focus on building another experience within ourselves. Your inner energy will match your outer experiences perfectly. Like a balancing act, what is ended inside of you will end outside of you. What is built up inside of your inner experiences will build outside of you.

Through the law of beginnings and endings, time structures energy inside of you to match energy outside of you. Otherwise, like an orchestra tuning up, energy inside of you would be creating outside events which would not make sense to you. Because this law organizes beginnings and endings through time, you can witness through your outer experiences the energy inside of you.

Solution Card

Take a deep breath and relax your body. Imagine this. Let's take you on a little trip. Your body has become weightless. You begin to float up to your ceiling, beyond your ceiling and out into the sky. You move higher and see your streets, the town below you, all becoming smaller, you continue to float and notice that as you past the clouds, you no longer have a physical body, but you still feel you as you. You turn around and look out at the expansiveness of the universe. Because you no longer have a physical body, you are not sure where you begin and where the universe begins. You begin to feel a connection with all the things around you. Because of this connection, you begin to see all sorts of things you did not see in your physical world in your physical body. You see different colors and different life forms that move around you, you see different planets that do not exist in the physical realm.

From this location, you have a very different experience of how energy lives. In a moment, you can be experiencing the green mist you noticed, a moment before, or traveling to, the pink planet you saw several moments previously. You can make your own intelligent choices, moment by moment, about what it is you wish to experience. You focus through your attention upon the experience, the experience builds within you, and as you begin to focus upon some other experience, your previous experiences begin to deplete. Your experience transforms, it builds up and depletes, just like breathing.

10. The Universal Law of Creation

When we are in the flow, we allow the resources of never ending energy to move through us to make what we see on the outside of us. The vessels of universal law provide us with life force to use in the creation of our personal reality. The law of creation allows the substance of our energy to be molded into reality. Through the shape or our flows and blocks, energy is presented through our minds to manifest our daily life.

Our emotions can block us or free us in our creation. It is our feelings which build or deplete our inner experiences and it is our beliefs which house our emotions. When we begin to change our inner participation with energy through experience, we change our outer participation with the concrete world of energy. Creative change occurs and we see something different.

Solution Card

Take a deep breath. We suggest you use your journal for this exercise. This exercise may take one day or several to complete. Focus inward on a problem that you feel needs healing. Write down the problem. Now, write down the mirrors outside of yourself that reflect your inner problem. Perhaps you feel you need a new job. One mirror may be problems with the new boss. Perhaps you are continually upset over your grown son's behavior. One mirror could possibly be conflicts with his wife. What are the mirrors communicating to you about your inner energy? What do you need to learn from the mirrors? What do you need to heal? What do you need to intentionally choose to make the change happen? Place this choice and new found awareness into your knowing. Trust that the change will happen. Note down synchronistic experiences from the world around you that begin to reflect your inward shift.

11. The Universal Law of Source

We define Source or God, Universal Mind. Universal Mind, in the form of energy within everything. Since we and everything else is made of energy, we are never alone. Because our energy is living, our connection to Universal Mind is alive as well. We have a built in connection to Universal Mind.

Our minds and Universal Mind are connected like twins to allow the energy of mind to live. Like Universal Mind, we have a desire to love, to be free, to create and to expand toward fulfillment. Together our energy and the energy of Universal Mind form each other's existence. Together we observe each other, our ties to one another is a mirror image of what we are. Universal Mind is humanity and all there is and we are energy in the form of mind. Because energy cannot be destroyed, our connection with Universal Mind is immortal. Our forever tie with Universal Mind cannot be severed. Energy continually flows from Universal Mind to us. Through our connection to one another, together we experience empowerment.

Because we have the energy of Universal Mind flowing into us, we have the energy available to expand our talents, skills and abilities. Through our constant connection, we can know more about Universal Mind through free expression and Universal Mind can know more about what it is through our form. The shape of reality, as we see it, becomes clear.

Solution Card

Remember the Christmas classic, *It's a Wonderful Life?* Clarence, the Angel, could not earn his wings until George recognized how important his life was. Take a deep breath. Just imagine how it would be for your loved ones if you were not around. What would it be like for your children? What would it be like for your spouse or your friends? What would it be like for perhaps your pet? How would your absence change their lives?

12. The Universal Law of Making

The universal law of making provides a road map for the energy flowing through us to manifest our personal reality. Energy through its vibration has an ability to talk. Energy talks through vibrating its experience. This law determines that through vibration, energy can become physical.

Making occurs through acknowledging a connection with Universal Mind through a felt experience of inner knowing, through Universal Mind's ability to hear the energy of your inward experience, healing emotional blocks, allowing flow and allowing yourself to receive the production of your energy coupled with Universal Mind.

And that is the point of our lives; to allow ourselves to continue to be in the flow of our energy and to allow experiences to happen without getting stuck.

The Law of Making provides a structure that is always present that assures our ability to create our world.

Solution Card

Take a deep breath and relax your body. Remember one of the happiest times in your life. Remember where you were at, how it felt, what was around you. Remember the physical smells and feelings. Now, tune into what you were experiencing: What you were thinking, how you were feeling, how you were actively engaged in the event?

As you tune into your emotions and feel the experience, tune into the pitch of the vibration of your experience. If joy could sing, how high would the notes be? Imagine that joy makes a sound. Tune into the joy within you. What does it sound like? Can you hear it?

Conclusion

Your life is not done. You are in a continuing flow, a process of growing closer to yourself and to Source. As you do so, you not only heal yourself, but you heal all those around you.

You have made the better choice: to expand your energy outward and touch the Universal Mind.

~Rochelle Sparrow and Cortney Kane

About the Authors

Rochelle Sparrow
Co-Author

There is such a thing as white slavery in the United States. It is not commonly discussed in our society, but every day, children are isolated from the world around them and suffer from abuse and neglect. Not just for a day, but for years.

I was one of those children. While I was growing up, I tried to spend as much time as possible outside of my house. I loved the woods, the ocean, the wind and the sky. I listened to the birds and heard the crickets sing.

The equality of the natural world around me taught me that something was terribly wrong with the abuse and oppression I was experiencing. When my stepfather began to rape me when I was a little girl, I knew life did not have to be this scary and sad. Although, like all abused children, I was told to keep the abuse a secret and that is was my fault, I experienced a deep longing for healing. I knew healing could happen. I knew other possibilities existed. I knew other outlooks of life were hidden from the current view I was being force fed.

I was born a shaman who could not articulate my ability to communicate with the natural world, yet those abilities were present. I heard the language of spirit. Nature became my teacher. The world around me showed me a different path. A path I could take to freedom. My life developed out of my desire to live and to live well.

When I tried to get back on the road to gaining back what was mine to have, I was twenty-four years old. I had been isolated and repeatedly raped for fourteen years. I was faced with serious issues that were not consciously in alignment with what I knew to be true. With the help of my natural connection to spirit and to talented healers, I stepped out of a reality that was not mine and stepped into a reality I was entitled to.

I recovered from clinical depression and post traumatic stress syndrome. I worked to become a therapist and went to school to get my masters degree in Social Work. I developed my skills as a shaman. I began my business as a psychic trance channel. I now have a closely connected, healthy family life and the best of friends. I work with Cortney Kane, within a transformative partnership which the whole is greater than the sum of its parts. All of this would not have been possible if it was not for the truth of my connection to spirit.

I want to teach you what I have learned about nature, energy, and healing. I want to show you how you can become empowered through connection to spirit and through your ability to heal from spirit. I want to help you see the possibilities that exist in your life.

I want to free you from what you have been taught. I want to lead you into the truth of who you are.

Cortney Kane
Co-Author / Artist

Bulbar Palsy is a form of amyotrophic lateral sclerosis disease and is rarely found in women. My mother was diagnosed with the disease when I was twelve. When other children were participating in cheerleading and dance classes, I was at home caring for my mother. My mother was dying. My father was numbing his pain through work. My twin sister and I had little adult support. I was alone and terrified of losing her. I was taught to be strong and to take care of others and not show how badly I was hurting. When people would ask how we were, I said, "Fine."

I was not fine. I was lifting my mother, feeding her through a feeding tube, and translating her words for her. On a daily basis I was taking her into the bathroom and physically helping her body pass her waste. In the evenings, I would journal and hide my deepest feelings away from the world. My mother passed after two years of caring for her and I was left with those unresolved emotions.

I recognized my potential for psychic abilities a week after my mother's death. She came to me while I slept and let me know that she was okay. She hugged me. Coming from a small Christian town in Oklahoma, this was evil. Through the next six years, I had many loved ones pass and all coming to me once they died. I still had many painful feelings surrounding my mother's death that I did not deal with. I tail-spun into a life of drugs and alcohol, with the excuses of being young and irresponsible. The last straw was driving drunk with my child and babysitter in the car. This was the end.

My belief in a better life and feeling my feelings for what they were began to aide me in my recovery. Through meditation and my healing I began to receive clear visions. My psychic abilities started to awaken. I started to receive messages from my guides to paint the information that I was receiving. This journey has led me to my partnership with my best friend. Rochelle and I now work together to bring you our understanding of our healing processes developed through a lifetime of recovery from suffering.

My goal is to help you see clarity though your layers of pain. I have come to realize that I could not heal without the impact of my psychic abilities. I want to help you recognize yours.

Solution (The Universal Law of Creation)

Take a deep breath. We suggest you use your journal for this exercise. This exercise may take one day or several to complete. Focus inward on a problem that you feel needs healing. Write down the problem. Now, write down the mirrors outside of yourself that reflect your inner problem. Perhaps you feel you need a new job. One mirror may be problems with the new boss. Perhaps you are continually upset over your grown son's behavior. One mirror could possibly be conflicts with his wife. What are the mirrors communicating to you about your inner energy? What do you need to learn from the mirrors? What do you need to heal? What do you need to intentionally choose to make the change happen? Place this choice and new found awareness into your knowing. Trust that the change will happen. Note down synchronistic experiences from the world around you that begin to reflect your inward shift.

The Universal Law of Creation

When we are in the flow, we allow the resources of energy to move through us to make what we see on the outside of us. The vessels of universal law provide us with life force to use in the creation of our personal reality. The law of creation allows the substance of our energy to be molded into reality. Through the shape or our flows and blocks, energy is presented through our minds to manifest our daily life.

Our emotions can block us or free us in our creation. It is our feelings which build or deplete our inner experiences and it is our beliefs which house our emotions. When we begin to change our inner participation with energy through experience, we change our outer participation with the concrete world of energy. Creative change occurs and we see something different.

Solution (The Universal Law of Endings and Beginnings)

Take a deep breath and relax your body. Imagine this. Let's take you on a little trip. Your body has become weightless. You begin to float up to your ceiling, beyond your ceiling and out into the sky. You move higher and see your streets, the town below you, all becoming smaller, you continue to float and notice that as you past the clouds, you no longer have a physical body, but you still feel you as you. You turn around and look out at the expansiveness of the universe. Because you no longer have a physical body, you are not sure where you begin and where the universe begins. You begin to feel a connection with all the things around you. Because of this connection, you begin to see all sorts of things you did not see in your physical world. You see different colors and different life forms that move around you, you see different planets that do not exist in the physical realm.

From this location, you have a very different experience of energy. In a moment, you can be experiencing the green mist you noticed, a moment before, or traveling to, the pink planet you saw several moments previously. You can make your own intelligent choices, moment by moment, about what it is you wish to experience. You focus through your attention upon the experience, the experience builds within you, and as you begin to focus upon some other experience, your previous experiences begin to deplete. Your experience transforms, it builds up and depletes, just like breathing.

The Universal Law of Endings and Beginnings

Beginnings and endings are a way to organize energy, so we can choose what we want to happen next.

Energy exists because of what it is experiencing within each moment. Energy builds and then depletes because of the experience itself. Like our breathing, energy experiences its own momentum, it knows when to pause, when to build and when to release energy. It is the release of energy that determines an ending to the energy and to the experience.

Through time, experiences build and release energy which create beginnings and endings. We can make choices as to what experience we want to build within our self or what experience we want to release. Through releasing energy, we deplete its experience. Its impact is no longer experienced and we can make room to focus on building another experience within ourselves. Your inner energy will match your outer experiences perfectly. Like a balancing act, what is ended inside of you will end outside of you. What is built up inside of your inner experiences will build outside of you.

Through the law of beginnings and endings, time structures energy inside of you to match energy outside of you. Otherwise, like an orchestra tuning up, energy inside of you would be creating outside events which would not make sense to you. Because this law organizes beginnings and endings through time, you can witness through your outer experiences the energy inside of you.

Solution (The Universal Law of Making)

Take a deep breath and relax your body. Remember one of the happiest times in your life. Remember where you were at, how it felt, what was around you. Remember the physical smells and feelings. Now, tune into what you were experiencing: What you were thinking, how you were feeling, how you were actively engaged in the event?

As you tune into your emotions and feel the experience, tune into the pitch of the vibration of your experience. If joy could sing, how high would the notes be? Imagine that joy makes a sound. Tune into the joy within you. What does it sound like? Can you hear it?

The Universal Law of Making

The universal law of making provides a road map for the energy flowing through us to manifest our reality. Energy through its vibration has an ability to talk. Energy talks through vibrating its experience. This law determines that through vibration, energy can become physical.

Making occurs through acknowledging a connection with Universal Mind through a felt experience of inner knowing, through Universal Mind's ability to hear the energy of your inward experience, healing emotional blocks, allowing flow and allowing yourself to receive the production of your energy coupled with Universal Mind.

And that is the point of our lives; to be in the flow of our energy and to allow experiences to happen without getting stuck.

The Law of Making provides a structure that is always present that assures our ability to create our world.

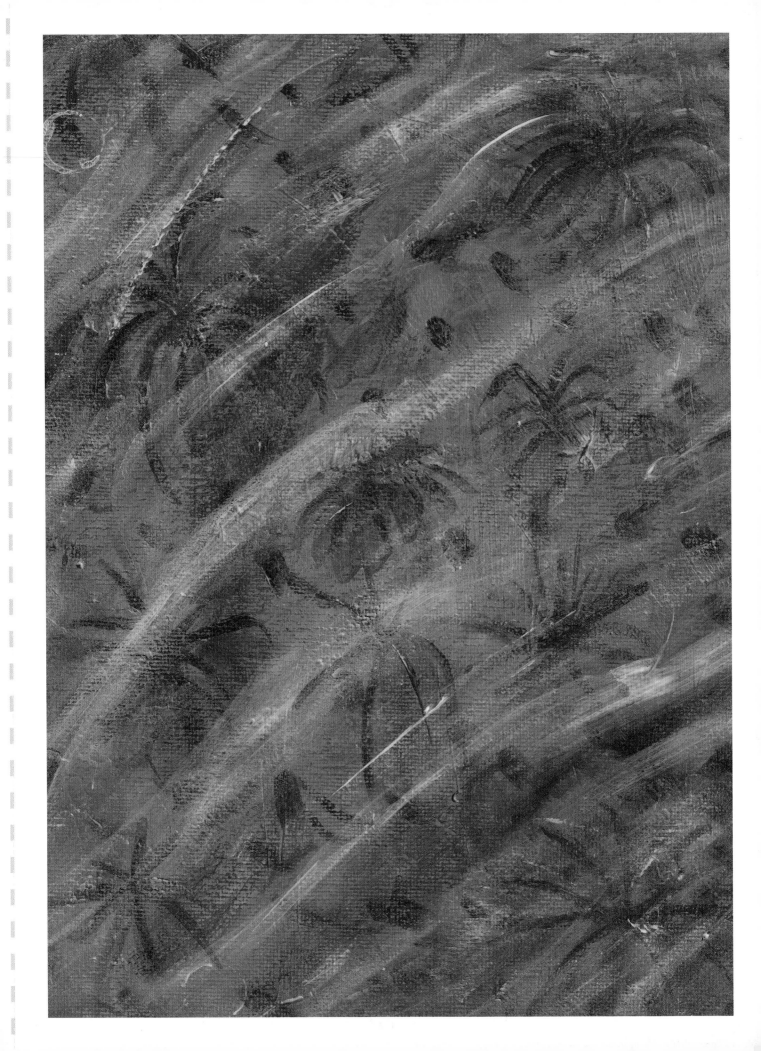

Solution (The Universal Law of Source)

Remember the Christmas classic, *It's a Wonderful Life?* Clarence, the Angel, could not earn his wings until George recognized how important his life was. Take a deep breath. Just imagine how it would be for your loved ones if you were not around. What would it be like for your children? What would it be like for your spouse or your friends? What would it be like for perhaps your pet? How would your absence change their lives?.

The Universal Law of Source

We define Source or God as Universal Mind. Universal Mind, in the form of energy within everything. Since we and everything else is made of energy, we are never alone. Because our energy is living, our connection to Universal Mind is alive as well. We have a built in connection to Universal Mind.

Our minds and Universal Mind are connected like twins to allow the energy of mind to live. Like Universal Mind, we have a desire to love, to be free, to create and to expand toward fulfillment. Together our energy and the energy of Universal Mind form each other's existence. Together we observe each other, our ties to one another is a mirror image of what we are. Universal Mind is humanity and all there is and we are energy in the form of mind. Because energy cannot be destroyed, our connection with Universal Mind is immortal. Our forever tie with Universal Mind cannot be severed. Energy continually flows from Universal Mind to us. Through our connection to one another, together we experience empowerment.

Because we have the energy of Universal Mind flowing into us, we have the energy available to expand our talents, skills and abilities. Through our constant connection, we can know more about Universal Mind through free expression and Universal Mind can know more about what it is through our form. The shape of reality becomes clear.

Solution (The Universal Law of Infinity)

Take a deep breath. Relax your body. Imagine that you can call all the animals to come to you that live upon earth. In your mind's eye, begin to form a line. See yourself surrounded by millions of animals. Now, imagine that you can become each animal. Which one would it be first? Perhaps you would become a bear? Maybe you would become a wolf? Imagine feeling as though you are a bear. What would it feel like? How large would you be? How would you move? Now, become the wolf. How fast can you run? How many others are with you? Imagine what it would be like to be a rhino or an elephant. If you ran out of choices to imagine becoming an animal from planet earth, could your mind develop more choices? How would that happen? Where would the ideas come from? How many choices could you develop?

Solution (The Universal Law of Love)

Do an experiment. Take a deep breath. You may want to journal this exercise. Think of a person who has angered you. Write now what you feel angry about. Is what you wrote down about something that they did to you? Or did not do? Take another deep breath. What happens that you personalize this situation. Take a deep breath and imagine feeling a sense of great love for yourself. Take another deep breath and imagine breathing in the energy of love and out the energy of love. What else could be happening in this situation? Are there other possibilities? Continue to ask yourself what could be underneath the anger. What happens to the energy inside of you?

Try this experiment on a daily basis. Experimenting on a daily basis will begin to help you change your viewpoint of yourself and the world.

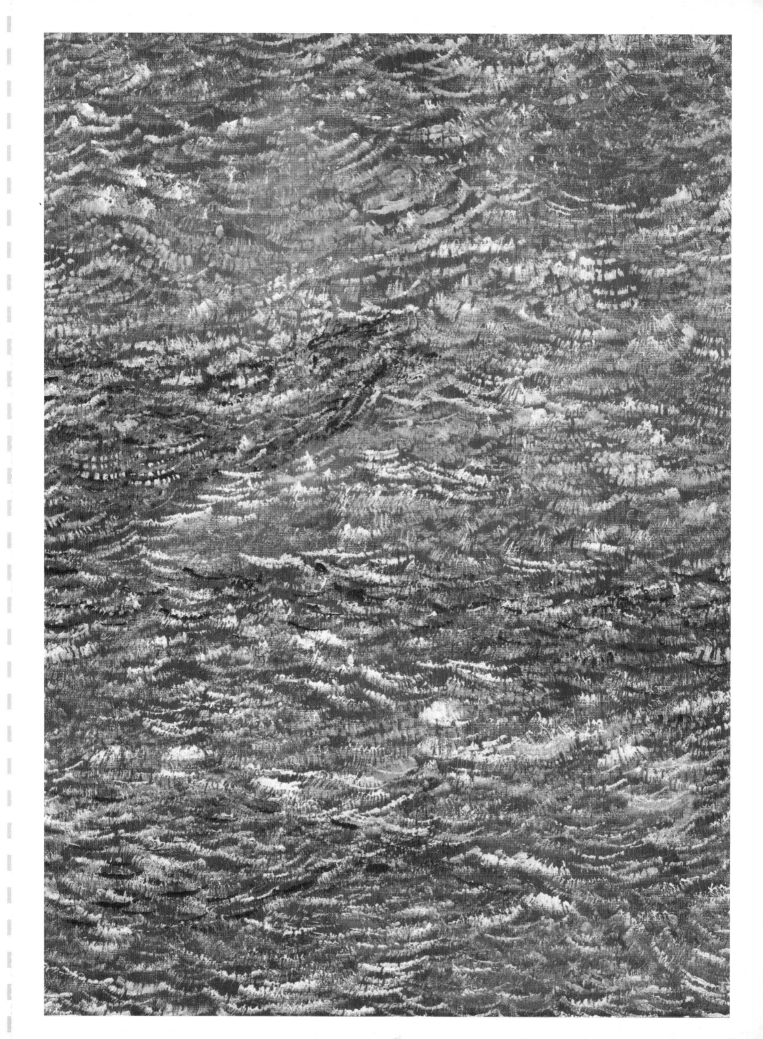

The Universal Law of Love

The easiest law to remember and practice each day is the law of love. We can open our hearts and allow this emotion of love to be in our lives every moment of every day. The law of love gives us emotional focus and direction for our daily actions. It allows us to understand that when we are operating in the energy of love, we are automatically aligned within the most primal energy of Universal Mind. Universal Mind cannot exist without the energy of love. Without the connective power of love, all of what we see in the universe would not materialize. Love unites all things.

Love is the fundamental building block in all creation and the original energy within Universal Mind. All things created were created from the energy of love. Love opens and allows energy to flow. It is the one emotional energy we can purposely use within our minds to open and broaden our perspective. When we look at ourselves or someone else with love, we automatically suspend judgment. We can see clearly what is, because we have accepted what exists.

Love broadens and releases the flow of energy. Love is creative and naturally manifests. Love helps to create, because love opens the gates of ideas. Love sets free our choices. We can then act because we have choices.

Solution (The Universal Law of Containment)

Take a deep breath and relax your body. Focus in on your ability to create. What do you like to do? Perhaps draw or paint? Perhaps write? Perhaps you have an ability to think up new ways to do things? Like an inventor? Are you musical? Do you like to sing? Intend to give yourself a window of time right now to experience what you like to do creatively. You may want to journal the answers to these questions after completing your experience. Where does your inspiration come from? How does it feel to you to create? Is it exciting or joyful? Did you feel a sense of energetic flow as you began your creation? Did you experience of sense of inner connection to something larger than you?

The Universal Law of Containment

The law of containment tells us that all the energy that ever was and ever will be already exists, that the energy resides within universal mind and that universal mind moves energy to create flow. Scientific law has proven that energy cannot be created or destroyed; it just changes form.

Universal Mind creates flow through change. New forms of energy are continually birthed through the womb of universal mind. The law of containment helps us to understand it is our right to continually progress in our lives.

Solution (The Universal Law of Variety)

You may want to grab your journal for this exercise. Take a deep breath. Focus on a pattern that reoccurs in your life. It could be a recurring problem with your mother. Perhaps you quit job after job without satisfaction. Again, you find yourself in the same old conflict with a coworker. Write down the pattern. Notice where the pattern occurs, what emotions it brings up, what happens before the pattern starts up. Write down your answers. Think back to your past. Are there any similarities in your pattern and events in your past? Write down the similarities. Now, write down the changes you need to make to help yourself heal the pattern. These changes are in your control. Perhaps you need to become less defensive when your mother criticizes you and begin to not buy into her comments about your child rearing. Maybe you need to stand up to your interfering coworker and let them know you do not appreciate their behavior. Perhaps you need to begin to believe that you are smart enough to further your education and to get the job you do want. What steps do you need to go through to help yourself make the changes? Write those down as well. You are now blocking the old energy from forming. Now, when do you begin?

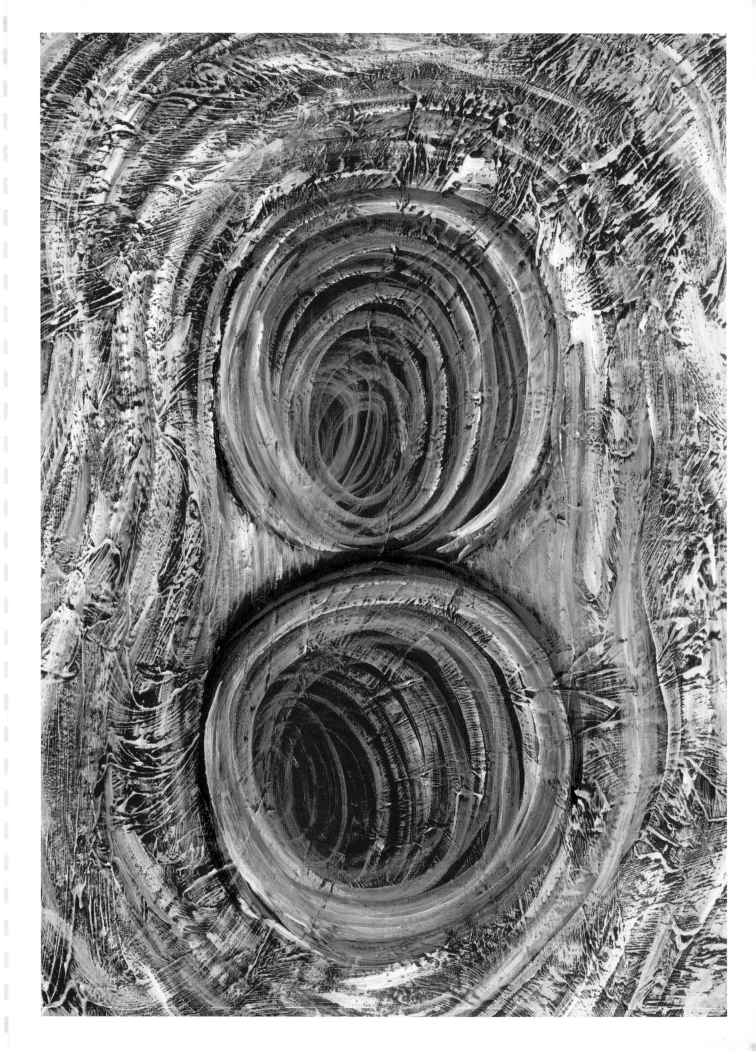

The Universal Law of Variety

Energy can take a broad range of forms. The varieties can as many styles of car handles as you can think of to fit as many styles of cars as you can imagine. The place you live in, whether it is an apartment or a house is one of several thousand, or perhaps millions of styles. There are several millions of varieties of insects, several species of animals and plants. The forms that energy can take appear infinite. The law of variety guarantees the presence of choice.

You can empower yourself to see the variety of choices in your life.

Solution (The Universal Law of Wholeness)

Breathe deeply. Relax. Feel the earth supporting your physical body. Now, notice that your body had everything it needs to support itself upon the earth. You can feel the stability of the ground below your feet. You can breath the air. There is food to nurture you. Notice that there is not one thing missing from your ability to support yourself within this moment. Now shift your awareness to a memory. It could be of a family member, when you were a child, or having a wonderful time on your birthday. Remember the warmth of this moment. During this time, you felt connected and you felt joy in your connection. Relive the moment in your memory, as though you were experiencing it now. Hold the moment in your mind. What is different in your experience as you went through this exercise in how you felt an hour ago? How much of your joyful experience can you recreate? Are you able to hold on this experience? Or are other experiences taking over? If other experiences are taking you away from your feeling of joy, what do you need to heal?

The Universal Law of Wholeness

Energy is whole just as it is no matter what it is. A car handle is not your car; however, it is a car handle nonetheless. There is nothing incomplete in its existence. The law of wholeness guarantees the completion of all energy in its smallest form or its largest form. Universal law guarantees your equality through your wholeness with every other thing in the universe. There is not one thing lacking within you, you are complete as you are.

Solution (The Universal Law of Opposites)

Find that space within your mind of knowing. Take a deep breath. Go deeper within your knowing. Imagine there is a road that travels into the experience of your knowing. You travel upon the road and you make the experience of knowing larger. You feel it even more. You feel the certainty and security of your knowing. Continue. Allow yourself to feel the totality of what it feels like to be within this emotional space. How would you describe it? What kinds of energy are there? How would you identify the energy? How many different types of energy is there? Is there information present for you in this space? Can the information help you to make choices? Continue to feel this space and breathe. How would you identify the energy of Universal Mind? What does Universal Mind feel like to you? Breathe in. Are you able to feel the energy of Universal Mind within the space of knowing?

The Universal Law of Opposites

There is a broad degree of difference which appears within the structure of energy. Just like paint can make a picture of an angel or a devil, energy can make opposing forms. There can exist in the same space of our world, emptiness and fulfillment, tropical forest and desert, illness and health, and many opposing energies that exist either in our minds, our bodies, or the world around us.

The law also reflects our inner world. Like a mirror image, the law of opposites forms a paradoxical structure so that we constantly create life outside of us through the choice of our inner experience. The opposite of our concrete outer world is our unseen inner energy. What we see outside of us is a reflection of what we see inside of us.

Solution (The Law of Relationship)

Breathe in deeply and become very quiet. Relax your body and meditate. What emotional experiences are you having? Ask yourself where these emotions stemmed from. Let the memories become apparent to you. Know that you are not responsible for whatever happened to you. Practice unconditional self regard. What you are now responsible for is creating a third solution. What emotional experience would be the third solution? Is it self acceptance? Love? What would it feel like?

The Law of Relationship

All energy everywhere has a built in relationship with itself. Energy recognizes its existence with other energy across the room or across the universe. It has an ability to communicate with itself, no matter what form it has taken. The law of relationships helps provide the structure for energy to form relationships with other energy. The energy of your thoughts and inner experiences will form a relationship with the same type of energy it is.

Solution (The Law of One)

Write down each situation that you currently feel unhappy with in your daily life. One example might be an unfulfilling job. Then write down all of your experiences, thoughts, beliefs, and feelings around this job. Sit back and close your eyes. Then imagine that you can change your job to any job you would like. Take a deep breath. Write down all of your experiences, thoughts, beliefs and feelings around changing your job to one you want. What conflicting experiences, thoughts, beliefs, and feelings come up that do not support the change? Especially notice thoughts that may have come up such as, "I am afraid if I change my job, ____ will happen." Those are the intentions and inner experiences that represent some past energetic wound that has not healed.

The Law of One

The law of one recognizes that everything everywhere is made up of energy. Energy is the core ingredient within this reality. Energy can exist in concrete reality as the chair in your living room or exist within your mind as the vision of your next art project. Regardless of the form it takes, energy is the basis of the form. It is the raw and essential ingredient of all things, seen or not seen.

The law of one recognizes energy within all things and within all dimensions in the universe. The law of one helps to bring all energy together as one. Once the needed energy is brought together, it can move into existence.